STAR WARS®

EPISODE I

THE PHANTOM MENACE™

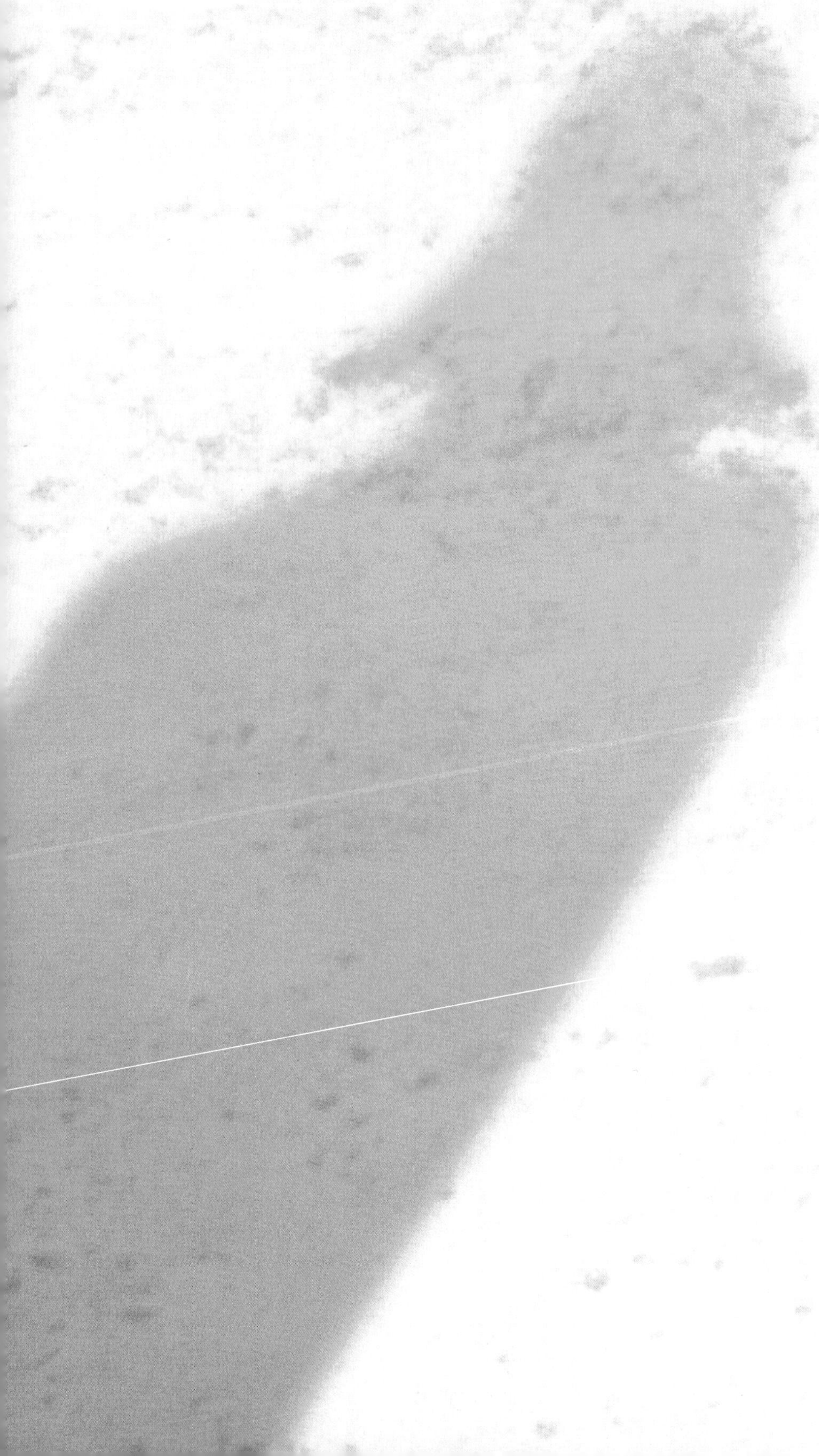

STAR WARS
EPISODE I
THE PHANTOM MENACE

Adapted by

HENRY GILROY

from an original story by

GEORGE LUCAS

Pencils by

RODOLFO DAMAGGIO

with inks by

AL WILLIAMSON

TITAN BOOKS

Episode I

THE PHANTOM MENACE

Turmoil has engulfed the
Galactic Republic. The taxation
of trade routes to outlying star
systems is in dispute.

Hoping to resolve the matter
with a blockade of deadly
battleships, the greedy Trade
Federation has stopped all
shipping to the small planet
of Naboo.

While the Congress of the
Republic endlessly debates
this alarming chain of events,
the Supreme Chancellor has
secretly dispatched two Jedi
Knights, the guardians of peace
and justice in the galaxy,
to settle the conflict. . . .

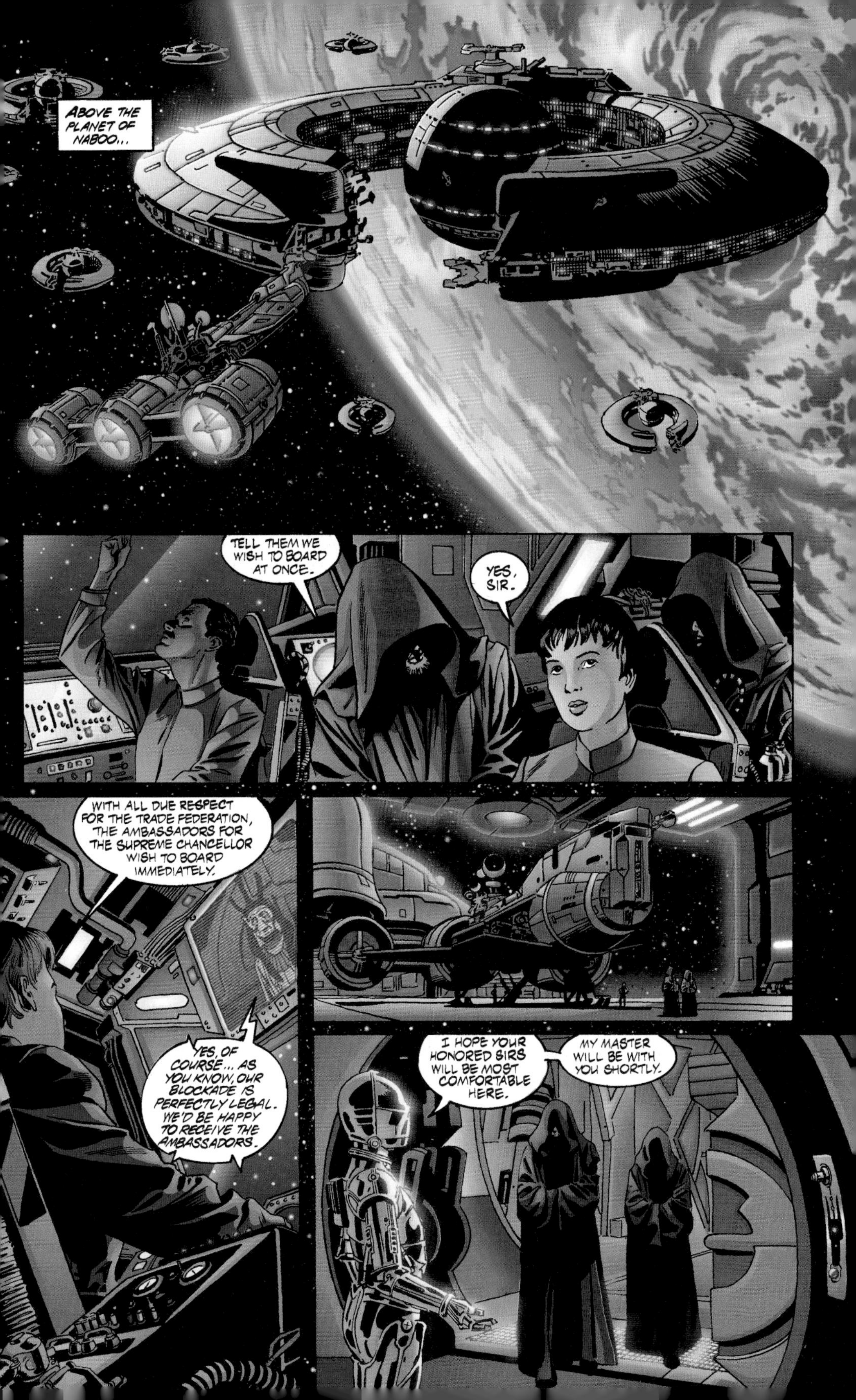

ABOVE THE PLANET OF NABOO...
TELL THEM WE WISH TO BOARD AT ONCE.
YES, SIR.
WITH ALL DUE RESPECT FOR THE TRADE FEDERATION, THE AMBASSADORS FOR THE SUPREME CHANCELLOR WISH TO BOARD IMMEDIATELY.
YES, OF COURSE... AS YOU KNOW, OUR BLOCKADE IS PERFECTLY LEGAL. WE'D BE HAPPY TO RECEIVE THE AMBASSADORS.
I HOPE YOUR HONORED SIRS WILL BE MOST COMFORTABLE HERE.
MY MASTER WILL BE WITH YOU SHORTLY.

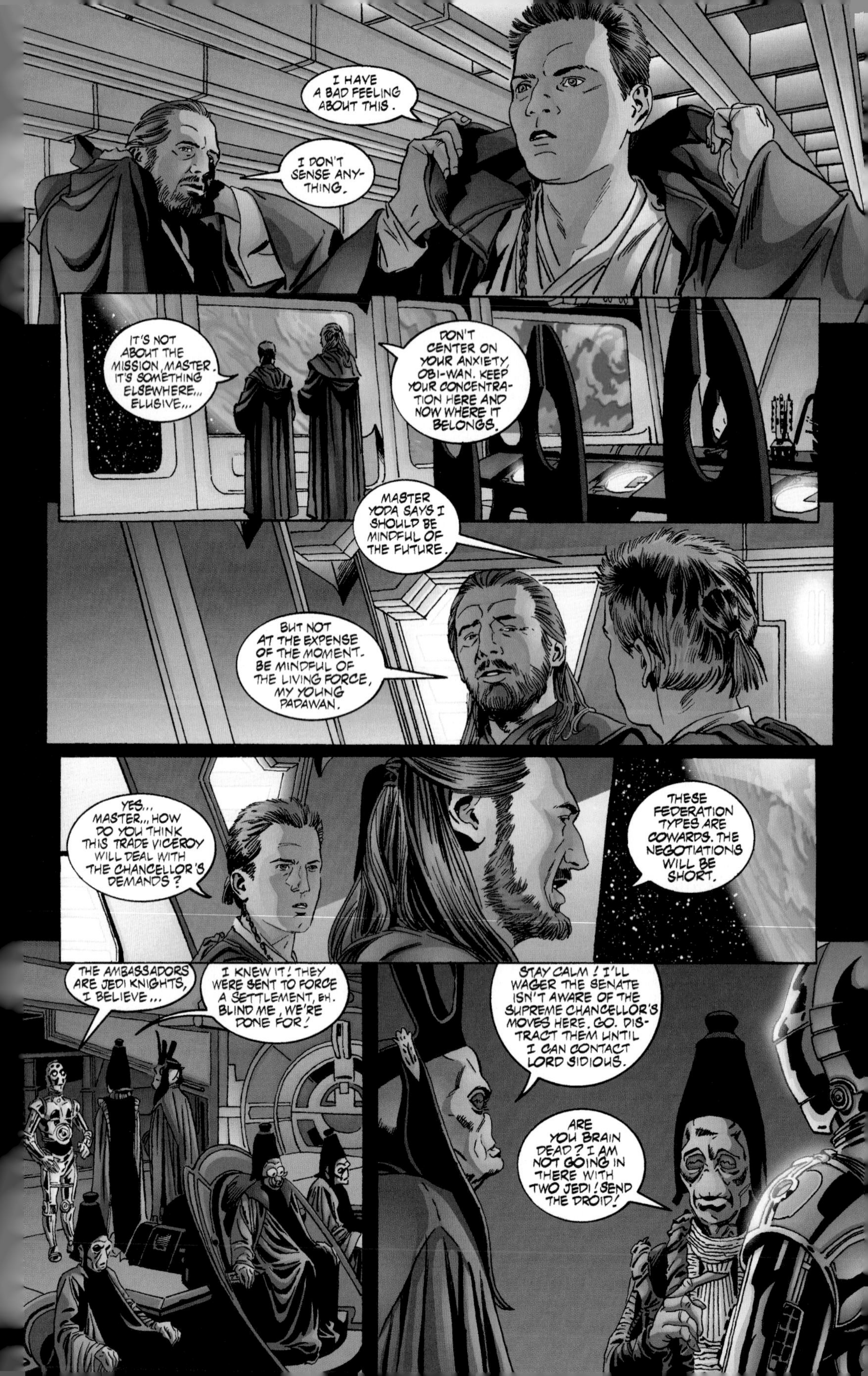
I HAVE A BAD FEELING ABOUT THIS.
I DON'T SENSE ANYTHING.
IT'S NOT ABOUT THE MISSION, MASTER. IT'S SOMETHING ELSEWHERE... ELUSIVE...
DON'T CENTER ON YOUR ANXIETY, OBI-WAN. KEEP YOUR CONCENTRATION HERE AND NOW WHERE IT BELONGS.
MASTER YODA SAYS I SHOULD BE MINDFUL OF THE FUTURE.
BUT NOT AT THE EXPENSE OF THE MOMENT. BE MINDFUL OF THE LIVING FORCE, MY YOUNG PADAWAN.
YES... MASTER... HOW DO YOU THINK THIS TRADE VICEROY WILL DEAL WITH THE CHANCELLOR'S DEMANDS?
THESE FEDERATION TYPES ARE COWARDS. THE NEGOTIATIONS WILL BE SHORT.
THE AMBASSADORS ARE JEDI KNIGHTS, I BELIEVE...
I KNEW IT! THEY WERE SENT TO FORCE A SETTLEMENT, EH. BLIND ME, WE'RE DONE FOR!
STAY CALM! I'LL WAGER THE SENATE ISN'T AWARE OF THE SUPREME CHANCELLOR'S MOVES HERE. GO. DISTRACT THEM UNTIL I CAN CONTACT LORD SIDIOUS.
ARE YOU BRAIN DEAD? I AM NOT GOING IN THERE WITH TWO JEDI! SEND THE DROID!

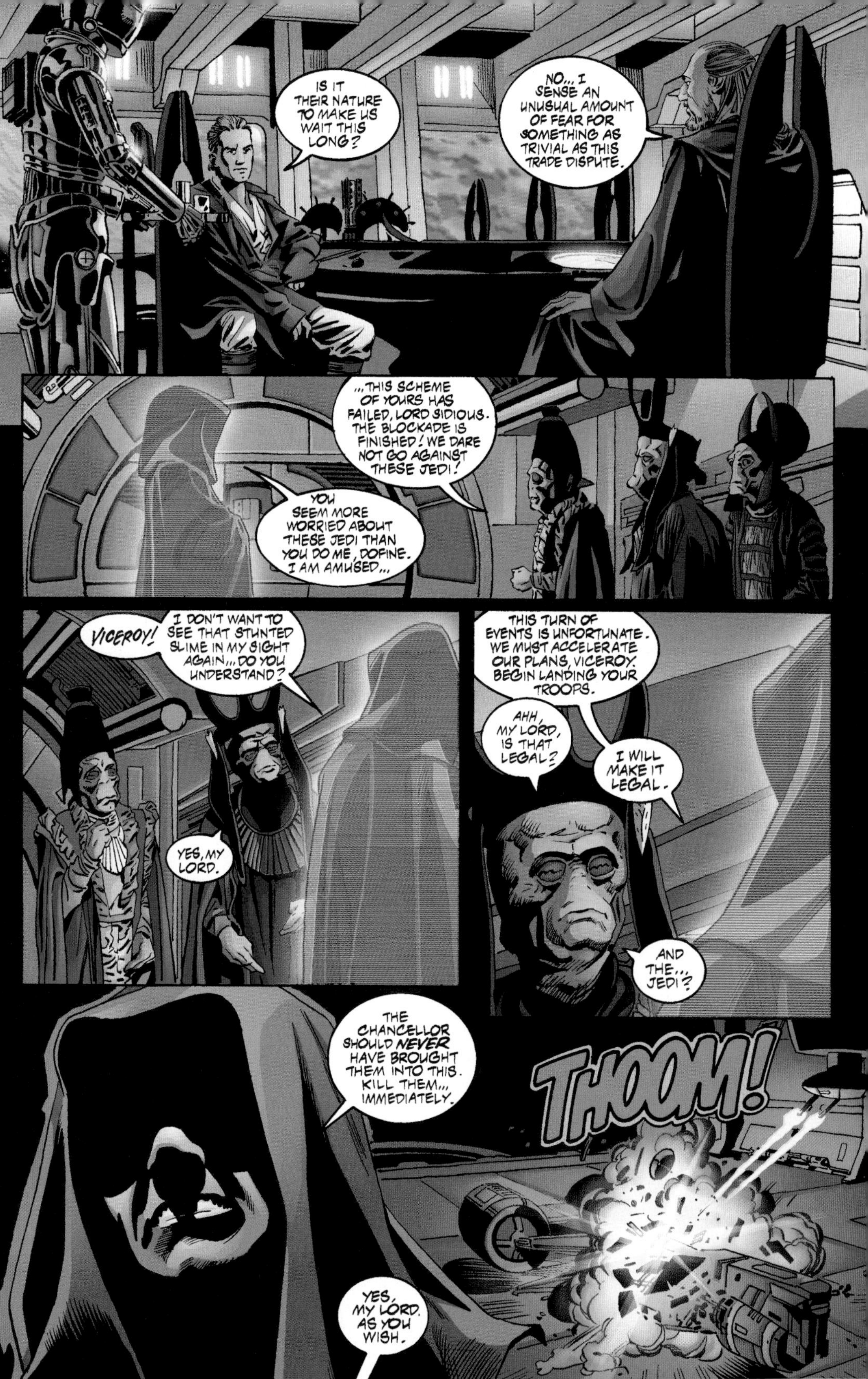
IS IT THEIR NATURE TO MAKE US WAIT THIS LONG?
NO... I SENSE AN UNUSUAL AMOUNT OF FEAR FOR SOMETHING AS TRIVIAL AS THIS TRADE DISPUTE.
...THIS SCHEME OF YOURS HAS FAILED, LORD SIDIOUS. THE BLOCKADE IS FINISHED! WE DARE NOT GO AGAINST THESE JEDI!
YOU SEEM MORE WORRIED ABOUT THESE JEDI THAN YOU DO ME, DOFINE. I AM AMUSED...
VICEROY!
I DON'T WANT TO SEE THAT STUNTED SLIME IN MY SIGHT AGAIN... DO YOU UNDERSTAND?
YES, MY LORD.
THIS TURN OF EVENTS IS UNFORTUNATE. WE MUST ACCELERATE OUR PLANS, VICEROY. BEGIN LANDING YOUR TROOPS.
AHH, MY LORD, IS THAT LEGAL?
I WILL MAKE IT LEGAL.
AND THE... JEDI?
THE CHANCELLOR SHOULD NEVER HAVE BROUGHT THEM INTO THIS. KILL THEM... IMMEDIATELY.
THOOM!
YES, MY LORD. AS YOU WISH.

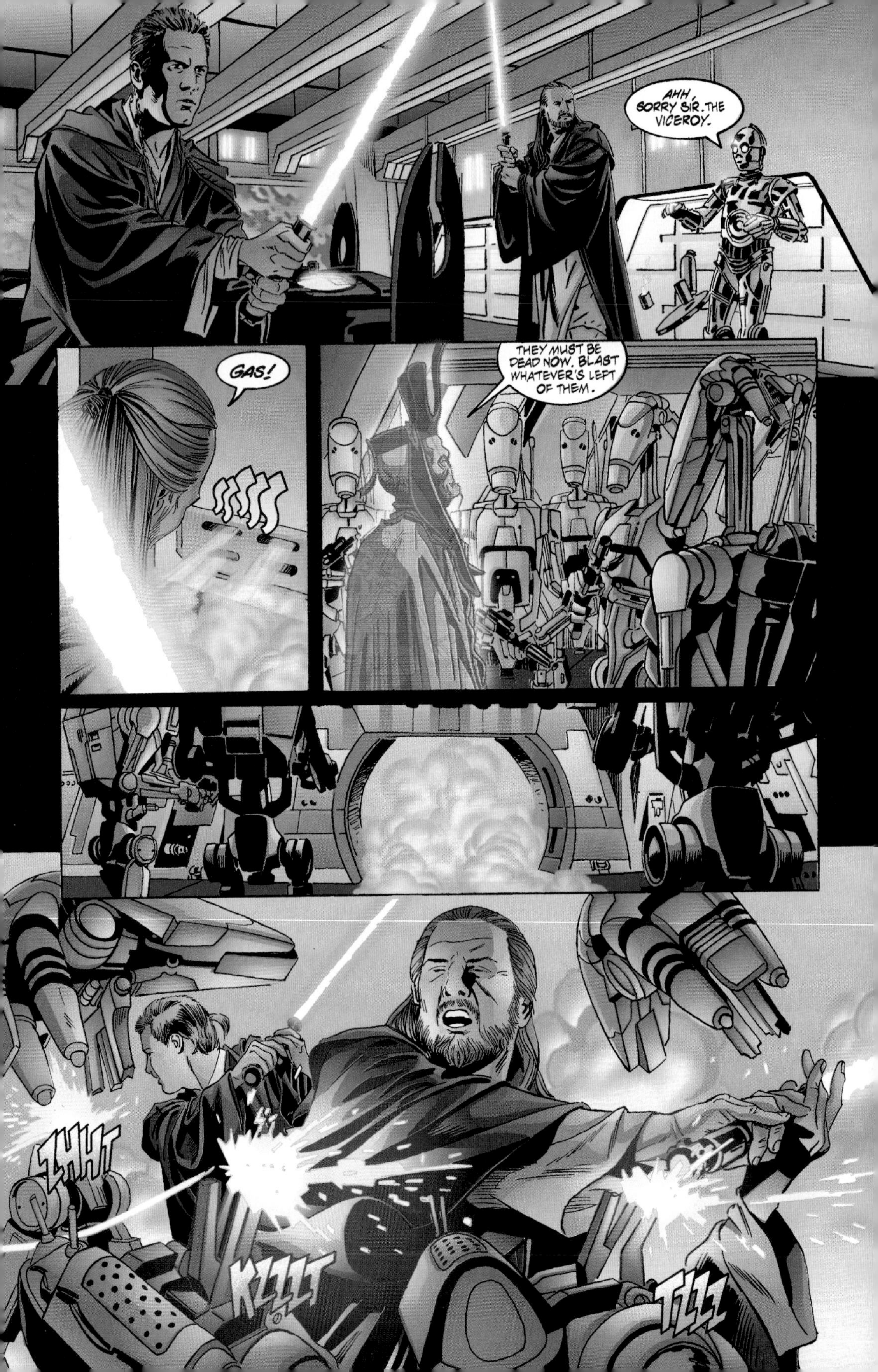
AHH, SORRY SIR. THE VICEROY.
GAS!
SSSS
THEY MUST BE DEAD NOW. BLAST WHATEVER'S LEFT OF THEM.
ZHHT
KZZZT
TZZZ

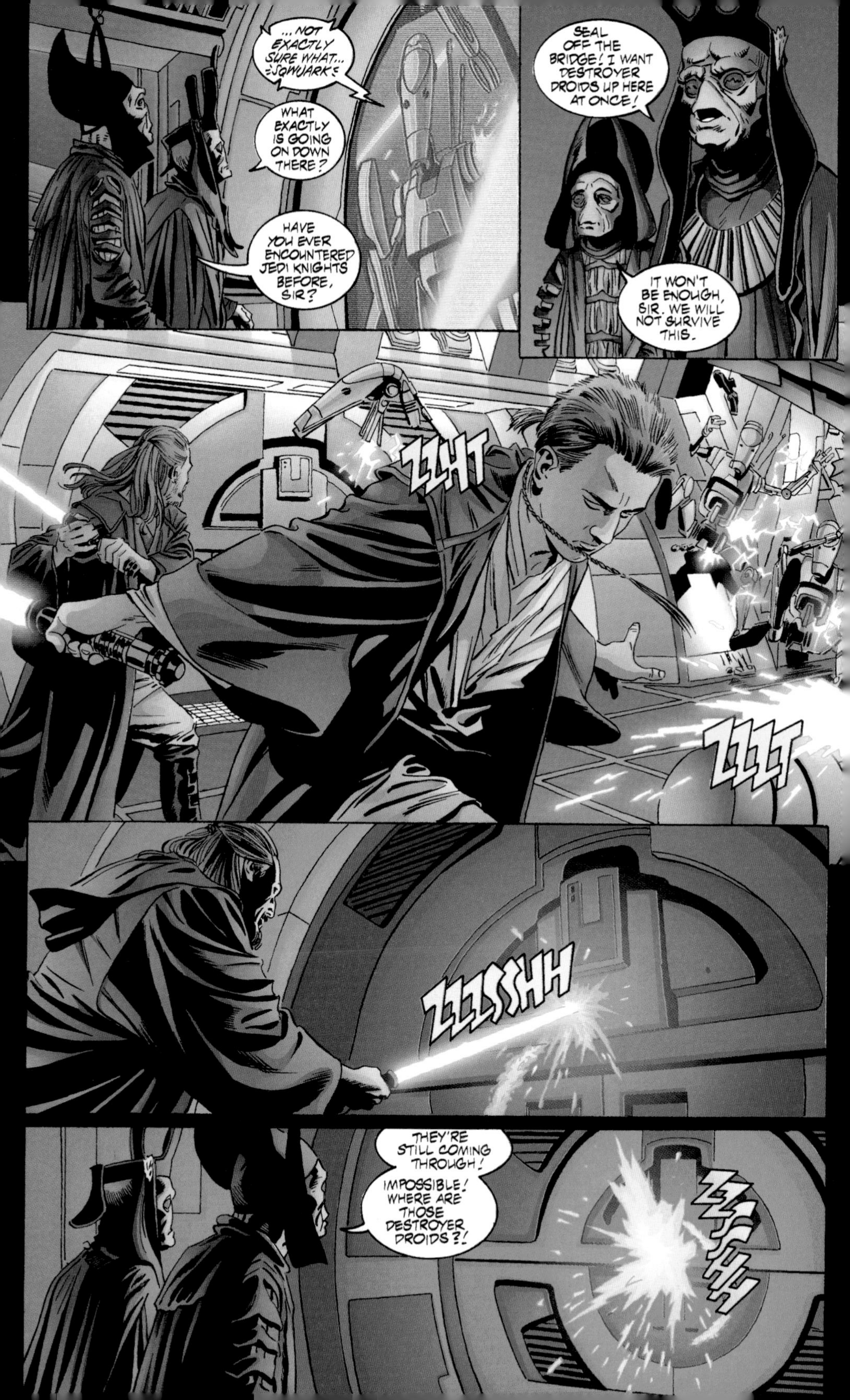

...NOT EXACTLY SURE WHAT... =SQWUARK=
WHAT EXACTLY IS GOING ON DOWN THERE?
HAVE YOU EVER ENCOUNTERED JEDI KNIGHTS BEFORE, SIR?
SEAL OFF THE BRIDGE! I WANT DESTROYER DROIDS UP HERE AT ONCE!
IT WON'T BE ENOUGH, SIR. WE WILL NOT SURVIVE THIS.
ZZHT
ZZZT
ZZZSSHH
THEY'RE STILL COMING THROUGH!
IMPOSSIBLE! WHERE ARE THOSE DESTROYER DROIDS?!
ZZSSHH

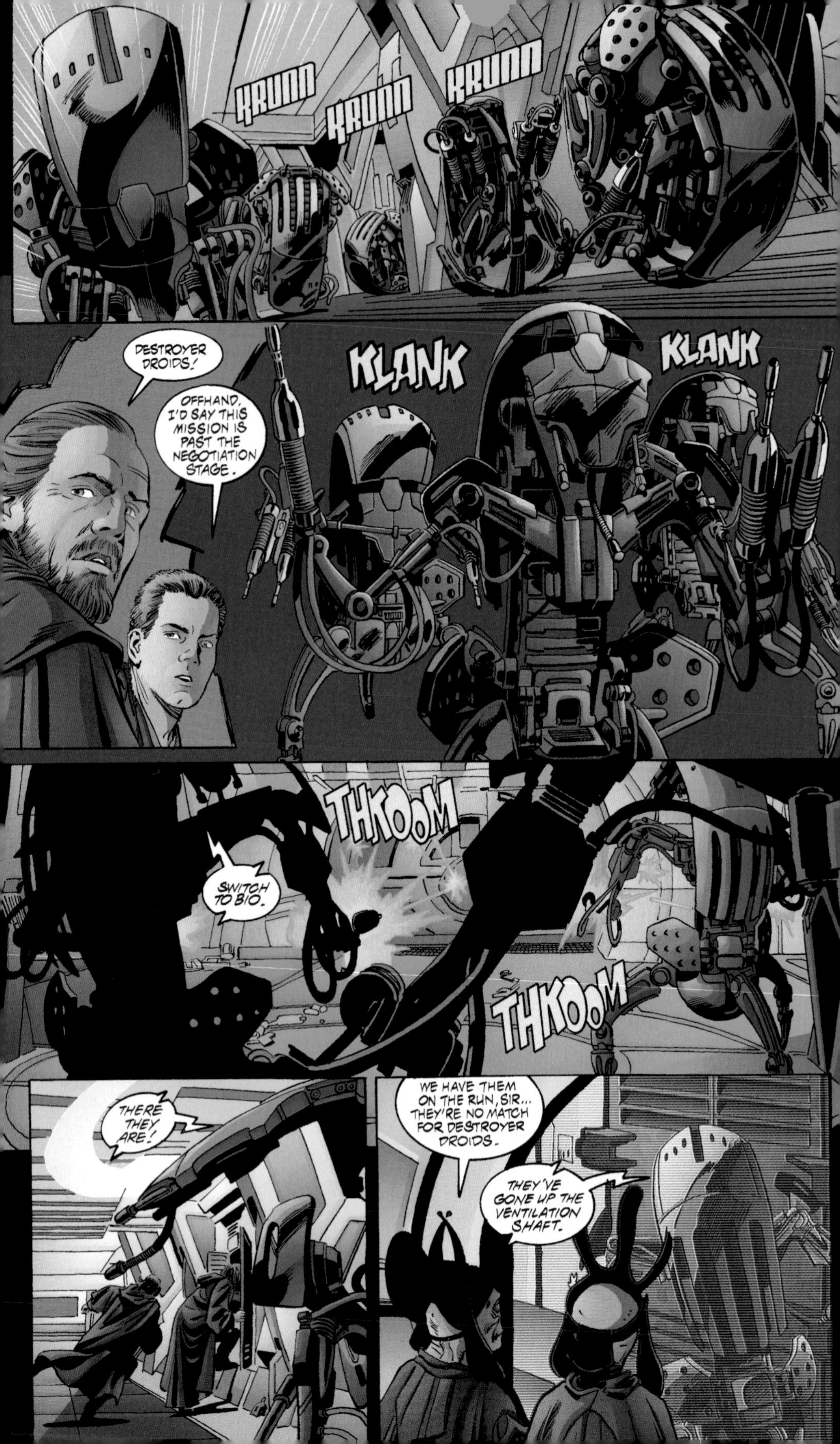
KRUNN
KRUNN
KRUNN
DESTROYER DROIDS!
OFFHAND, I'D SAY THIS MISSION IS PAST THE NEGOTIATION STAGE.
KLANK
KLANK
THKOOM
SWITCH TO BIO.
THKOOM
THERE THEY ARE!
WE HAVE THEM ON THE RUN, SIR... THEY'RE NO MATCH FOR DESTROYER DROIDS.
THEY'VE GONE UP THE VENTILATION SHAFT.

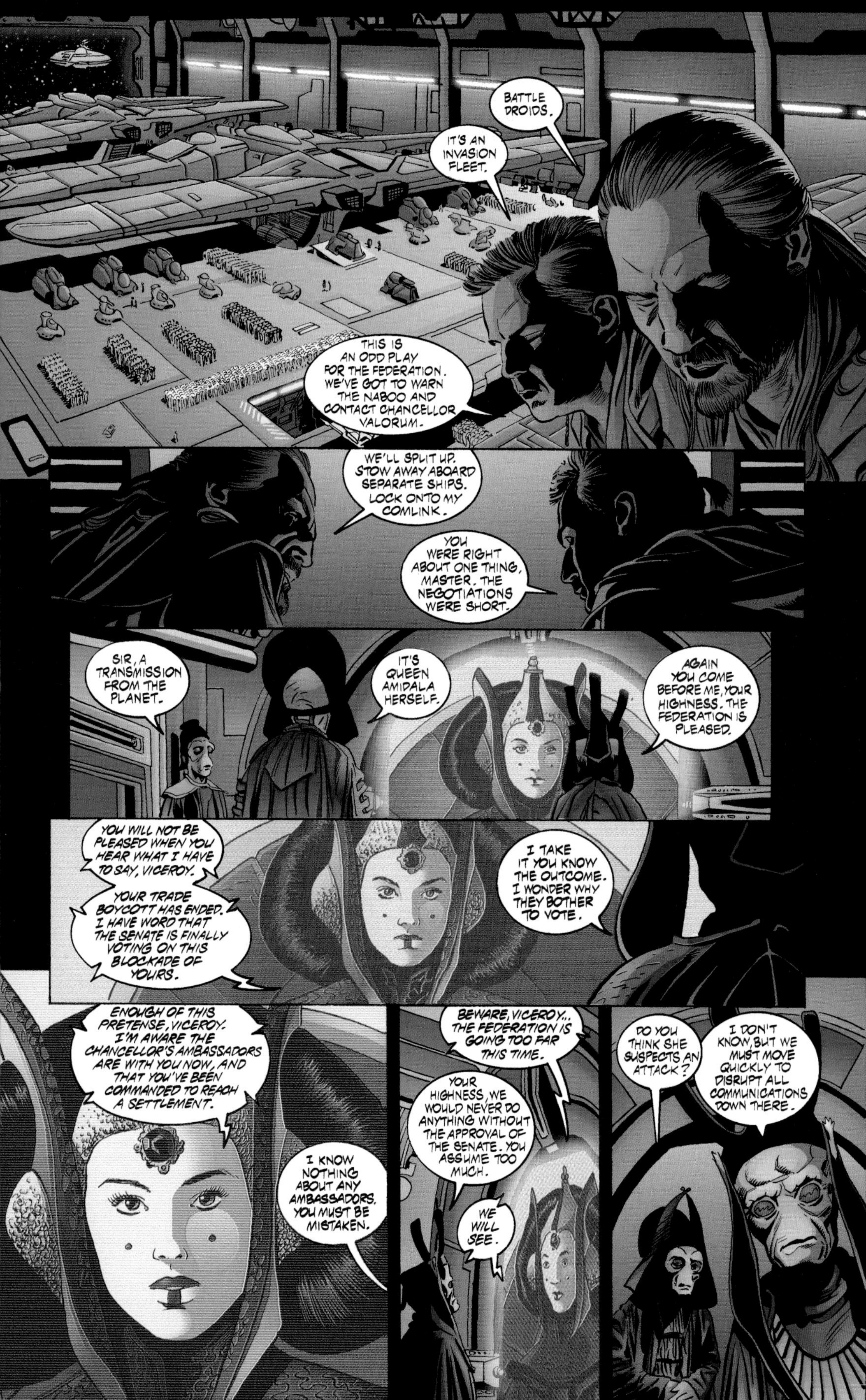
BATTLE DROIDS.
IT'S AN INVASION FLEET.
THIS IS AN ODD PLAY FOR THE FEDERATION. WE'VE GOT TO WARN THE NABOO AND CONTACT CHANCELLOR VALORUM.
WE'LL SPLIT UP. STOW AWAY ABOARD SEPARATE SHIPS. LOCK ONTO MY COMLINK.
YOU WERE RIGHT ABOUT ONE THING, MASTER. THE NEGOTIATIONS WERE SHORT.
SIR, A TRANSMISSION FROM THE PLANET.
IT'S QUEEN AMIDALA HERSELF.
AGAIN YOU COME BEFORE ME, YOUR HIGHNESS. THE FEDERATION IS PLEASED.
YOU WILL NOT BE PLEASED WHEN YOU HEAR WHAT I HAVE TO SAY, VICEROY.
YOUR TRADE BOYCOTT HAS ENDED. I HAVE WORD THAT THE SENATE IS FINALLY VOTING ON THIS BLOCKADE OF YOURS.
I TAKE IT YOU KNOW THE OUTCOME. I WONDER WHY THEY BOTHER TO VOTE.
ENOUGH OF THIS PRETENSE, VICEROY. I'M AWARE THE CHANCELLOR'S AMBASSADORS ARE WITH YOU NOW, AND THAT YOU'VE BEEN COMMANDED TO REACH A SETTLEMENT.
I KNOW NOTHING ABOUT ANY AMBASSADORS. YOU MUST BE MISTAKEN.
BEWARE, VICEROY... THE FEDERATION IS GOING TOO FAR THIS TIME.
YOUR HIGHNESS, WE WOULD NEVER DO ANYTHING WITHOUT THE APPROVAL OF THE SENATE. YOU ASSUME TOO MUCH.
WE WILL SEE.
DO YOU THINK SHE SUSPECTS AN ATTACK?
I DON'T KNOW, BUT WE MUST MOVE QUICKLY TO DISRUPT ALL COMMUNICATIONS DOWN THERE.

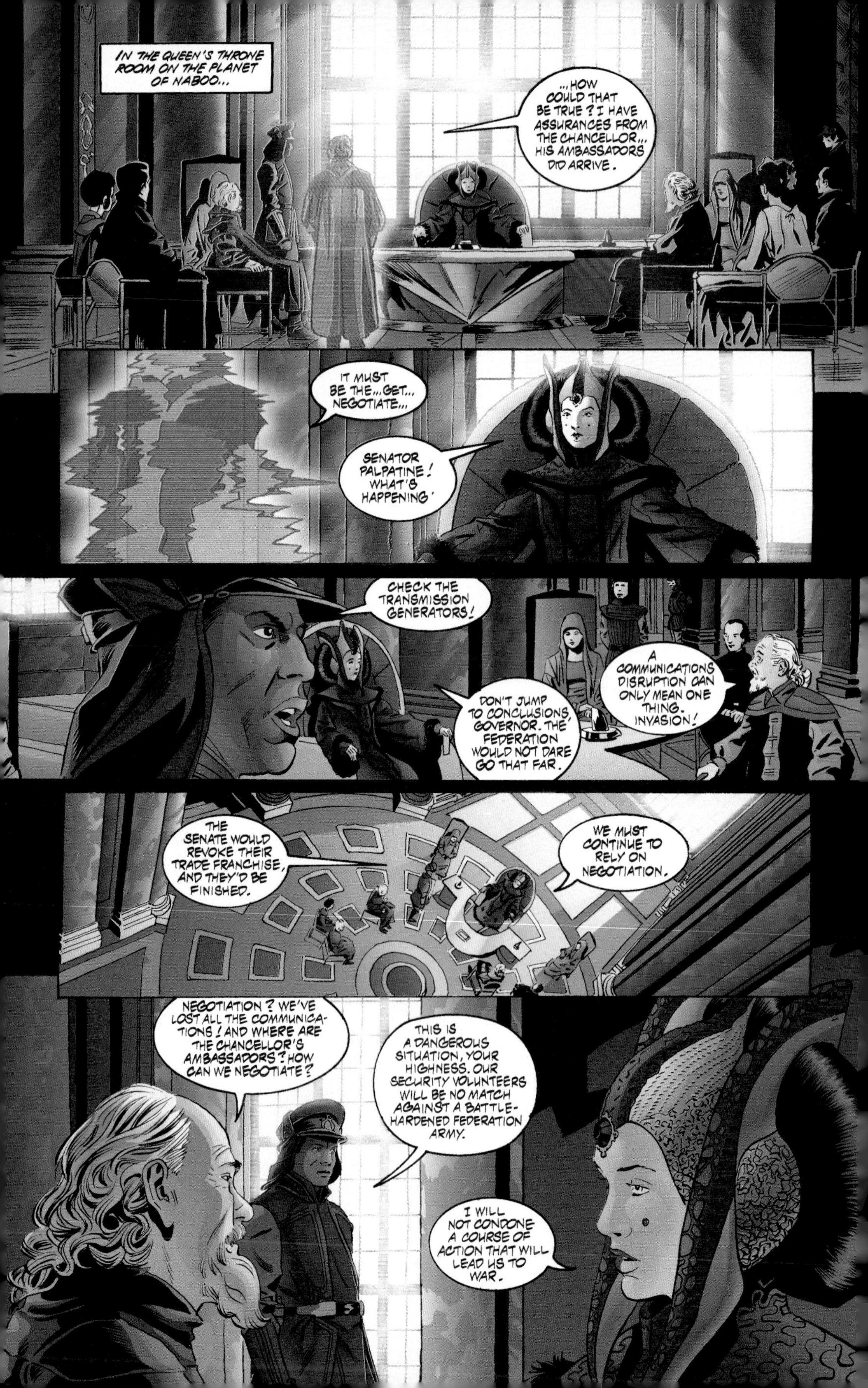
IN THE QUEEN'S THRONE ROOM ON THE PLANET OF NABOO...
...HOW COULD THAT BE TRUE? I HAVE ASSURANCES FROM THE CHANCELLOR... HIS AMBASSADORS DID ARRIVE.
IT MUST BE THE... GET... NEGOTIATE...
SENATOR PALPATINE! WHAT'S HAPPENING'
CHECK THE TRANSMISSION GENERATORS!
DON'T JUMP TO CONCLUSIONS, GOVERNOR. THE FEDERATION WOULD NOT DARE GO THAT FAR.
A COMMUNICATIONS DISRUPTION CAN ONLY MEAN ONE THING. INVASION!
THE SENATE WOULD REVOKE THEIR TRADE FRANCHISE, AND THEY'D BE FINISHED.
WE MUST CONTINUE TO RELY ON NEGOTIATION.
NEGOTIATION? WE'VE LOST ALL THE COMMUNICATIONS! AND WHERE ARE THE CHANCELLOR'S AMBASSADORS? HOW CAN WE NEGOTIATE?
THIS IS A DANGEROUS SITUATION, YOUR HIGHNESS. OUR SECURITY VOLUNTEERS WILL BE NO MATCH AGAINST A BATTLE-HARDENED FEDERATION ARMY.
I WILL NOT CONDONE A COURSE OF ACTION THAT WILL LEAD US TO WAR.

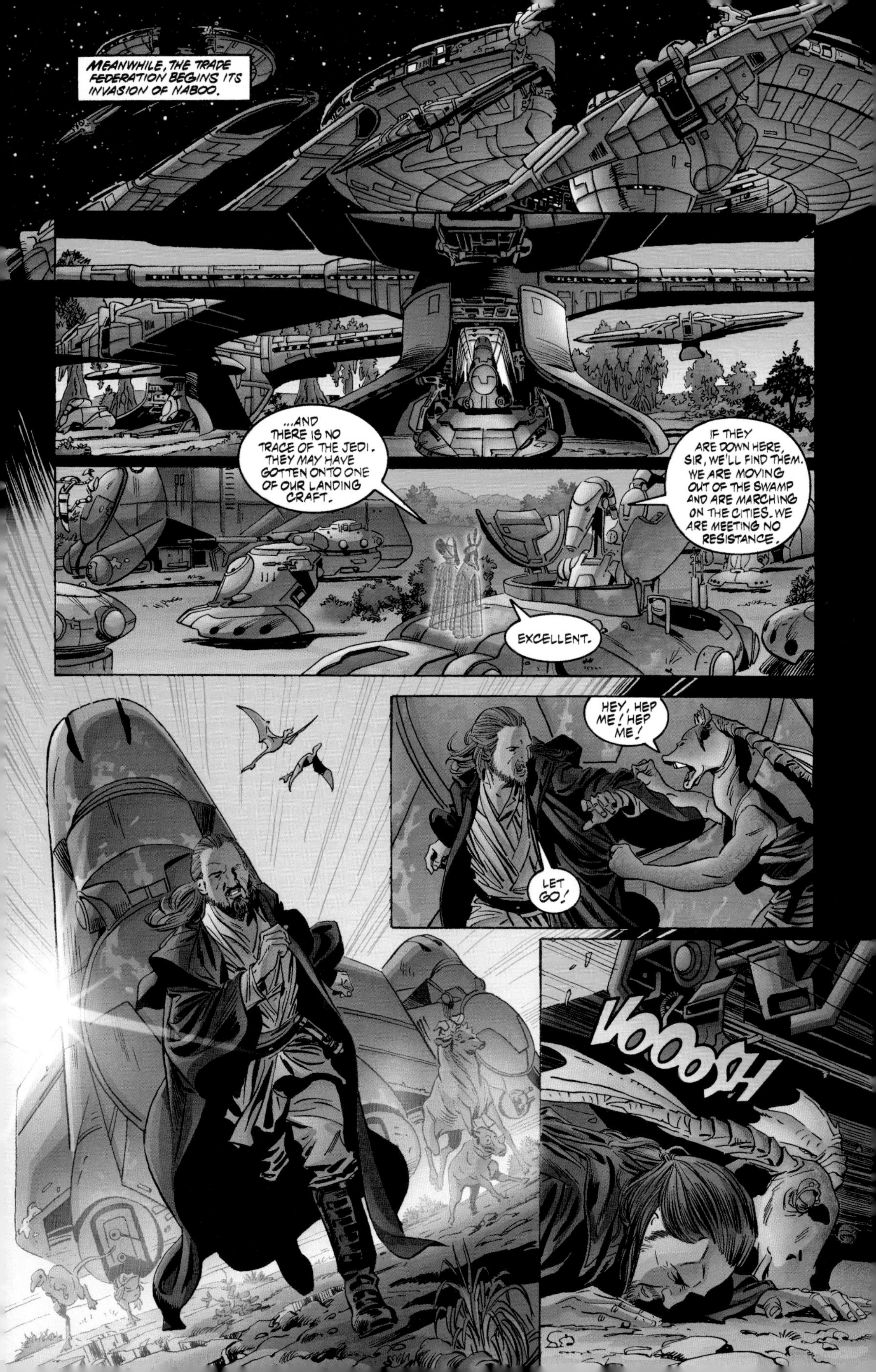
MEANWHILE, THE TRADE FEDERATION BEGINS ITS INVASION OF NABOO.
...AND THERE IS NO TRACE OF THE JEDI. THEY MAY HAVE GOTTEN ONTO ONE OF OUR LANDING CRAFT.
IF THEY ARE DOWN HERE, SIR, WE'LL FIND THEM. WE ARE MOVING OUT OF THE SWAMP AND ARE MARCHING ON THE CITIES. WE ARE MEETING NO RESISTANCE.
EXCELLENT.
HEY, HEP ME! HEP ME!
LET GO!
VOOOSH

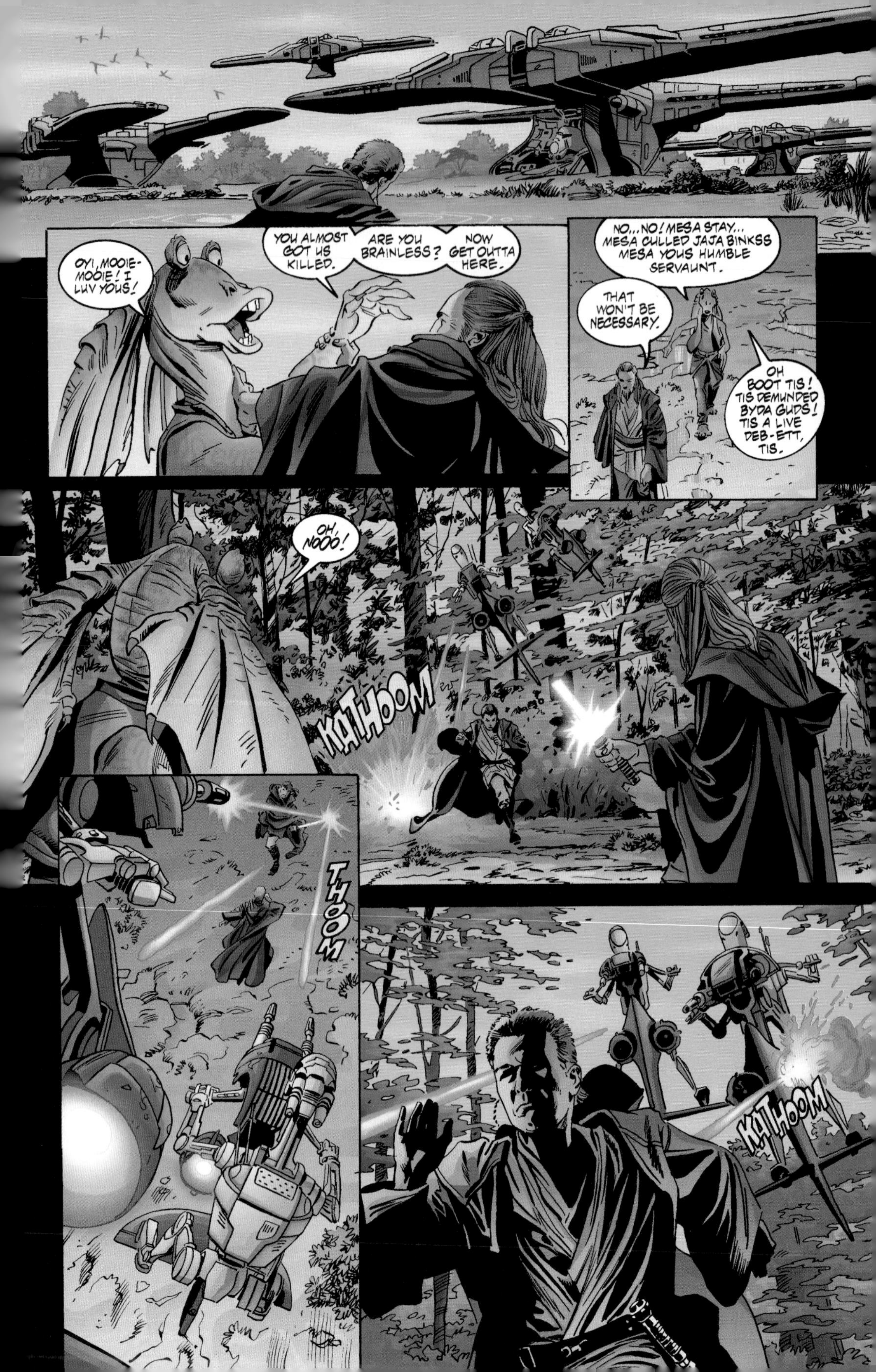
OY!, MOOIE-MOOIE! I LUV YOUS!
YOU ALMOST GOT US KILLED.
ARE YOU BRAINLESS?
NOW GET OUTTA HERE.
NO...NO! MESA STAY... MESA CULLED JAJA BINKSS MESA YOUS HUMBLE SERVAUNT.
THAT WON'T BE NECESSARY.
OH BOOT TIS! TIS DEMUNDED BYDA GUDS! TIS A LIVE DEB-ETT, TIS.
OH, NOOO!
KATHOOM
THOOOM
KATHOOM

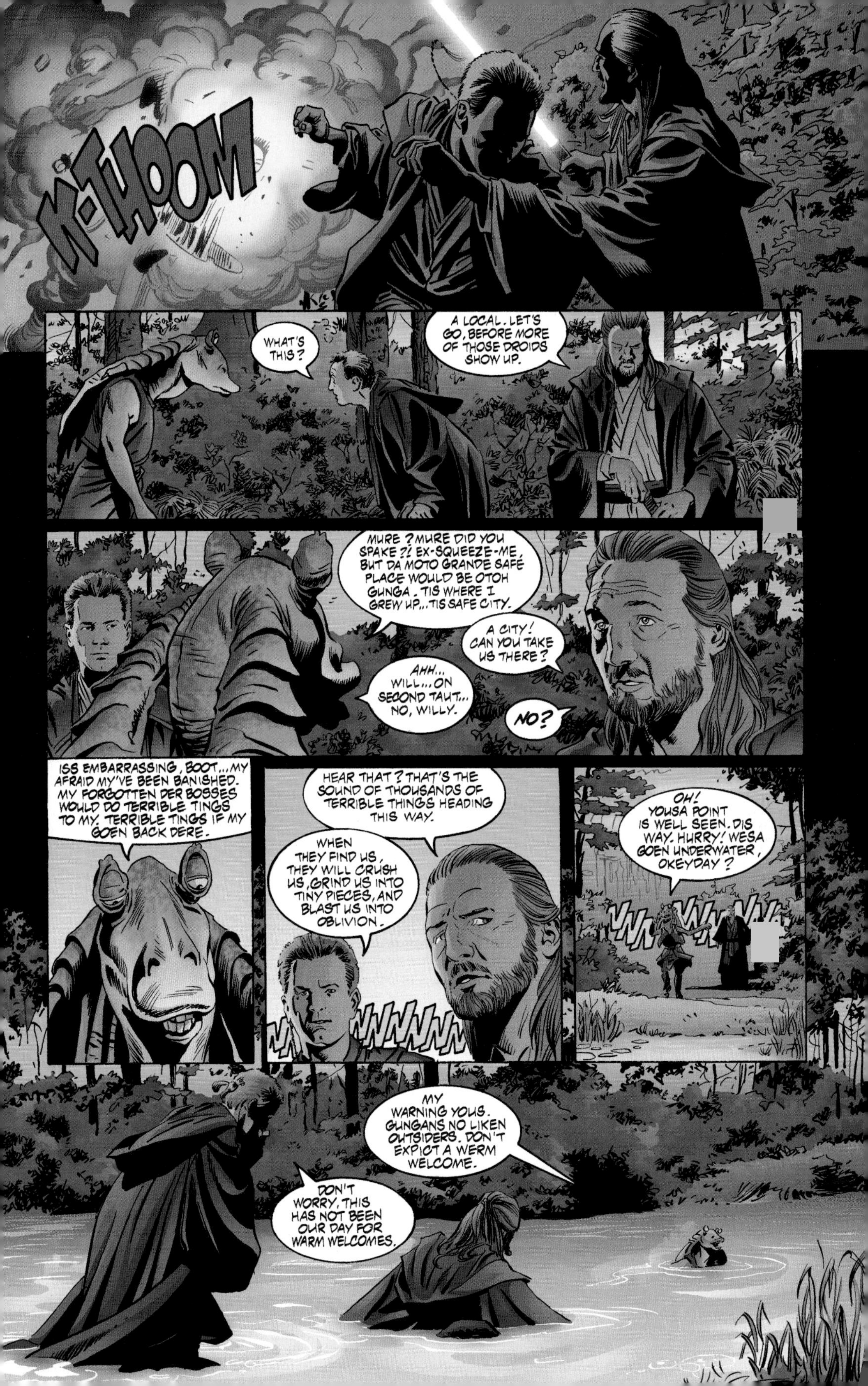
K-THOOM
WHAT'S THIS?
A LOCAL. LET'S GO, BEFORE MORE OF THOSE DROIDS SHOW UP.
MURE? MURE DID YOU SPAKE?! EX-SQUEEZE-ME, BUT DA MOTO GRANDE SAFE PLACE WOULD BE OTOH GUNGA. TIS WHERE I GREW UP... TIS SAFE CITY.
A CITY! CAN YOU TAKE US THERE?
AHH... WILL... ON SECOND TAUT... NO, WILLY.
NO?
ISS EMBARRASSING, BOOT... MY AFRAID MY'VE BEEN BANISHED. MY FORGOTTEN DER BOSSES WOULD DO TERRIBLE TINGS TO MY. TERRIBLE TINGS IF MY GOEN BACK DERE.
HEAR THAT? THAT'S THE SOUND OF THOUSANDS OF TERRIBLE THINGS HEADING THIS WAY.
WHEN THEY FIND US, THEY WILL CRUSH US, GRIND US INTO TINY PIECES, AND BLAST US INTO OBLIVION.
OH! YOUSA POINT IS WELL SEEN. DIS WAY. HURRY! WESA GOEN UNDERWATER, OKEYDAY?
MY WARNING YOUS. GUNGANS NO LIKEN OUTSIDERS. DON'T EXPICT A WERM WELCOME.
DON'T WORRY, THIS HAS NOT BEEN OUR DAY FOR WARM WELCOMES.

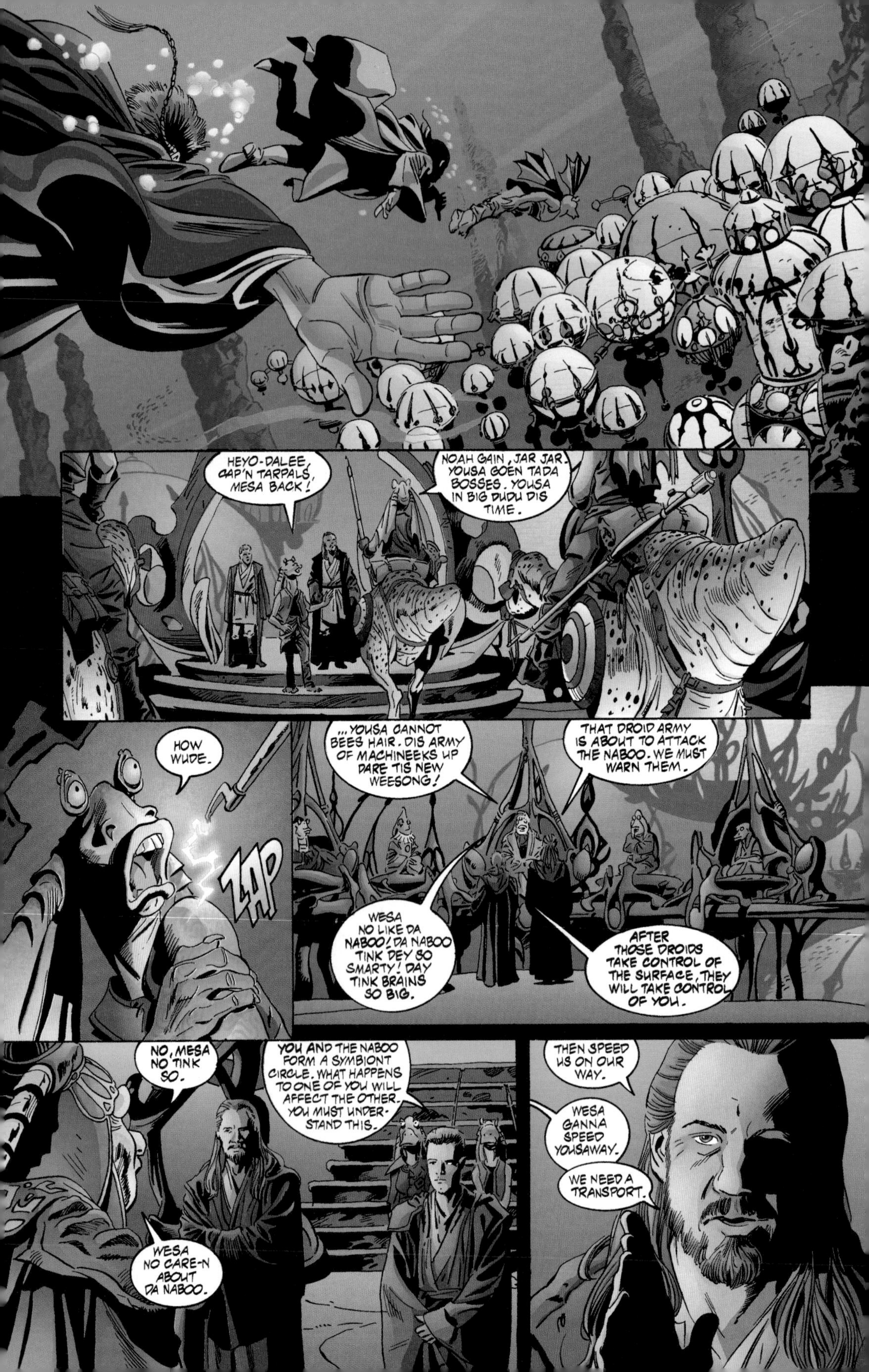
HEYO-DALEE, CAP'N TARPALS, MESA BACK!
NOAH GAIN, JAR JAR. YOUSA GOEN TADA BOSSES. YOUSA IN BIG DUDU DIS TIME.
HOW WUDE.
ZAP
...YOUSA CANNOT BEES HAIR. DIS ARMY OF MACHINEEKS UP DARE TIS NEW WEESONG!
THAT DROID ARMY IS ABOUT TO ATTACK THE NABOO. WE MUST WARN THEM.
WESA NO LIKE DA NABOO! DA NABOO TINK DEY SO SMARTY! DAY TINK BRAINS SO BIG.
AFTER THOSE DROIDS TAKE CONTROL OF THE SURFACE, THEY WILL TAKE CONTROL OF YOU.
NO, MESA NO TINK SO.
WESA NO CARE-N ABOUT DA NABOO.
YOU AND THE NABOO FORM A SYMBIONT CIRCLE. WHAT HAPPENS TO ONE OF YOU WILL AFFECT THE OTHER. YOU MUST UNDERSTAND THIS.
THEN SPEED US ON OUR WAY.
WESA GANNA SPEED YOUSAWAY.
WE NEED A TRANSPORT.

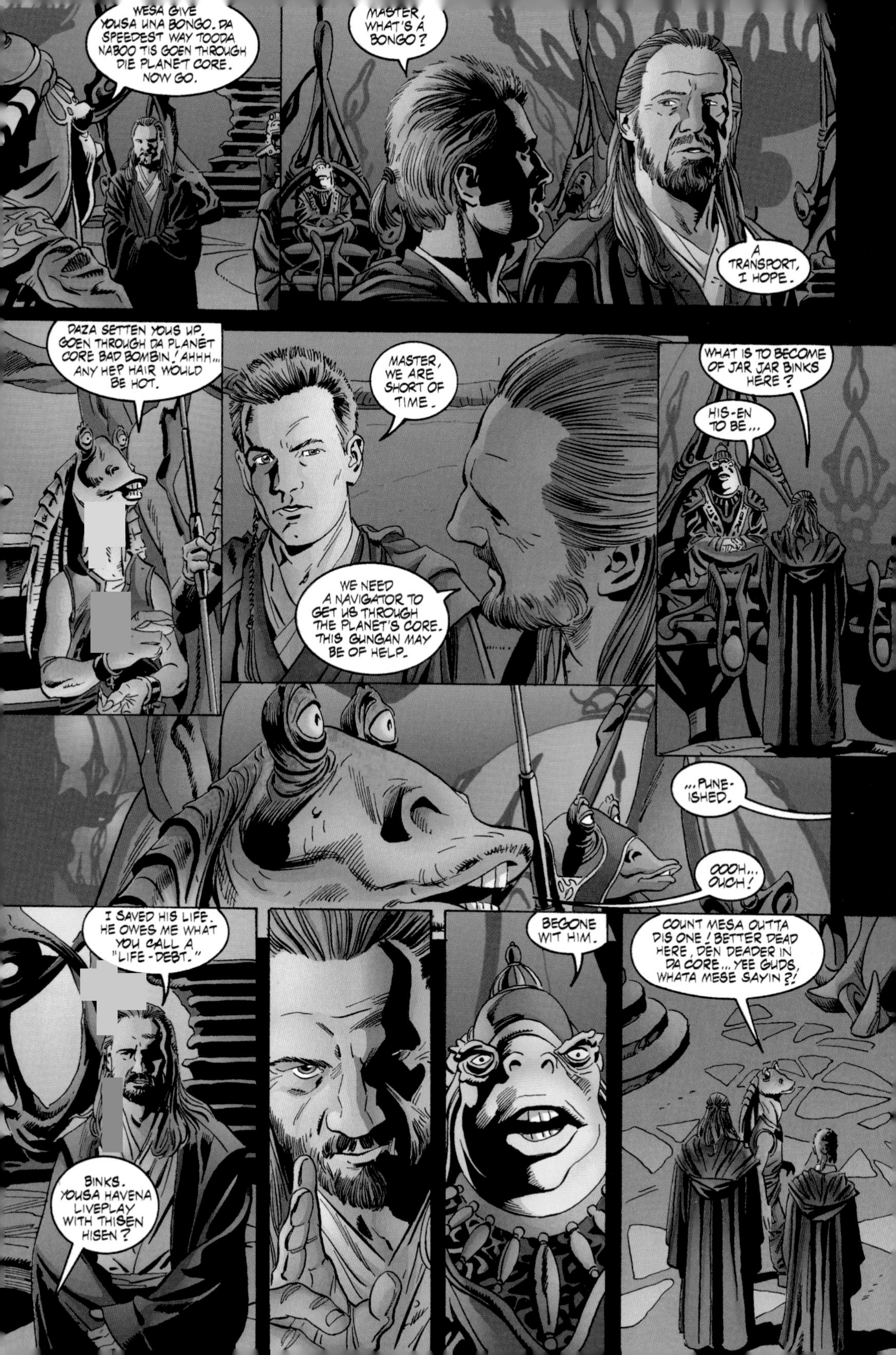
WESA GIVE YOUSA UNA BONGO. DA SPEEDEST WAY TOODA NABOO TIS GOEN THROUGH DIE PLANET CORE. NOW GO.
MASTER, WHAT'S A BONGO?
A TRANSPORT, I HOPE.
DAZA SETTEN YOUS UP. GOEN THROUGH DA PLANET CORE BAD BOMBIN! AHHH... ANY HEP HAIR WOULD BE HOT.
MASTER, WE ARE SHORT OF TIME.
WE NEED A NAVIGATOR TO GET US THROUGH THE PLANET'S CORE. THIS GUNGAN MAY BE OF HELP.
WHAT IS TO BECOME OF JAR JAR BINKS HERE?
HIS-EN TO BE...
...PUNE-ISHED.
OOOH... OUCH!
I SAVED HIS LIFE. HE OWES ME WHAT YOU CALL A "LIFE-DEBT."
BINKS. YOUSA HAVENA LIVEPLAY WITH THISEN HISEN?
BEGONE WIT HIM.
COUNT MESA OUTTA DIS ONE! BETTER DEAD HERE, DEN DEADER IN DA CORE... YEE GUDS, WHATA MESE SAYIN?!

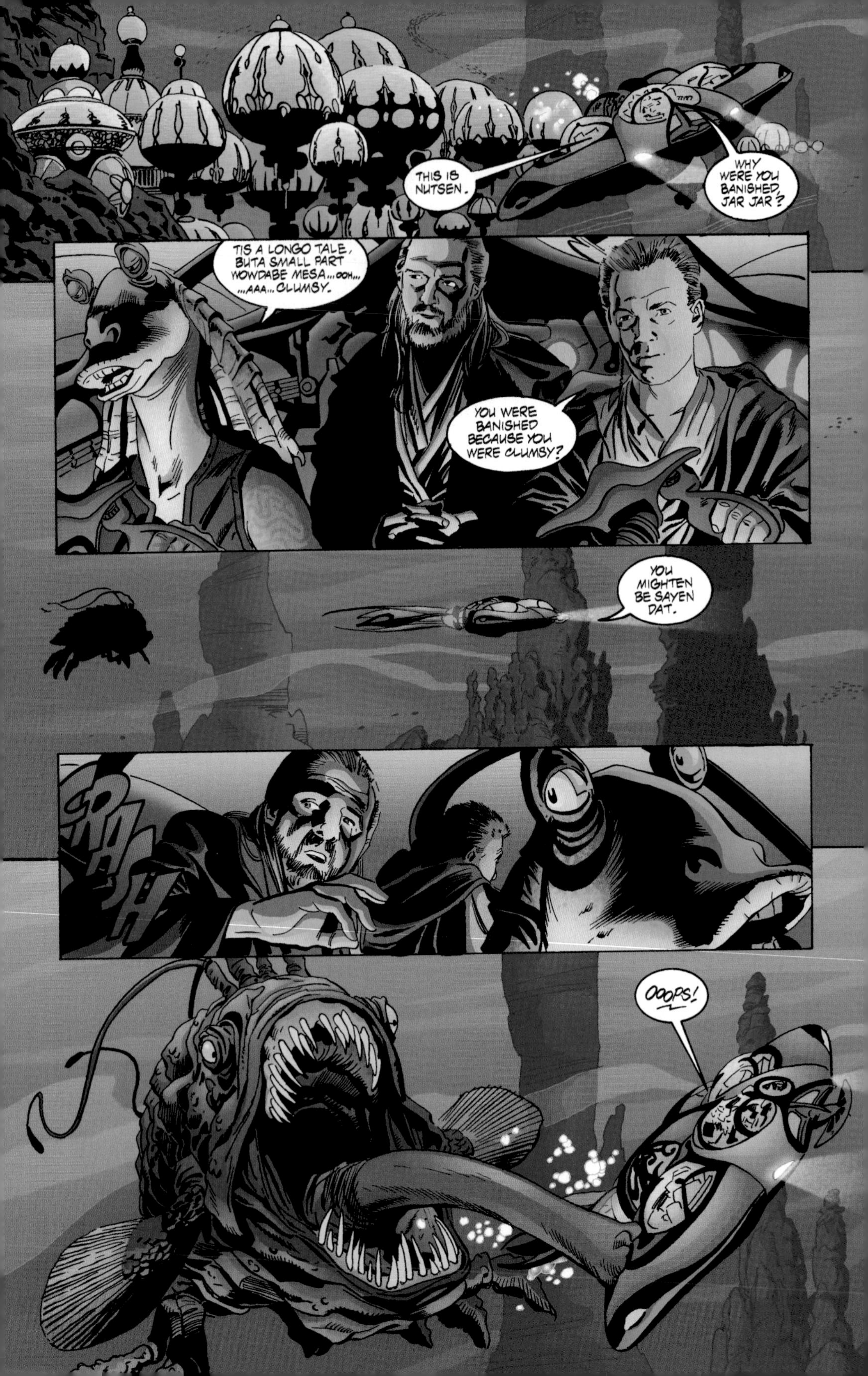
THIS IS NUTSEN.
WHY WERE YOU BANISHED, JAR JAR?
TIS A LONGO TALE, BUTA SMALL PART WOWDABE MESA...OOH... ...AAA...CLUMSY.
YOU WERE BANISHED BECAUSE YOU WERE CLUMSY?
YOU MIGHTEN BE SAYEN DAT.
CRASH
OOOPS!

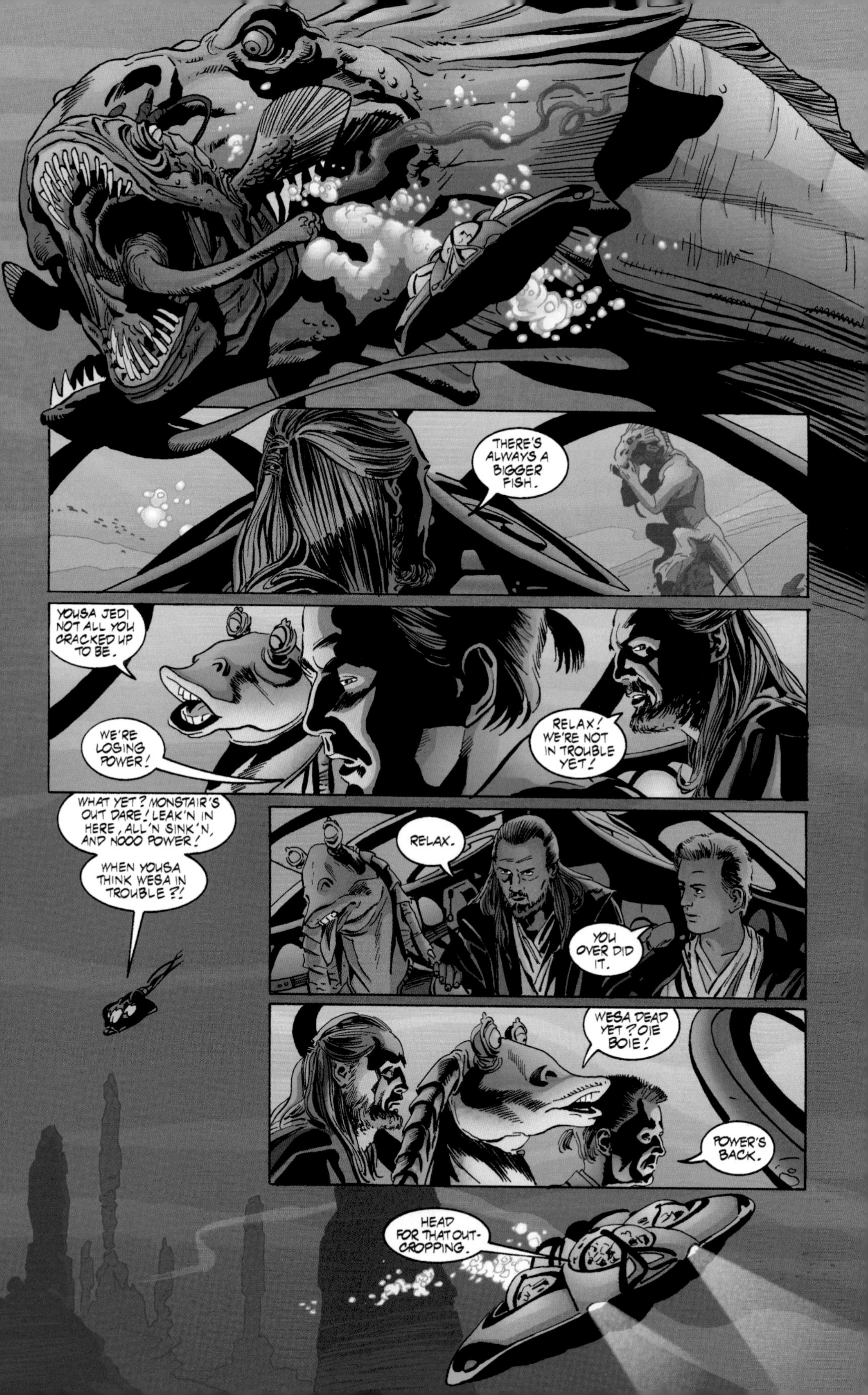
THERE'S ALWAYS A BIGGER FISH.
YOUSA JEDI NOT ALL YOU CRACKED UP TO BE.
WE'RE LOSING POWER!
RELAX! WE'RE NOT IN TROUBLE YET!
WHAT YET? MONSTAIR'S OUT DARE! LEAK'N IN HERE, ALL'N SINK'N, AND NOOO POWER!
WHEN YOUSA THINK WESA IN TROUBLE?!
RELAX.
YOU OVER DID IT.
WESA DEAD YET? OIE BOIE!
POWER'S BACK.
HEAD FOR THAT OUT-CROPPING.

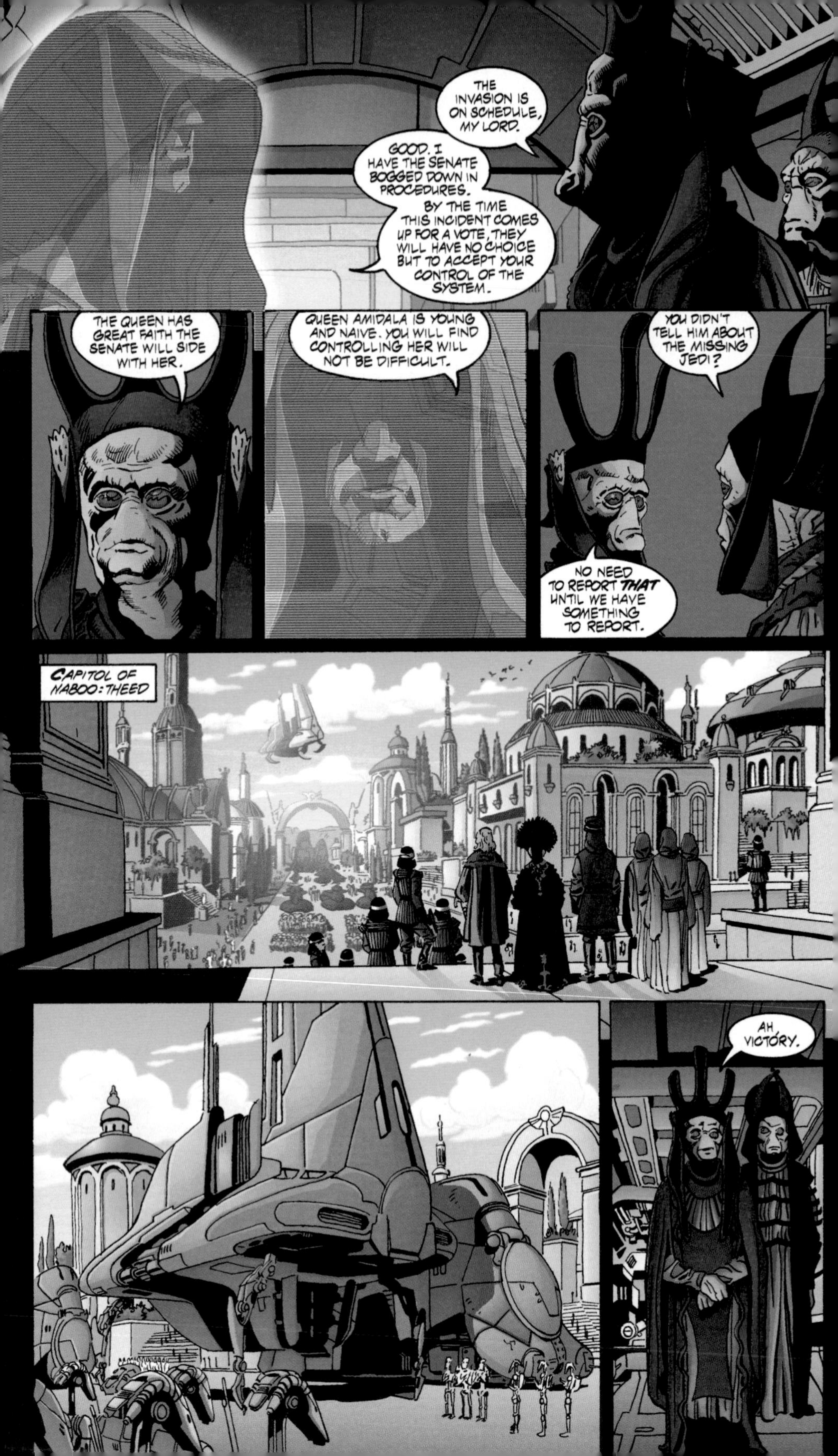
THE INVASION IS ON SCHEDULE, MY LORD.
GOOD. I HAVE THE SENATE BOGGED DOWN IN PROCEDURES.
BY THE TIME THIS INCIDENT COMES UP FOR A VOTE, THEY WILL HAVE NO CHOICE BUT TO ACCEPT YOUR CONTROL OF THE SYSTEM.
THE QUEEN HAS GREAT FAITH THE SENATE WILL SIDE WITH HER.
QUEEN AMIDALA IS YOUNG AND NAIVE. YOU WILL FIND CONTROLLING HER WILL NOT BE DIFFICULT.
YOU DIDN'T TELL HIM ABOUT THE MISSING JEDI?
NO NEED TO REPORT THAT UNTIL WE HAVE SOMETHING TO REPORT.
CAPITOL OF NABOO: THEED
AH VICTORY.

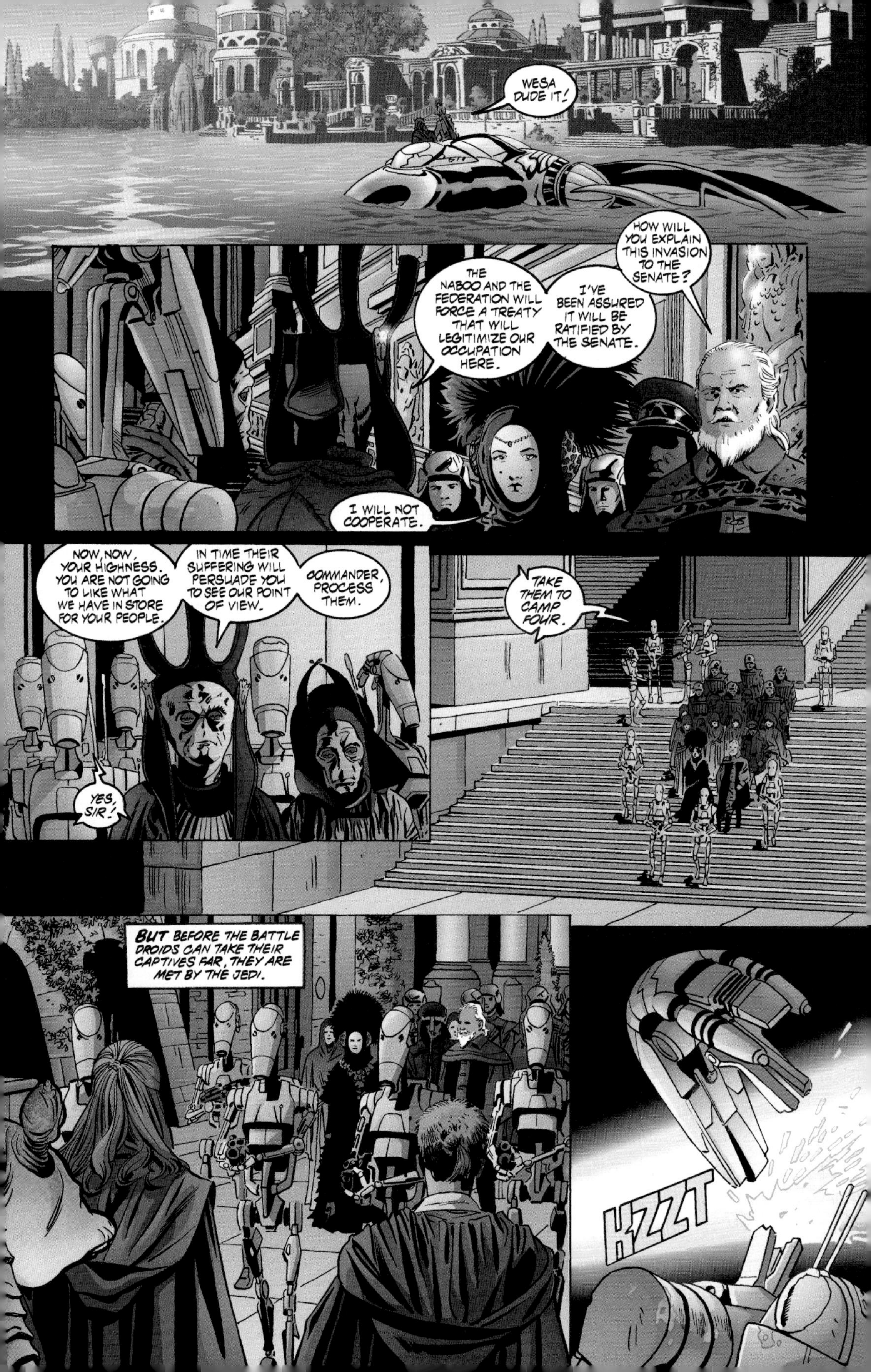
WESA DUDE IT!
HOW WILL YOU EXPLAIN THIS INVASION TO THE SENATE?
I'VE BEEN ASSURED IT WILL BE RATIFIED BY THE SENATE.
THE NABOO AND THE FEDERATION WILL FORCE A TREATY THAT WILL LEGITIMIZE OUR OCCUPATION HERE.
I WILL NOT COOPERATE.
NOW, NOW, YOUR HIGHNESS. YOU ARE NOT GOING TO LIKE WHAT WE HAVE IN STORE FOR YOUR PEOPLE.
IN TIME THEIR SUFFERING WILL PERSUADE YOU TO SEE OUR POINT OF VIEW.
COMMANDER, PROCESS THEM.
YES, SIR!
TAKE THEM TO CAMP FOUR.
BUT BEFORE THE BATTLE DROIDS CAN TAKE THEIR CAPTIVES FAR, THEY ARE MET BY THE JEDI.
HZZT

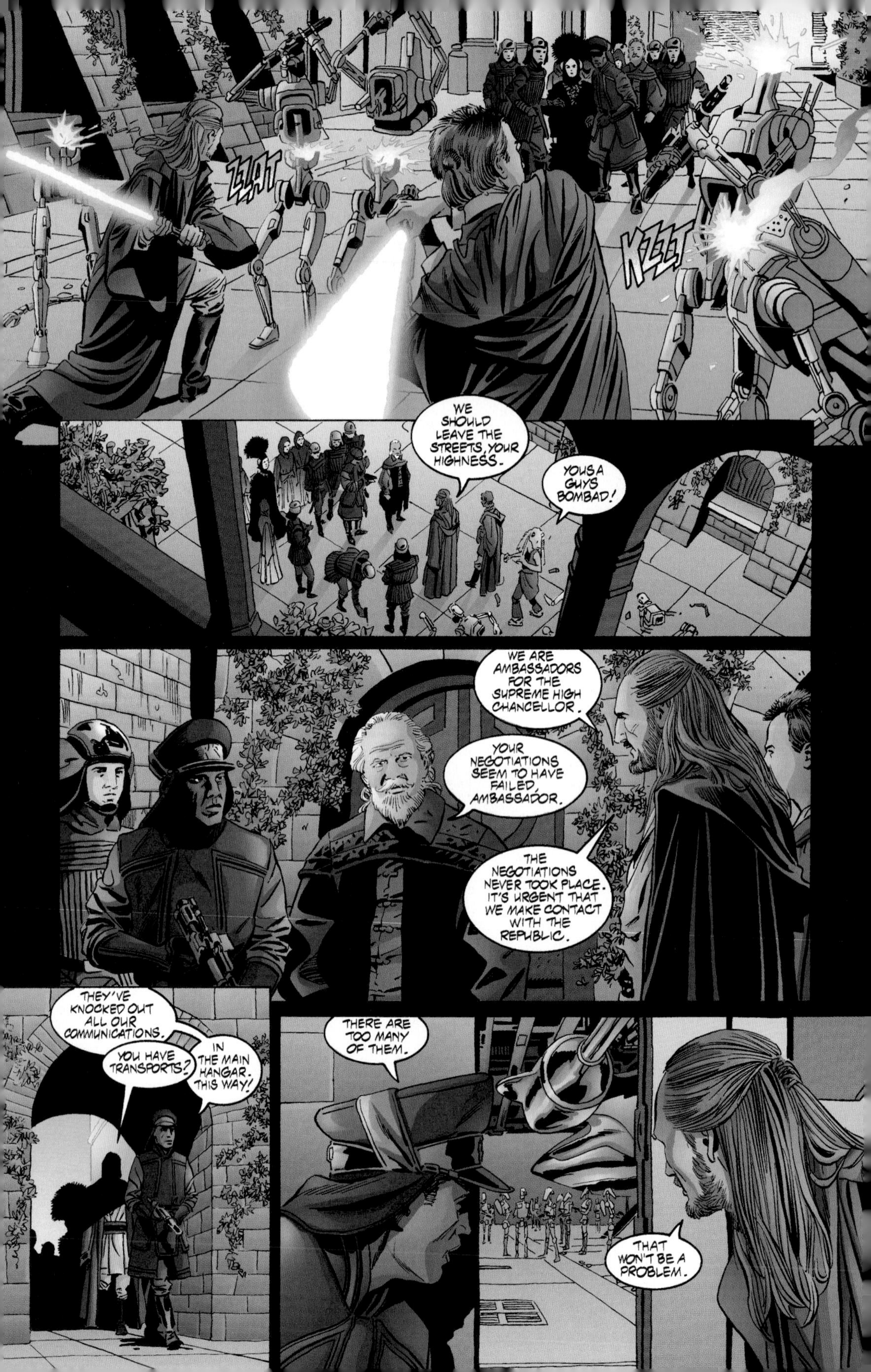

ZZAT
KZEET
WE SHOULD LEAVE THE STREETS, YOUR HIGHNESS.
YOUSA GUYS BOMBAD!
WE ARE AMBASSADORS FOR THE SUPREME HIGH CHANCELLOR.
YOUR NEGOTIATIONS SEEM TO HAVE FAILED, AMBASSADOR.
THE NEGOTIATIONS NEVER TOOK PLACE. IT'S URGENT THAT WE MAKE CONTACT WITH THE REPUBLIC.
THEY'VE KNOCKED OUT ALL OUR COMMUNICATIONS.
YOU HAVE TRANSPORTS?
IN THE MAIN HANGAR. THIS WAY!
THERE ARE TOO MANY OF THEM.
THAT WON'T BE A PROBLEM.

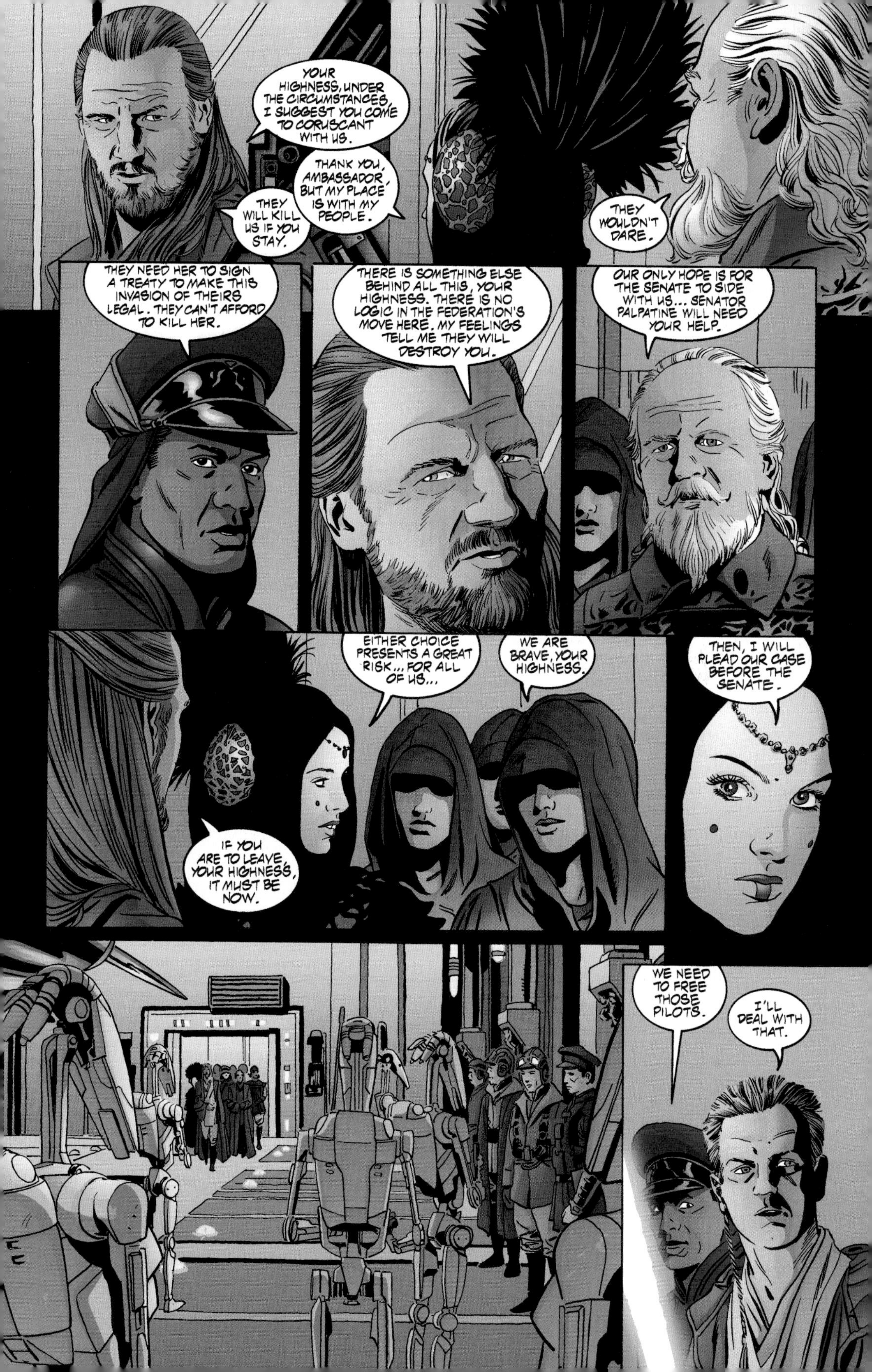

YOUR HIGHNESS, UNDER THE CIRCUMSTANCES, I SUGGEST YOU COME TO CORUSCANT WITH US.
THANK YOU, AMBASSADOR, BUT MY PLACE IS WITH MY PEOPLE.
THEY WILL KILL US IF YOU STAY.
THEY WOULDN'T DARE.
THEY NEED HER TO SIGN A TREATY TO MAKE THIS INVASION OF THEIRS LEGAL. THEY CAN'T AFFORD TO KILL HER.
THERE IS SOMETHING ELSE BEHIND ALL THIS, YOUR HIGHNESS. THERE IS NO LOGIC IN THE FEDERATION'S MOVE HERE. MY FEELINGS TELL ME THEY WILL DESTROY YOU.
OUR ONLY HOPE IS FOR THE SENATE TO SIDE WITH US... SENATOR PALPATINE WILL NEED YOUR HELP.
IF YOU ARE TO LEAVE, YOUR HIGHNESS, IT MUST BE NOW.
EITHER CHOICE PRESENTS A GREAT RISK... FOR ALL OF US...
WE ARE BRAVE, YOUR HIGHNESS.
THEN, I WILL PLEAD OUR CASE BEFORE THE SENATE.
WE NEED TO FREE THOSE PILOTS.
I'LL DEAL WITH THAT.

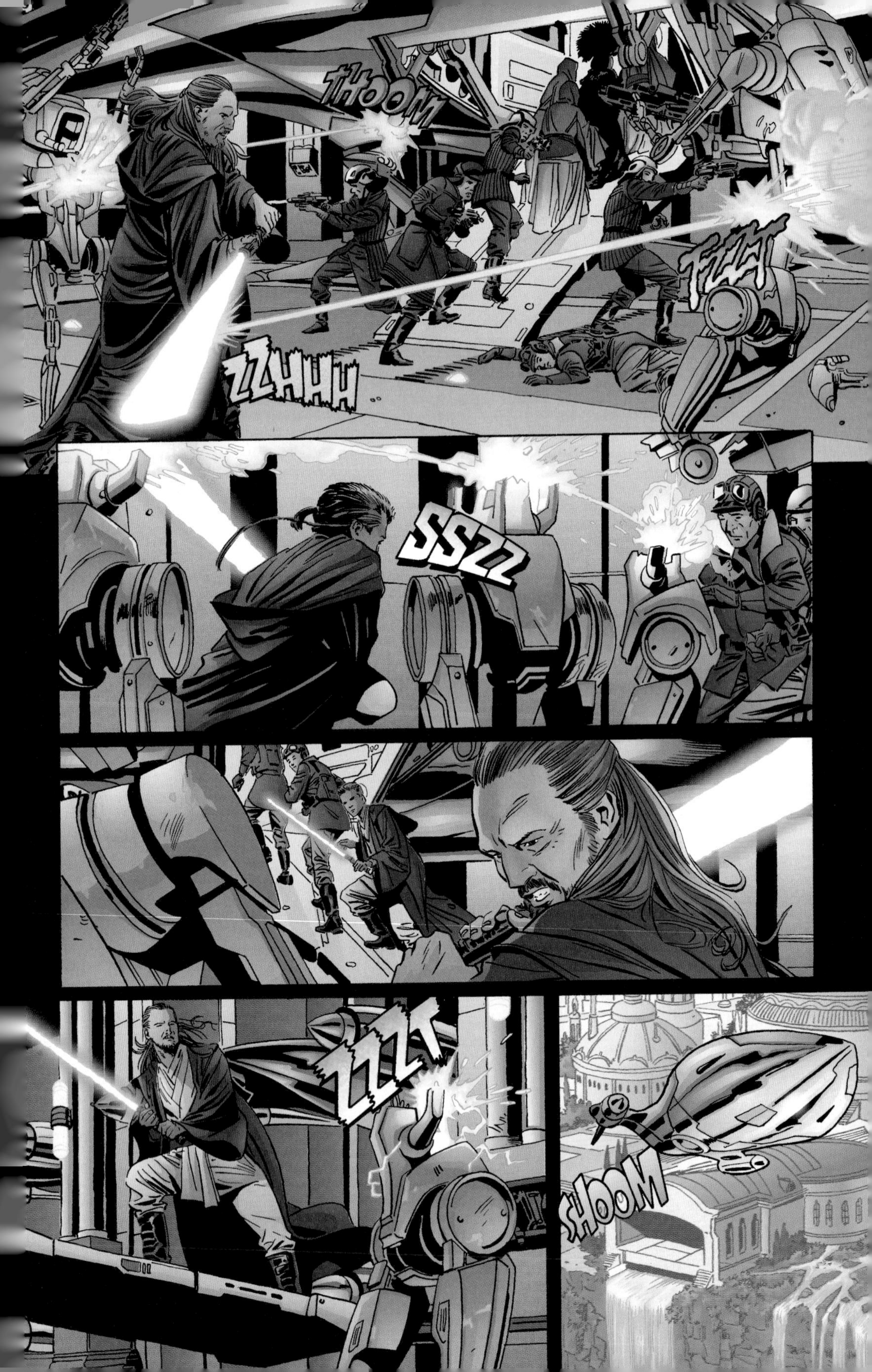
THOOM
FZZT
ZZHHH
SSZZ
ZZZT
SHOOM

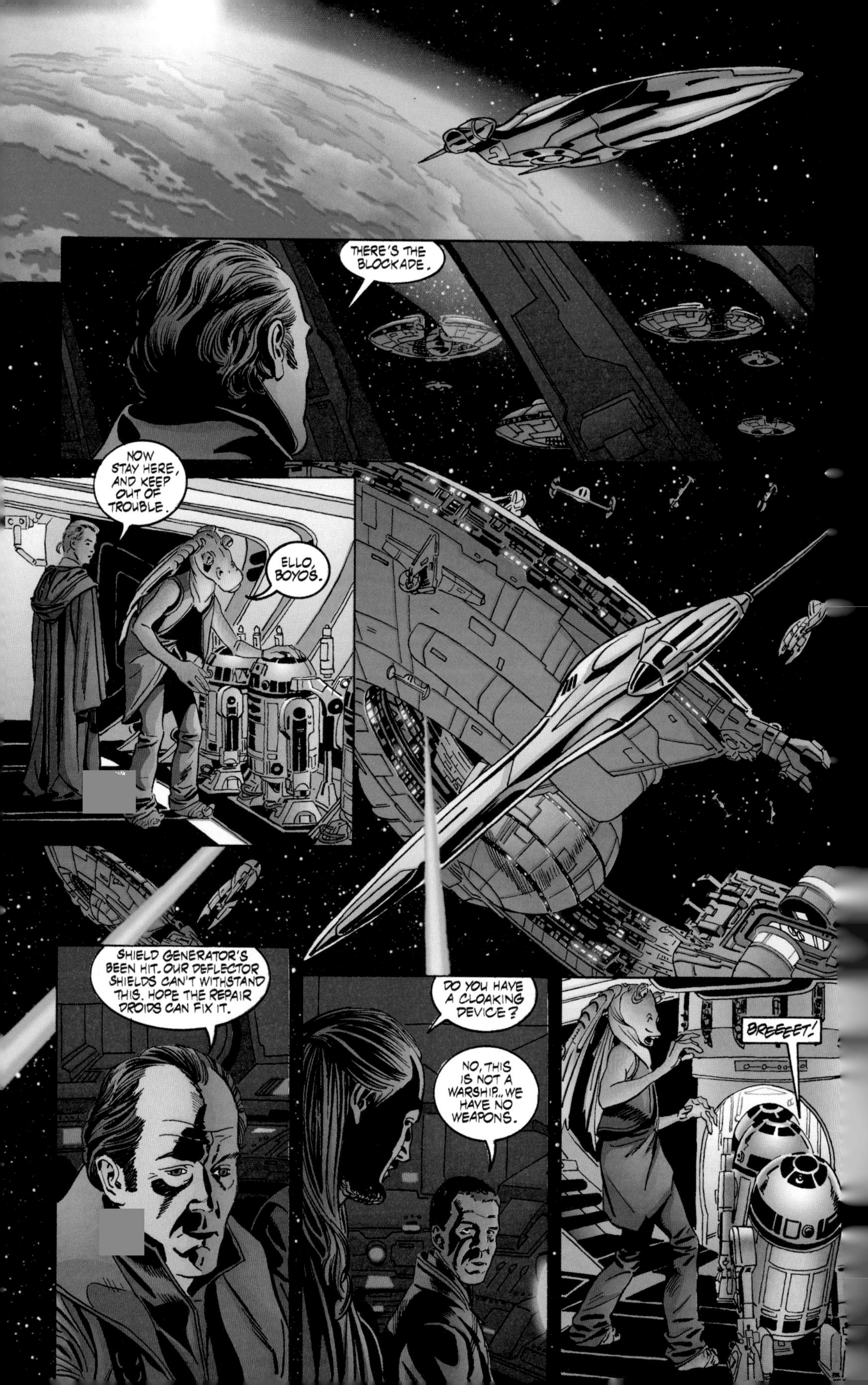
THERE'S THE BLOCKADE.
NOW STAY HERE, AND KEEP OUT OF TROUBLE.
ELLO, BOYOS.
SHIELD GENERATOR'S BEEN HIT. OUR DEFLECTOR SHIELDS CAN'T WITHSTAND THIS. HOPE THE REPAIR DROIDS CAN FIX IT.
DO YOU HAVE A CLOAKING DEVICE?
NO, THIS IS NOT A WARSHIP... WE HAVE NO WEAPONS.
BREEEEET!

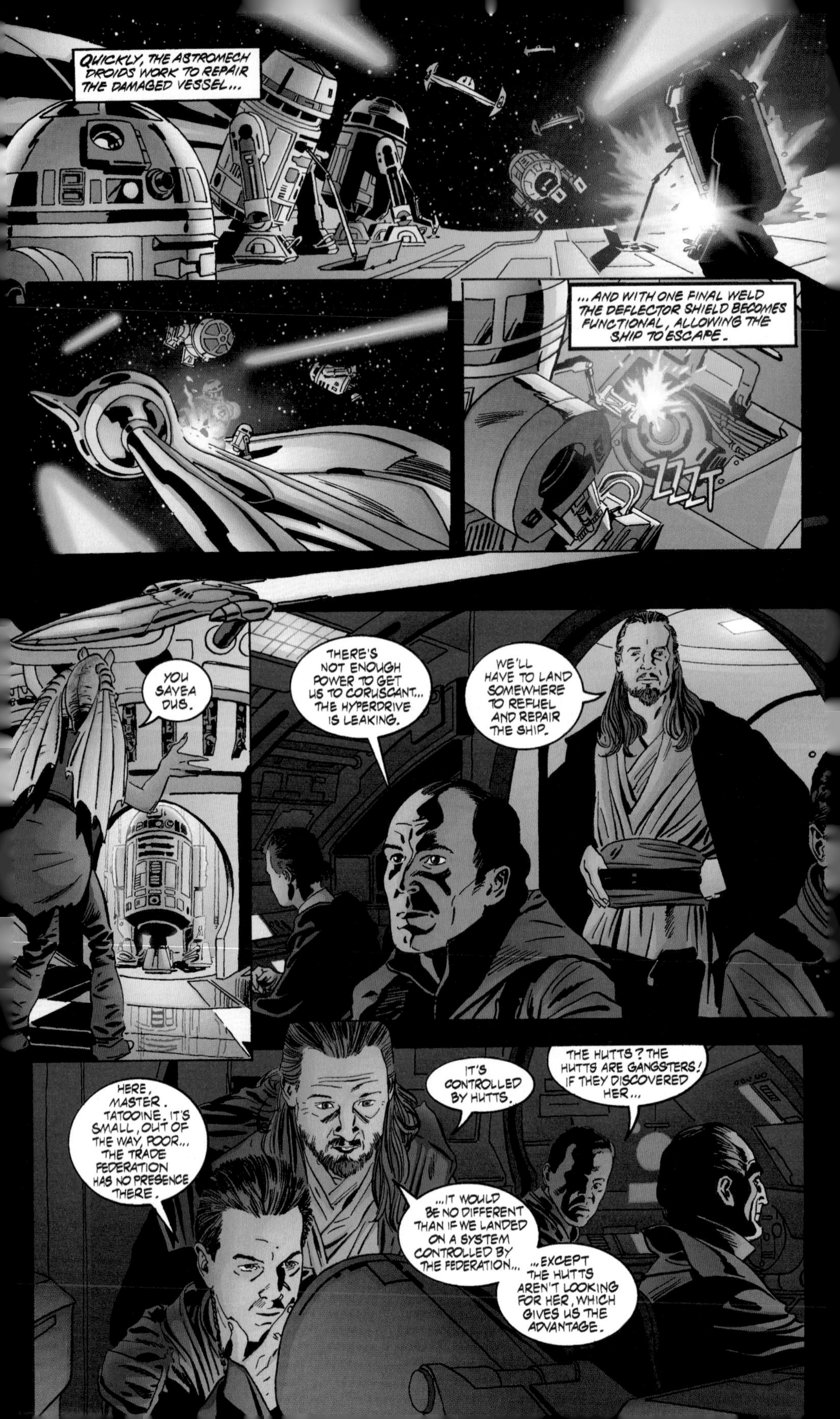
QUICKLY, THE ASTROMECH DROIDS WORK TO REPAIR THE DAMAGED VESSEL...
...AND WITH ONE FINAL WELD THE DEFLECTOR SHIELD BECOMES FUNCTIONAL, ALLOWING THE SHIP TO ESCAPE.
ZZZT
YOU SAYEA DUS.
THERE'S NOT ENOUGH POWER TO GET US TO CORUSCANT... THE HYPERDRIVE IS LEAKING.
WE'LL HAVE TO LAND SOMEWHERE TO REFUEL AND REPAIR THE SHIP.
HERE, MASTER. TATOOINE. IT'S SMALL, OUT OF THE WAY, POOR... THE TRADE FEDERATION HAS NO PRESENCE THERE.
IT'S CONTROLLED BY HUTTS.
THE HUTTS? THE HUTTS ARE GANGSTERS! IF THEY DISCOVERED HER...
...IT WOULD BE NO DIFFERENT THAN IF WE LANDED ON A SYSTEM CONTROLLED BY THE FEDERATION...
...EXCEPT THE HUTTS AREN'T LOOKING FOR HER, WHICH GIVES US THE ADVANTAGE.

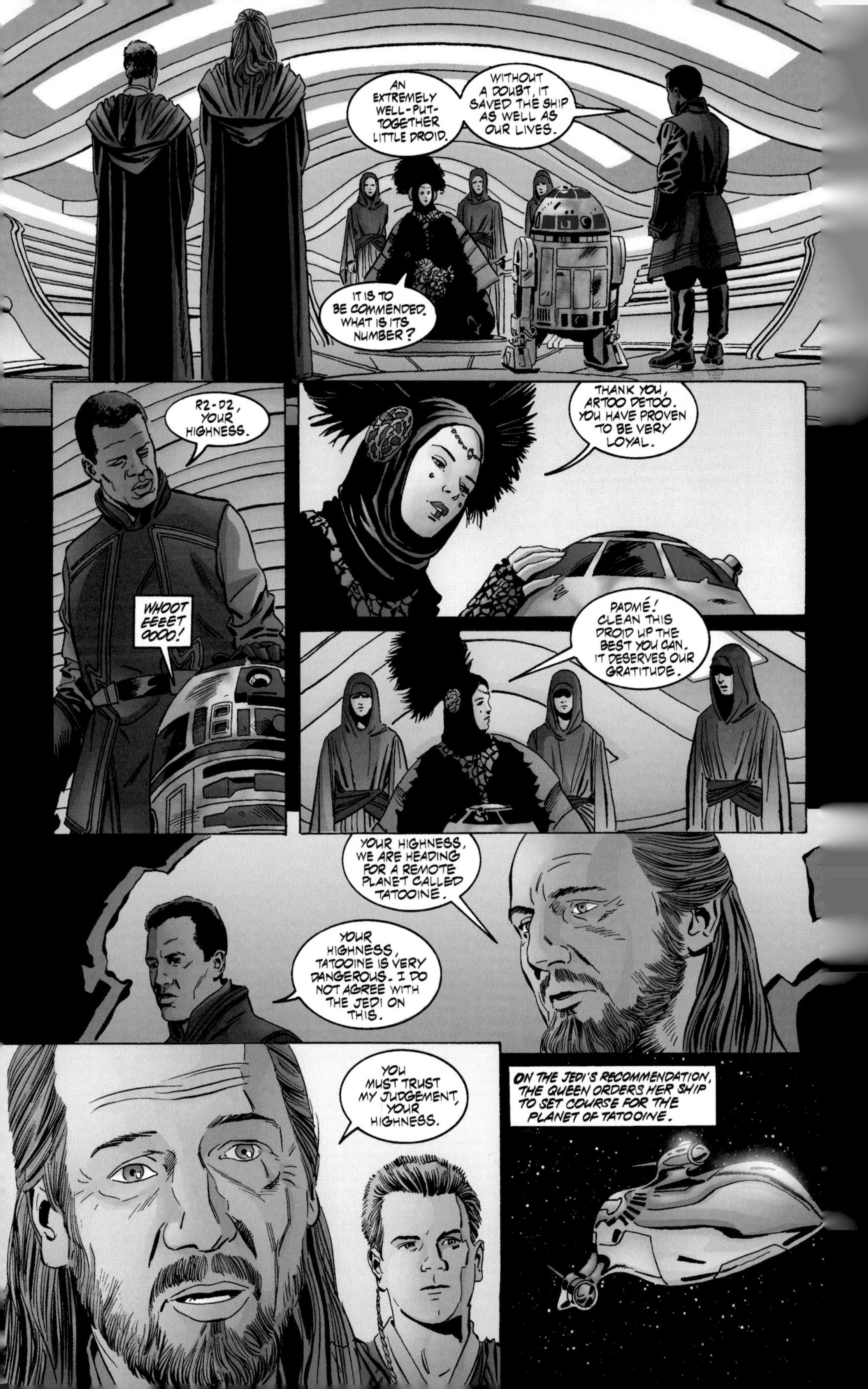
AN EXTREMELY WELL-PUT-TOGETHER LITTLE DROID.
WITHOUT A DOUBT, IT SAVED THE SHIP AS WELL AS OUR LIVES.
IT IS TO BE COMMENDED. WHAT IS ITS NUMBER?
R2-D2, YOUR HIGHNESS.
WHOOT EEEET OOOO!
THANK YOU, ARTOO DETOO. YOU HAVE PROVEN TO BE VERY LOYAL.
PADMÉ! CLEAN THIS DROID UP THE BEST YOU CAN. IT DESERVES OUR GRATITUDE.
YOUR HIGHNESS, WE ARE HEADING FOR A REMOTE PLANET CALLED TATOOINE.
YOUR HIGHNESS, TATOOINE IS VERY DANGEROUS. I DO NOT AGREE WITH THE JEDI ON THIS.
YOU MUST TRUST MY JUDGEMENT, YOUR HIGHNESS.
ON THE JEDI'S RECOMMENDATION, THE QUEEN ORDERS HER SHIP TO SET COURSE FOR THE PLANET OF TATOOINE.

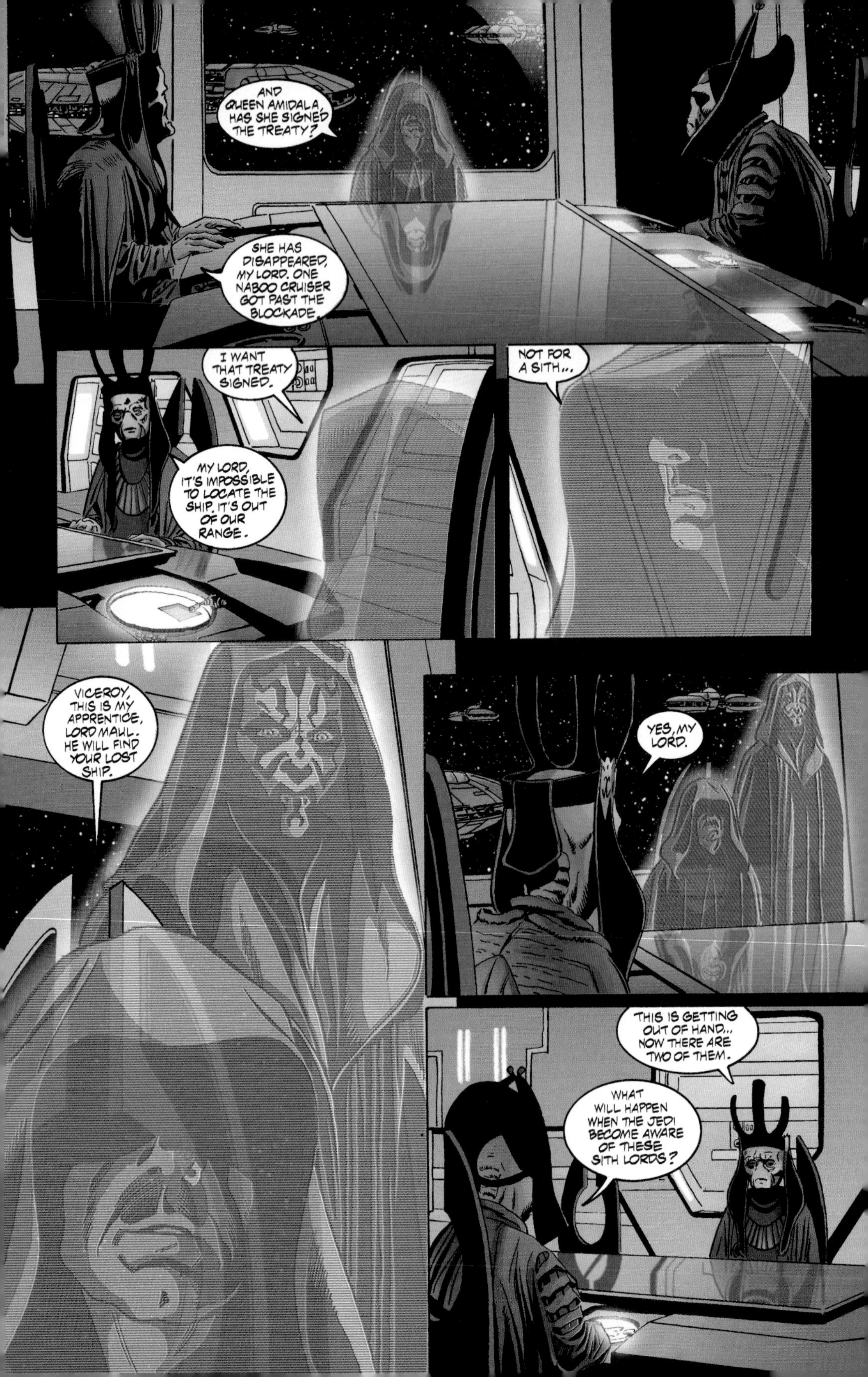
AND QUEEN AMIDALA, HAS SHE SIGNED THE TREATY?
SHE HAS DISAPPEARED, MY LORD. ONE NABOO CRUISER GOT PAST THE BLOCKADE.
I WANT THAT TREATY SIGNED.
MY LORD, IT'S IMPOSSIBLE TO LOCATE THE SHIP. IT'S OUT OF OUR RANGE.
NOT FOR A SITH...
VICEROY, THIS IS MY APPRENTICE, LORD MAUL. HE WILL FIND YOUR LOST SHIP.
YES, MY LORD.
THIS IS GETTING OUT OF HAND... NOW THERE ARE TWO OF THEM.
WHAT WILL HAPPEN WHEN THE JEDI BECOME AWARE OF THESE SITH LORDS?

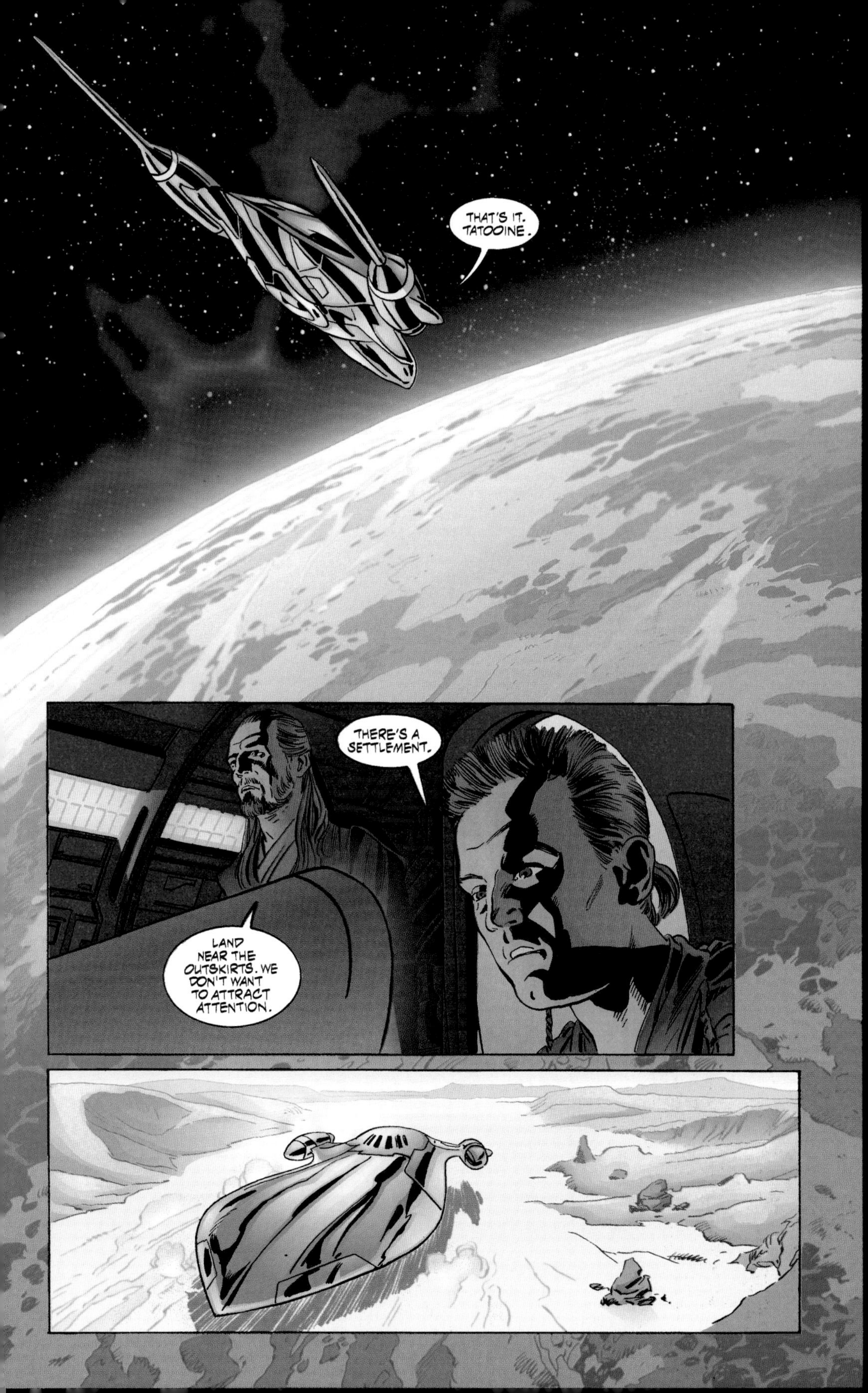
THAT'S IT. TATOOINE.
THERE'S A SETTLEMENT.
LAND NEAR THE OUTSKIRTS. WE DON'T WANT TO ATTRACT ATTENTION.

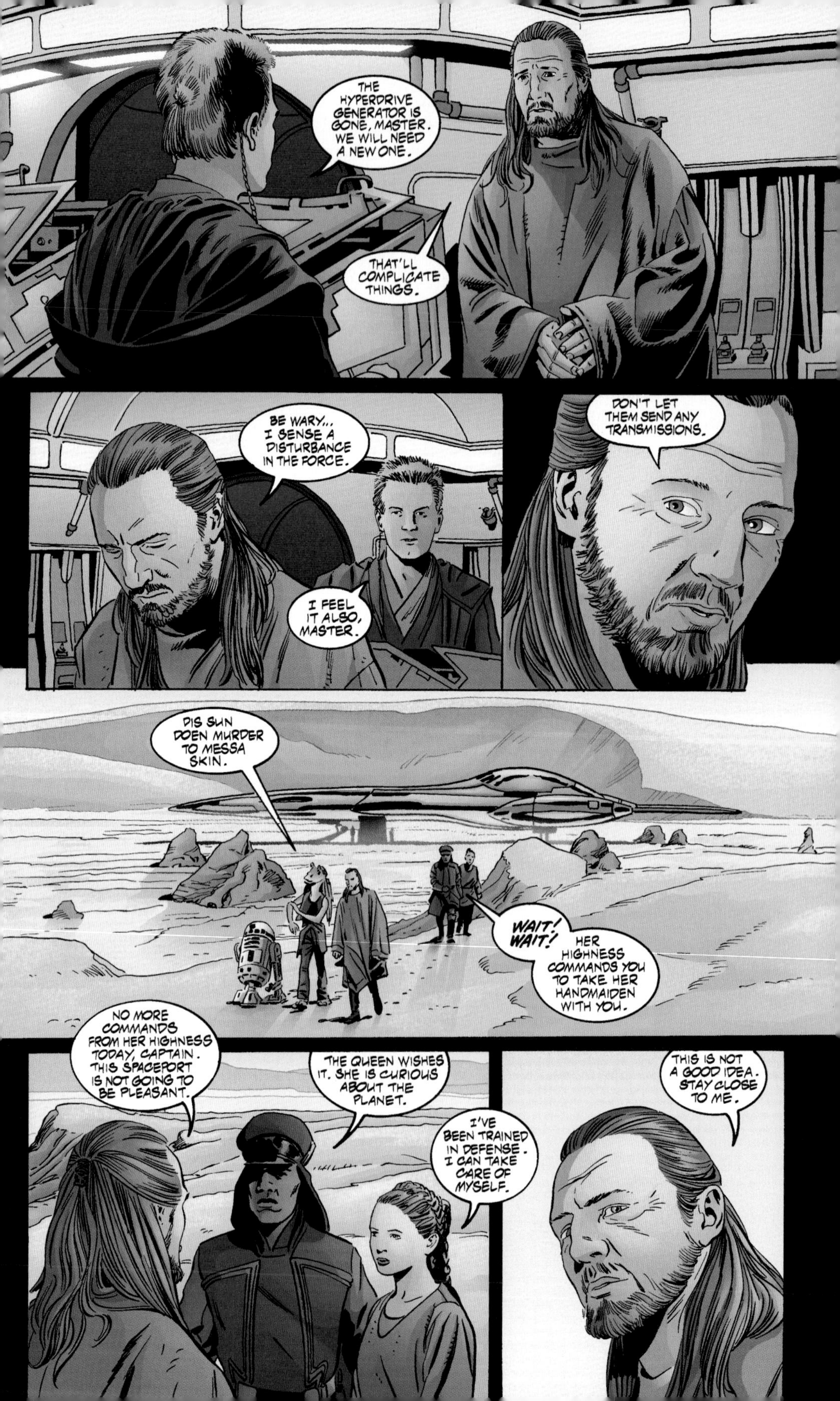
THE HYPERDRIVE GENERATOR IS GONE, MASTER. WE WILL NEED A NEW ONE.
THAT'LL COMPLICATE THINGS.
BE WARY... I SENSE A DISTURBANCE IN THE FORCE.
I FEEL IT ALSO, MASTER.
DON'T LET THEM SEND ANY TRANSMISSIONS.
DIS SUN DOEN MURDER TO MESSA SKIN.
WAIT! WAIT! HER HIGHNESS COMMANDS YOU TO TAKE HER HANDMAIDEN WITH YOU.
NO MORE COMMANDS FROM HER HIGHNESS TODAY, CAPTAIN. THIS SPACEPORT IS NOT GOING TO BE PLEASANT.
THE QUEEN WISHES IT. SHE IS CURIOUS ABOUT THE PLANET.
I'VE BEEN TRAINED IN DEFENSE. I CAN TAKE CARE OF MYSELF.
THIS IS NOT A GOOD IDEA. STAY CLOSE TO ME.

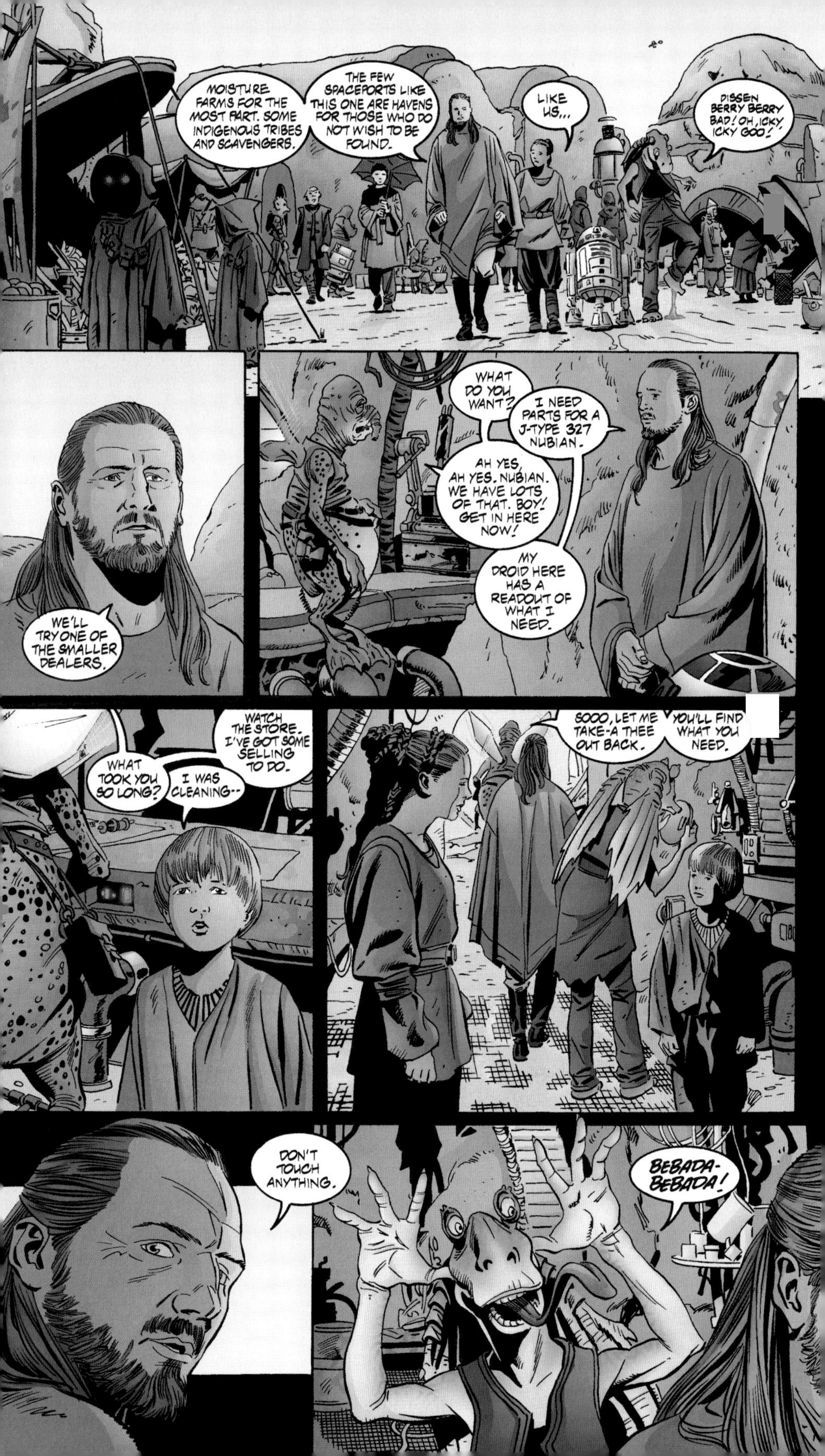
MOISTURE FARMS FOR THE MOST PART. SOME INDIGENOUS TRIBES AND SCAVENGERS.
THE FEW SPACEPORTS LIKE THIS ONE ARE HAVENS FOR THOSE WHO DO NOT WISH TO BE FOUND.
LIKE US...
DISSEN BERRY BERRY BAD! OH, ICKY, ICKY GOO!
WE'LL TRY ONE OF THE SMALLER DEALERS.
WHAT DO YOU WANT?
I NEED PARTS FOR A J-TYPE 327 NUBIAN.
AH YES, AH YES. NUBIAN. WE HAVE LOTS OF THAT. BOY! GET IN HERE NOW!
MY DROID HERE HAS A READOUT OF WHAT I NEED.
WATCH THE STORE. I'VE GOT SOME SELLING TO DO.
WHAT TOOK YOU SO LONG?
I WAS CLEANING--
SOOO, LET ME TAKE-A THEE OUT BACK.
YOU'LL FIND WHAT YOU NEED.
DON'T TOUCH ANYTHING.
BEBADA-BEBADA!

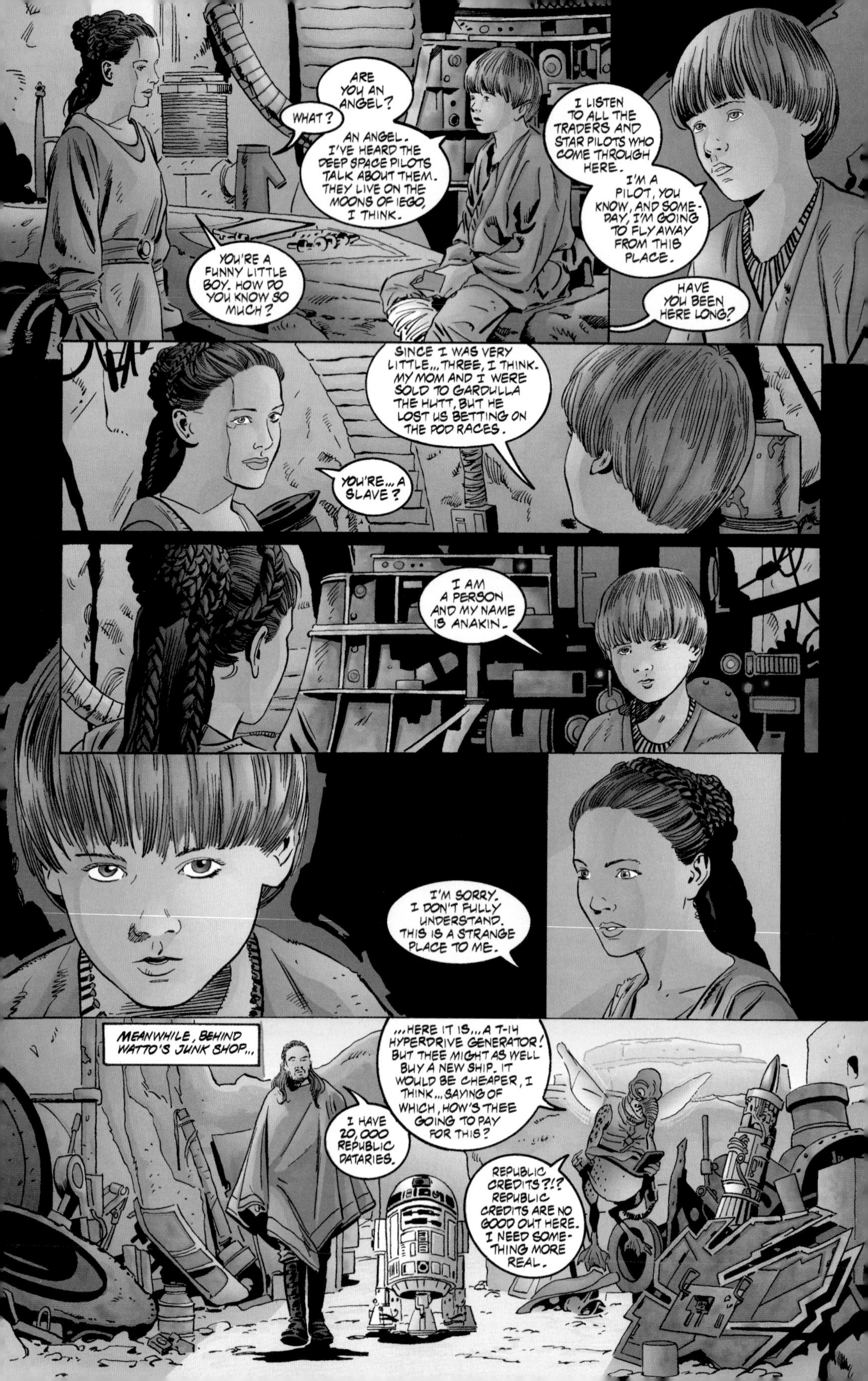
ARE YOU AN ANGEL?
WHAT?
AN ANGEL. I'VE HEARD THE DEEP SPACE PILOTS TALK ABOUT THEM. THEY LIVE ON THE MOONS OF IEGO, I THINK.
I LISTEN TO ALL THE TRADERS AND STAR PILOTS WHO COME THROUGH HERE.
I'M A PILOT, YOU KNOW, AND SOME-DAY, I'M GOING TO FLY AWAY FROM THIS PLACE.
YOU'RE A FUNNY LITTLE BOY. HOW DO YOU KNOW SO MUCH?
HAVE YOU BEEN HERE LONG?
SINCE I WAS VERY LITTLE... THREE, I THINK. MY MOM AND I WERE SOLD TO GARDULLA THE HUTT, BUT HE LOST US BETTING ON THE POD RACES.
YOU'RE... A SLAVE?
I AM A PERSON AND MY NAME IS ANAKIN.
I'M SORRY. I DON'T FULLY UNDERSTAND. THIS IS A STRANGE PLACE TO ME.
MEANWHILE, BEHIND WATTO'S JUNK SHOP...
...HERE IT IS... A T-14 HYPERDRIVE GENERATOR! BUT THEE MIGHT AS WELL BUY A NEW SHIP. IT WOULD BE CHEAPER, I THINK... SAYING OF WHICH, HOW'S THEE GOING TO PAY FOR THIS?
I HAVE 20,000 REPUBLIC DATARIES.
REPUBLIC CREDITS?!? REPUBLIC CREDITS ARE NO GOOD OUT HERE. I NEED SOME-THING MORE REAL.

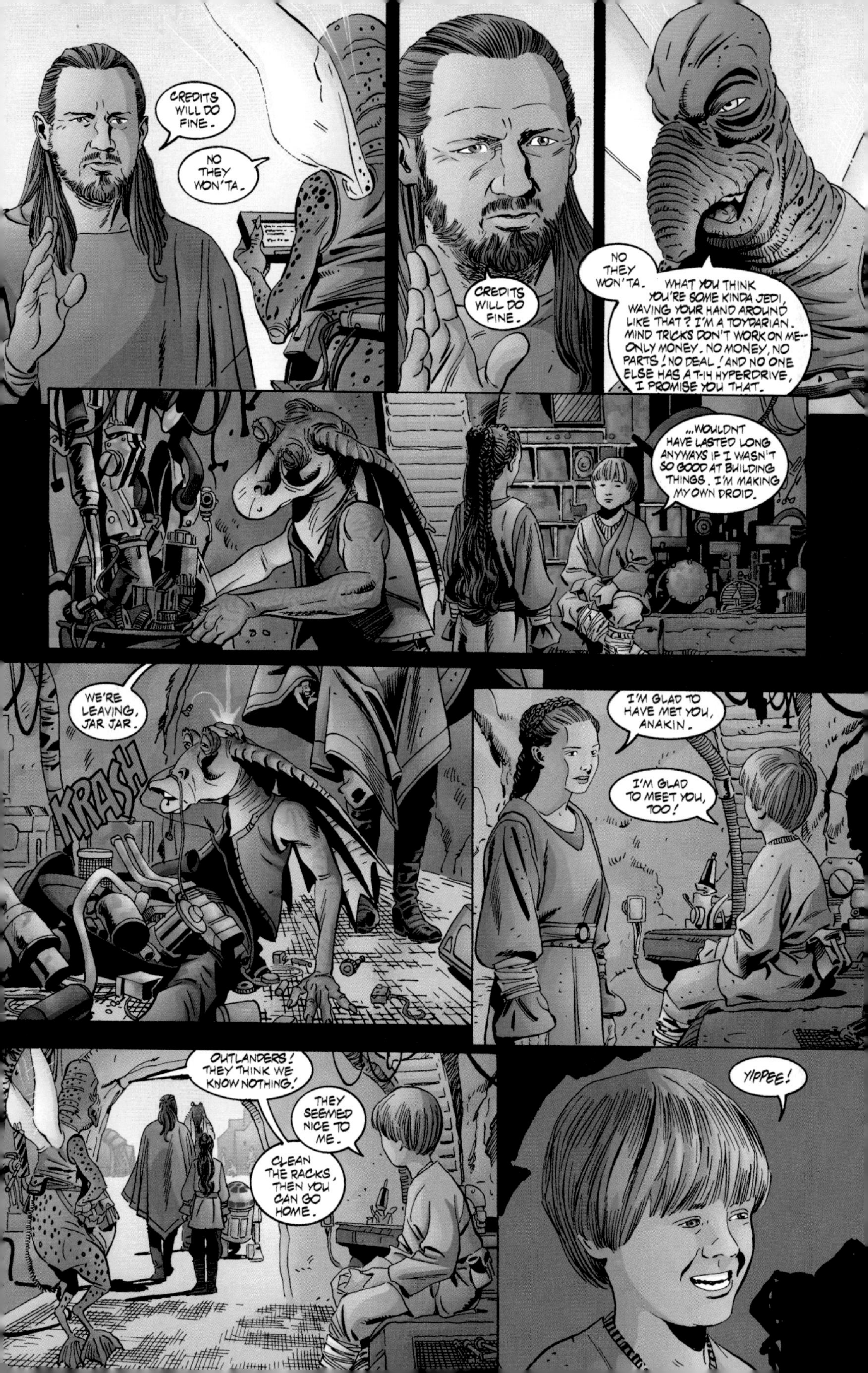
CREDITS WILL DO FINE.
NO THEY WON'TA.
CREDITS WILL DO FINE.
NO THEY WON'TA.
WHAT YOU THINK YOU'RE SOME KINDA JEDI, WAVING YOUR HAND AROUND LIKE THAT? I'M A TOYDARIAN. MIND TRICKS DON'T WORK ON ME-- ONLY MONEY. NO MONEY, NO PARTS! NO DEAL! AND NO ONE ELSE HAS A T-14 HYPERDRIVE, I PROMISE YOU THAT.
...WOULDN'T HAVE LASTED LONG ANYWAYS IF I WASN'T SO GOOD AT BUILDING THINGS. I'M MAKING MY OWN DROID.
WE'RE LEAVING, JAR JAR.
KRASH
I'M GLAD TO HAVE MET YOU, ANAKIN.
I'M GLAD TO MEET YOU, TOO!
OUTLANDERS! THEY THINK WE KNOW NOTHING!
THEY SEEMED NICE TO ME.
CLEAN THE RACKS, THEN YOU CAN GO HOME.
YIPPEE!

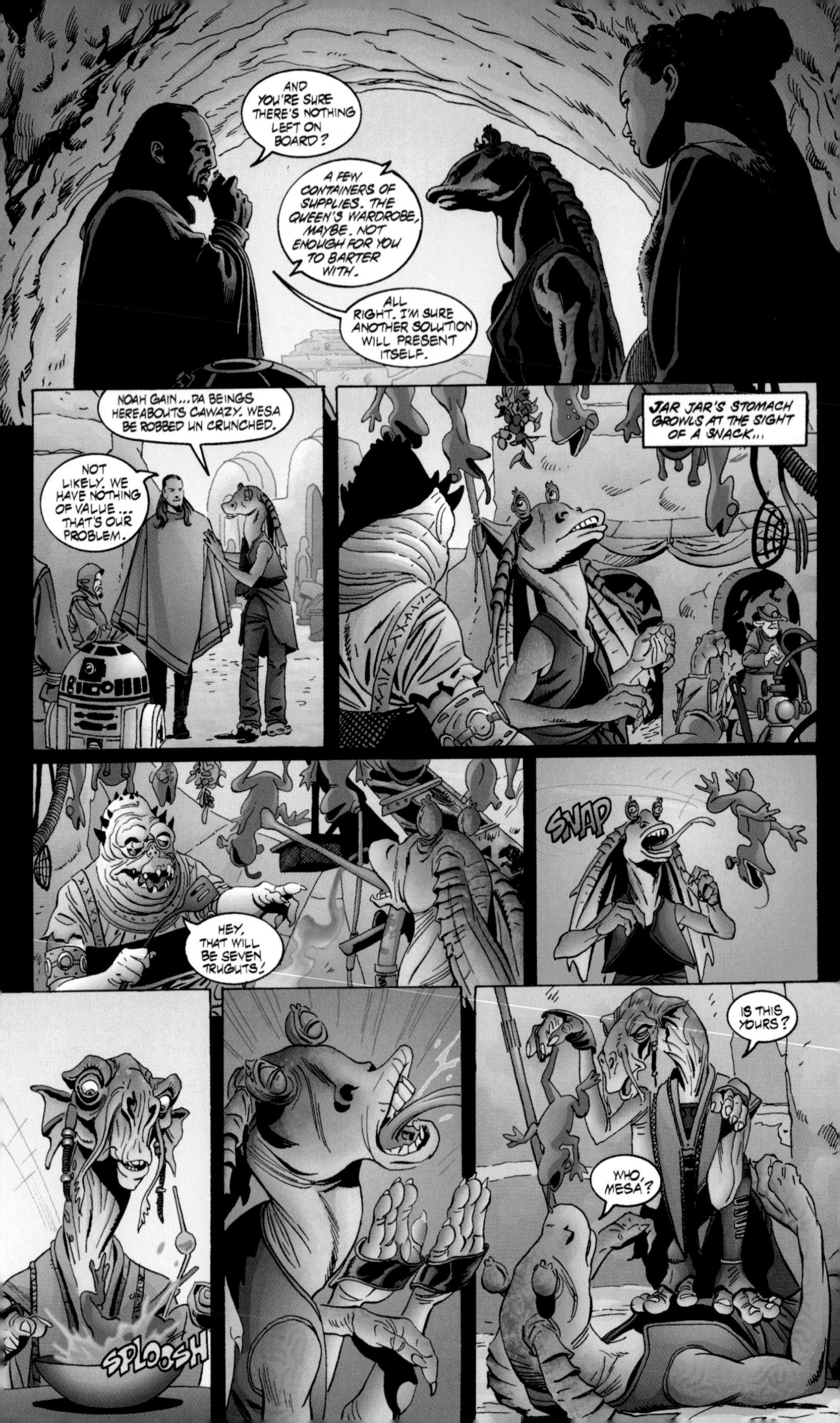
AND YOU'RE SURE THERE'S NOTHING LEFT ON BOARD?
A FEW CONTAINERS OF SUPPLIES. THE QUEEN'S WARDROBE, MAYBE. NOT ENOUGH FOR YOU TO BARTER WITH.
ALL RIGHT. I'M SURE ANOTHER SOLUTION WILL PRESENT ITSELF.
NOAH GAIN... DA BEINGS HEREABOUTS CAWAZY. WESA BE ROBBED UN CRUNCHED.
NOT LIKELY. WE HAVE NOTHING OF VALUE... THAT'S OUR PROBLEM.
JAR JAR'S STOMACH GROWLS AT THE SIGHT OF A SNACK...
HEY, THAT WILL BE SEVEN TRUGUTS!
SNAP
SPLOOSH
IS THIS YOURS?
WHO, MESA?

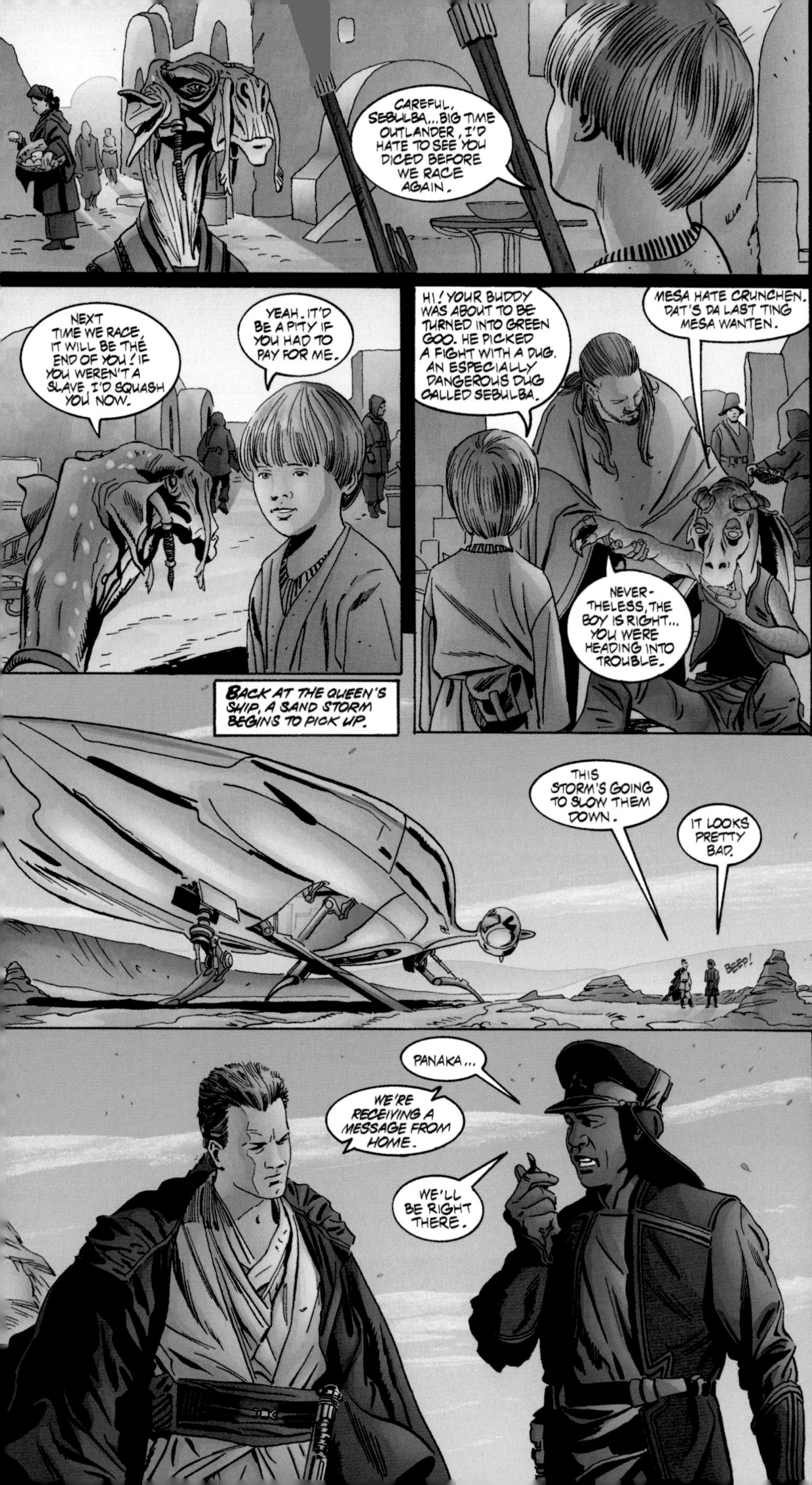
CAREFUL, SEBULBA... BIG TIME OUTLANDER, I'D HATE TO SEE YOU DICED BEFORE WE RACE AGAIN.
NEXT TIME WE RACE, IT WILL BE THE END OF YOU! IF YOU WEREN'T A SLAVE, I'D SQUASH YOU NOW.
YEAH. IT'D BE A PITY IF YOU HAD TO PAY FOR ME.
HI! YOUR BUDDY WAS ABOUT TO BE TURNED INTO GREEN GOO. HE PICKED A FIGHT WITH A DUG. AN ESPECIALLY DANGEROUS DUG CALLED SEBULBA.
MESA HATE CRUNCHEN. DAT'S DA LAST TING MESA WANTEN.
NEVER-THELESS, THE BOY IS RIGHT... YOU WERE HEADING INTO TROUBLE.
BACK AT THE QUEEN'S SHIP, A SAND STORM BEGINS TO PICK UP.
THIS STORM'S GOING TO SLOW THEM DOWN.
IT LOOKS PRETTY BAD.
BEEP!
PANAKA...
WE'RE RECEIVING A MESSAGE FROM HOME.
WE'LL BE RIGHT THERE.

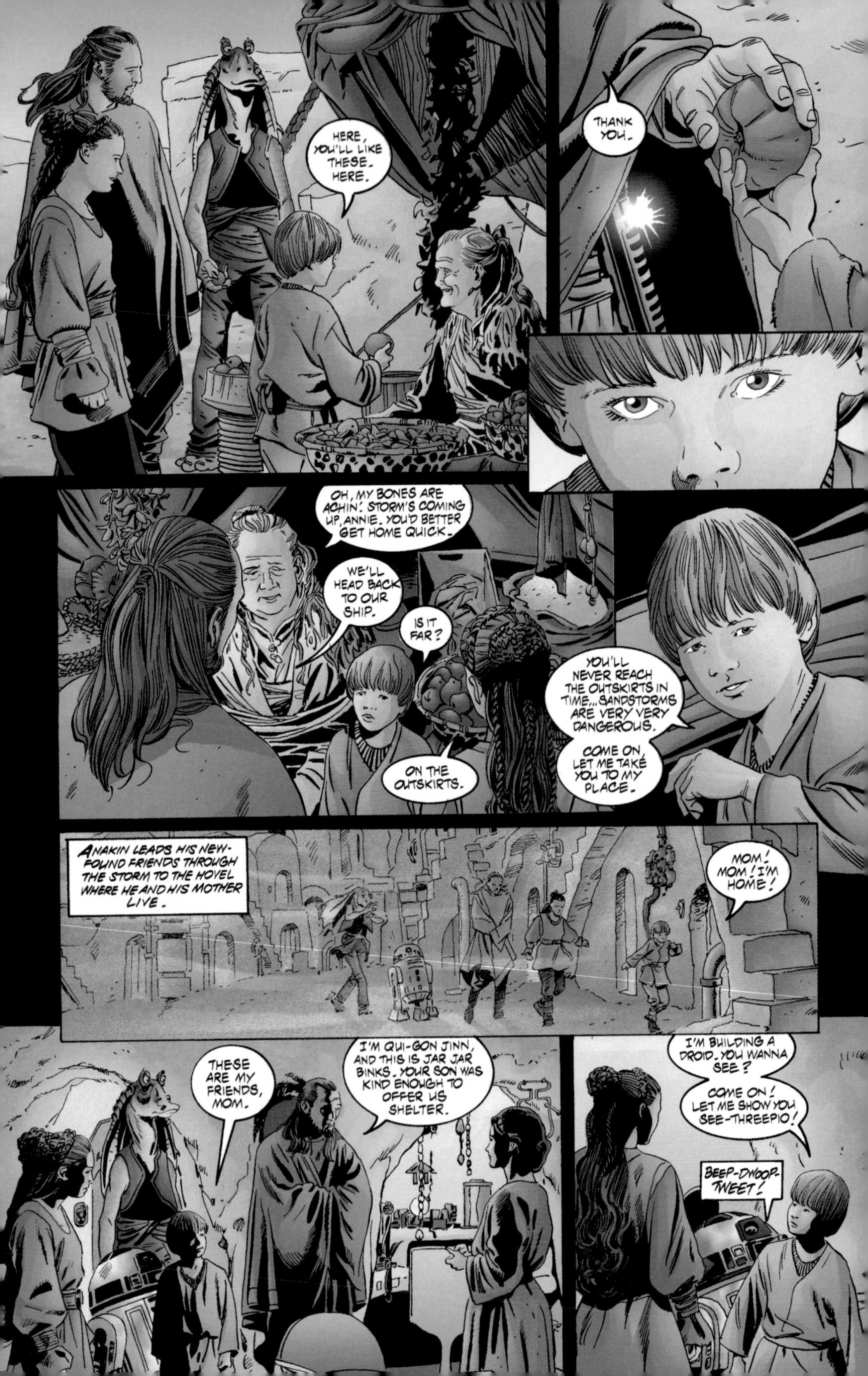
HERE, YOU'LL LIKE THESE. HERE.
THANK YOU.
OH, MY BONES ARE ACHIN'. STORM'S COMING UP, ANNIE. YOU'D BETTER GET HOME QUICK.
WE'LL HEAD BACK TO OUR SHIP.
IS IT FAR?
ON THE OUTSKIRTS.
YOU'LL NEVER REACH THE OUTSKIRTS IN TIME... SANDSTORMS ARE VERY VERY DANGEROUS.
COME ON, LET ME TAKE YOU TO MY PLACE.
ANAKIN LEADS HIS NEW-FOUND FRIENDS THROUGH THE STORM TO THE HOVEL WHERE HE AND HIS MOTHER LIVE.
MOM! MOM! I'M HOME!
THESE ARE MY FRIENDS, MOM.
I'M QUI-GON JINN, AND THIS IS JAR JAR BINKS. YOUR SON WAS KIND ENOUGH TO OFFER US SHELTER.
I'M BUILDING A DROID. YOU WANNA SEE?
COME ON! LET ME SHOW YOU SEE-THREEPIO!
BEEP-DWOOP-TWEET!

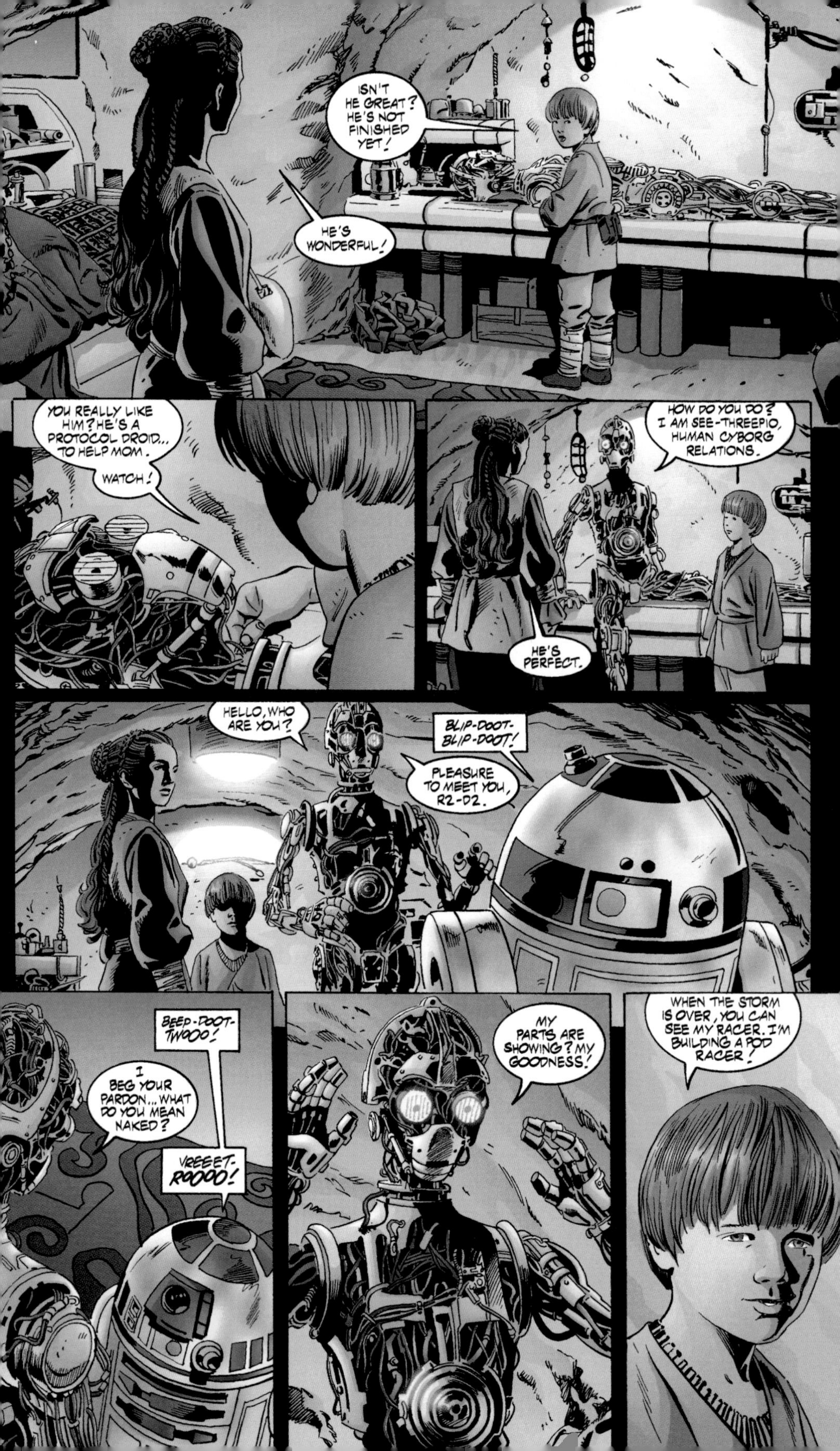
ISN'T HE GREAT? HE'S NOT FINISHED YET!
HE'S WONDERFUL!
YOU REALLY LIKE HIM? HE'S A PROTOCOL DROID... TO HELP MOM.
WATCH!
HOW DO YOU DO? I AM SEE-THREEPIO, HUMAN CYBORG RELATIONS.
HE'S PERFECT.
HELLO, WHO ARE YOU?
BLIP-DOOT-BLIP-DOOT!
PLEASURE TO MEET YOU, R2-D2.
BEEP-DOOT-TWOOO!
I BEG YOUR PARDON... WHAT DO YOU MEAN NAKED?
VREEEET-ROOOO!
MY PARTS ARE SHOWING? MY GOODNESS!
WHEN THE STORM IS OVER, YOU CAN SEE MY RACER. I'M BUILDING A POD RACER!

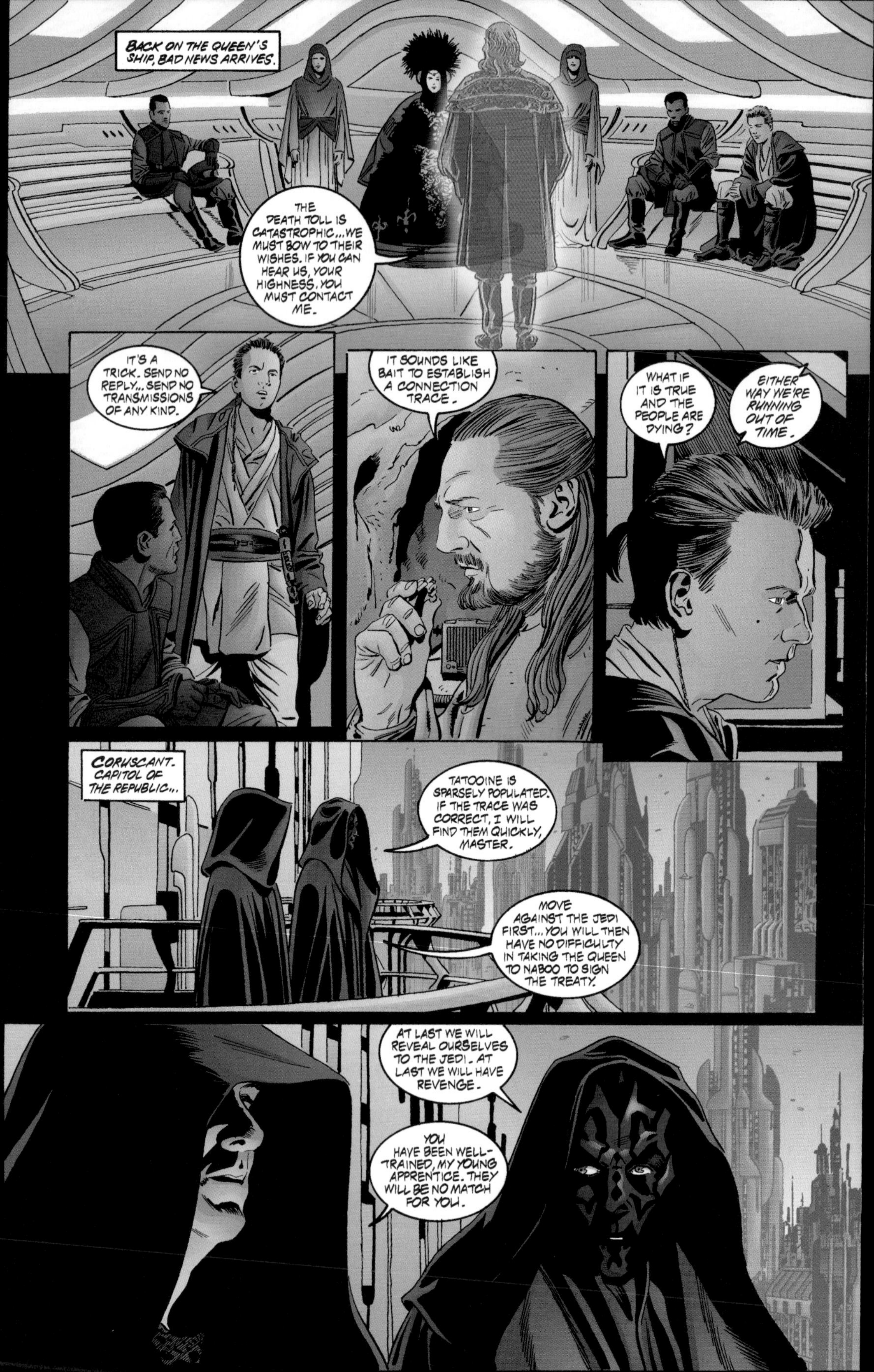
BACK ON THE QUEEN'S SHIP, BAD NEWS ARRIVES.
THE DEATH TOLL IS CATASTROPHIC... WE MUST BOW TO THEIR WISHES. IF YOU CAN HEAR US, YOUR HIGHNESS, YOU MUST CONTACT ME.
IT'S A TRICK. SEND NO REPLY... SEND NO TRANSMISSIONS OF ANY KIND.
IT SOUNDS LIKE BAIT TO ESTABLISH A CONNECTION TRACE.
WHAT IF IT IS TRUE AND THE PEOPLE ARE DYING?
EITHER WAY WE'RE RUNNING OUT OF TIME.
CORUSCANT. CAPITOL OF THE REPUBLIC...
TATOOINE IS SPARSELY POPULATED. IF THE TRACE WAS CORRECT, I WILL FIND THEM QUICKLY, MASTER.
MOVE AGAINST THE JEDI FIRST... YOU WILL THEN HAVE NO DIFFICULTY IN TAKING THE QUEEN TO NABOO TO SIGN THE TREATY.
AT LAST WE WILL REVEAL OURSELVES TO THE JEDI. AT LAST WE WILL HAVE REVENGE.
YOU HAVE BEEN WELL-TRAINED, MY YOUNG APPRENTICE. THEY WILL BE NO MATCH FOR YOU.

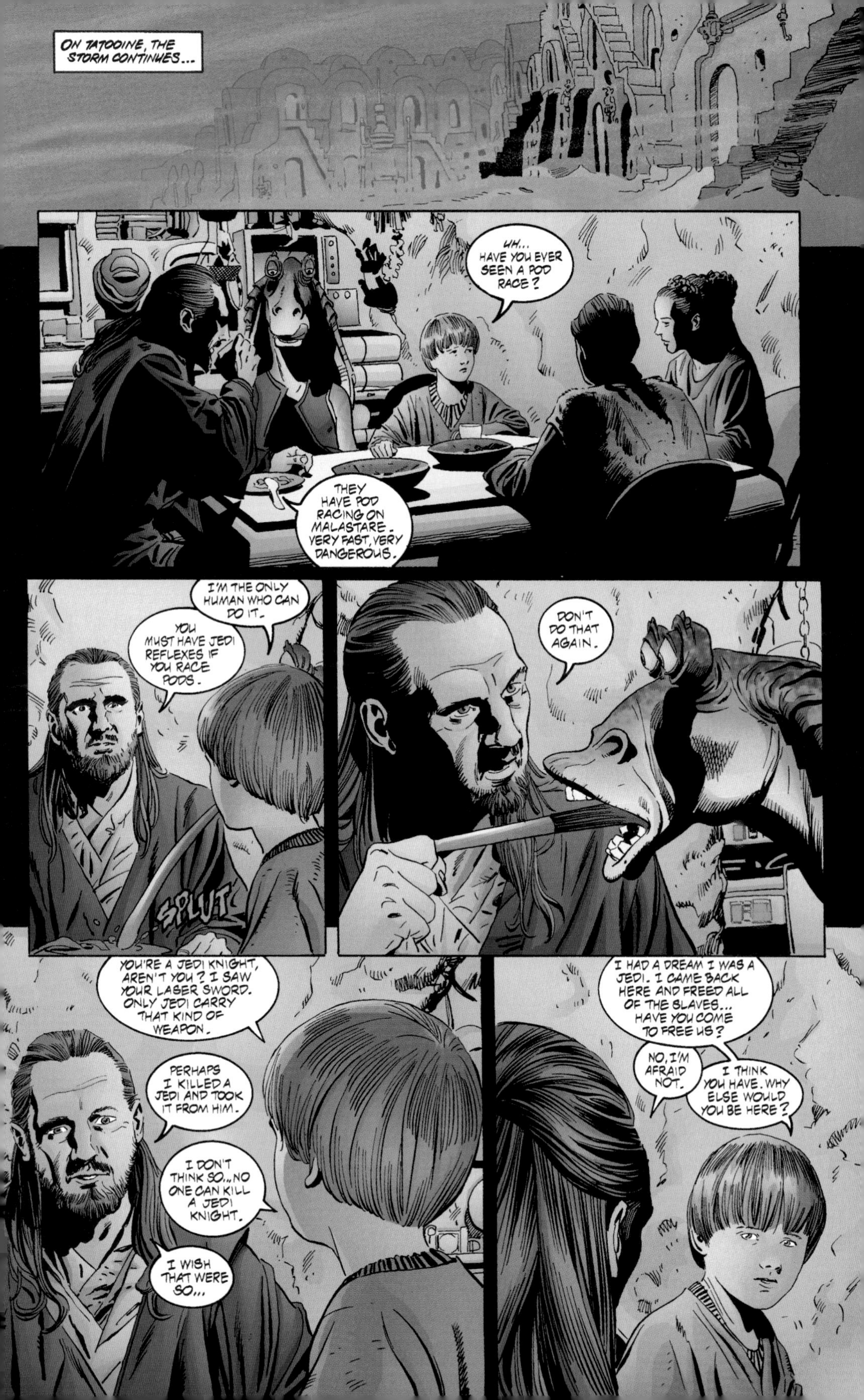

ON TATOOINE, THE STORM CONTINUES...
UH... HAVE YOU EVER SEEN A POD RACE?
THEY HAVE POD RACING ON MALASTARE. VERY FAST, VERY DANGEROUS.
I'M THE ONLY HUMAN WHO CAN DO IT.
YOU MUST HAVE JEDI REFLEXES IF YOU RACE PODS.
SPLUT
DON'T DO THAT AGAIN.
YOU'RE A JEDI KNIGHT, AREN'T YOU? I SAW YOUR LASER SWORD. ONLY JEDI CARRY THAT KIND OF WEAPON.
PERHAPS I KILLED A JEDI AND TOOK IT FROM HIM.
I DON'T THINK SO...NO ONE CAN KILL A JEDI KNIGHT.
I WISH THAT WERE SO...
I HAD A DREAM I WAS A JEDI. I CAME BACK HERE AND FREED ALL OF THE SLAVES... HAVE YOU COME TO FREE US?
NO, I'M AFRAID NOT.
I THINK YOU HAVE. WHY ELSE WOULD YOU BE HERE?

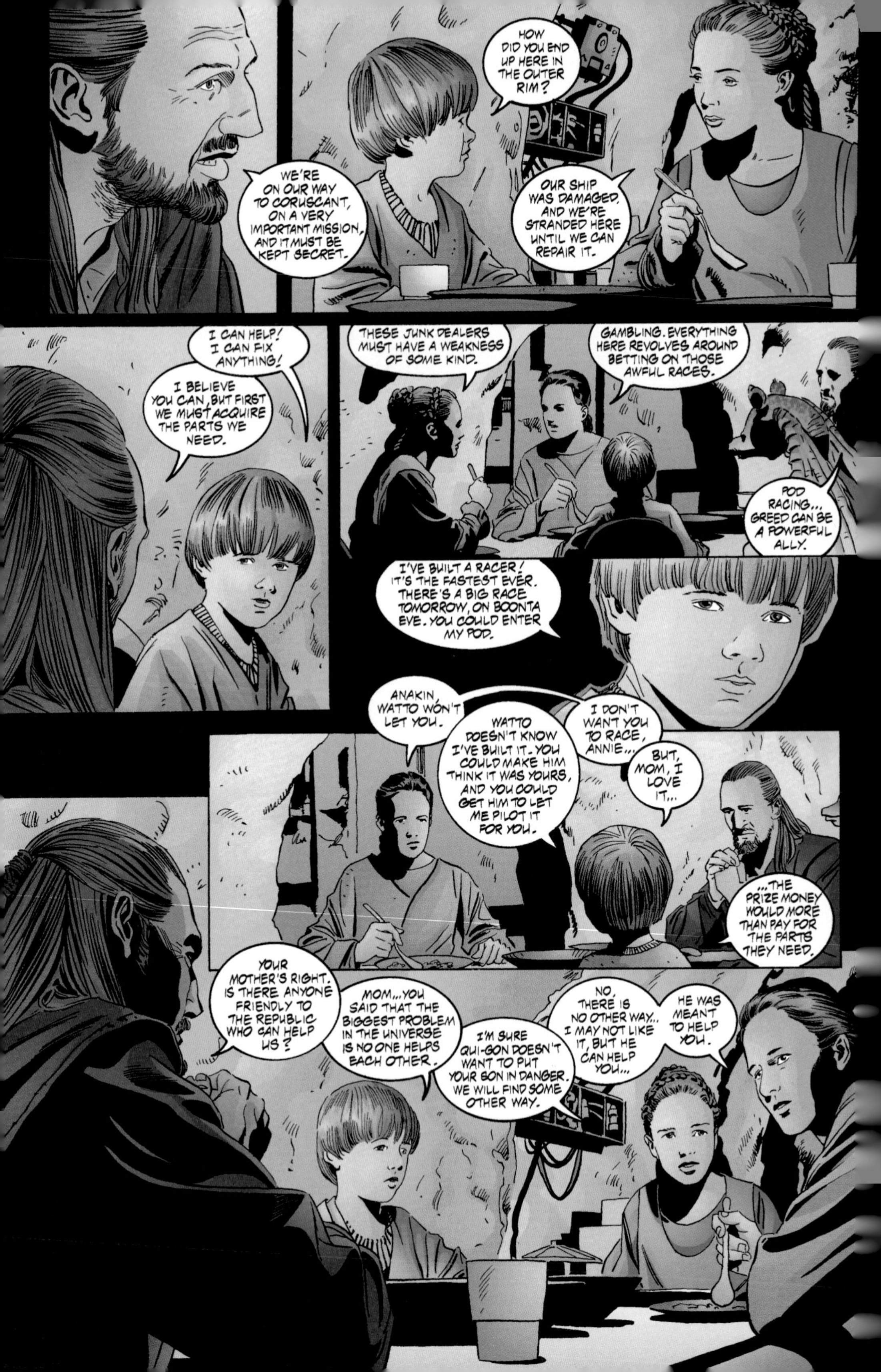

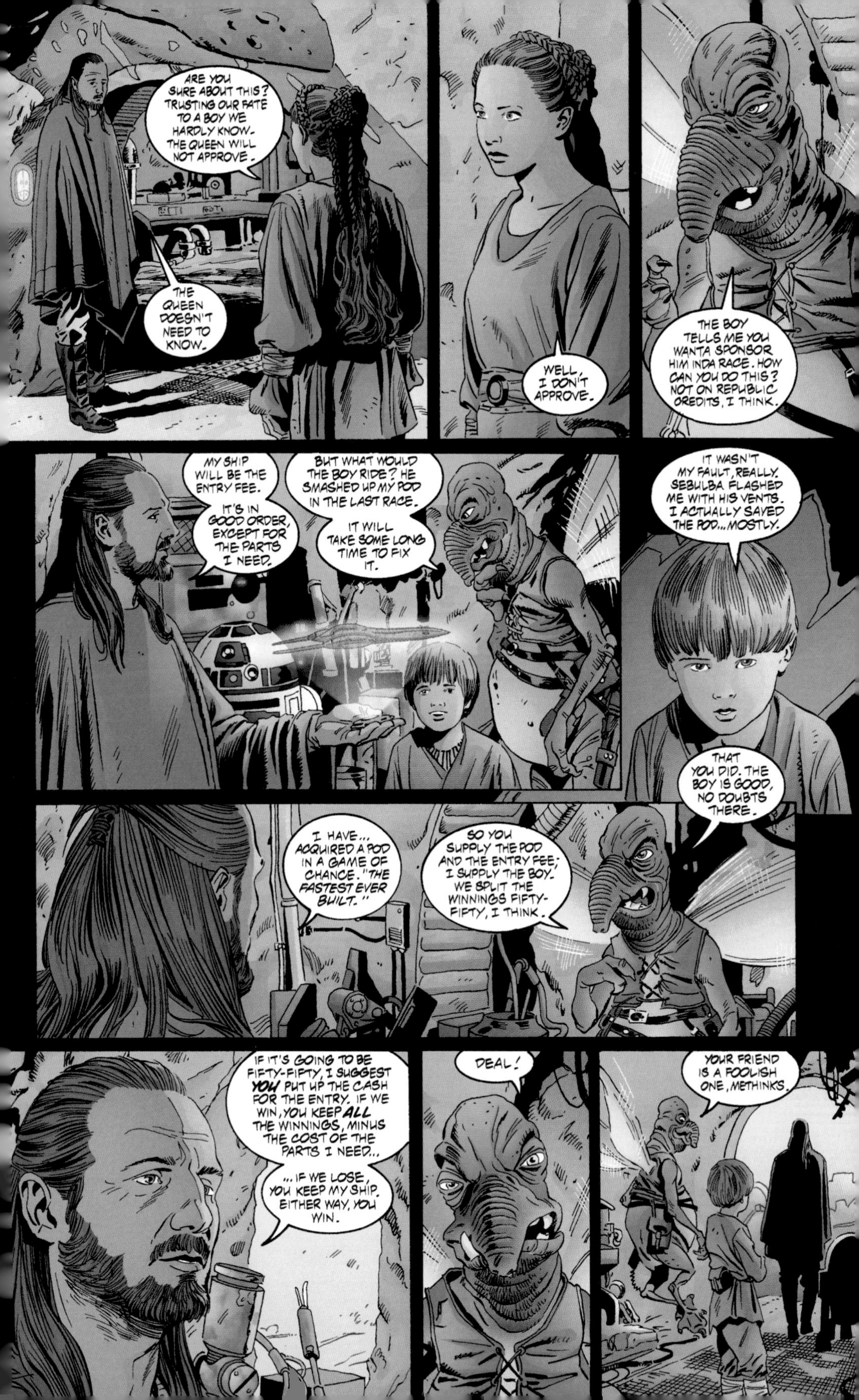
ARE YOU SURE ABOUT THIS? TRUSTING OUR FATE TO A BOY WE HARDLY KNOW. THE QUEEN WILL NOT APPROVE.
THE QUEEN DOESN'T NEED TO KNOW.
WELL, I DON'T APPROVE.
THE BOY TELLS ME YOU WANTA SPONSOR HIM INDA RACE. HOW CAN YOU DO THIS? NOT ON REPUBLIC CREDITS, I THINK.
MY SHIP WILL BE THE ENTRY FEE.
IT'S IN GOOD ORDER, EXCEPT FOR THE PARTS I NEED.
BUT WHAT WOULD THE BOY RIDE? HE SMASHED UP MY POD IN THE LAST RACE.
IT WILL TAKE SOME LONG TIME TO FIX IT.
IT WASN'T MY FAULT, REALLY. SEBULBA FLASHED ME WITH HIS VENTS. I ACTUALLY SAVED THE POD... MOSTLY.
THAT YOU DID. THE BOY IS GOOD, NO DOUBTS THERE.
I HAVE... ACQUIRED A POD IN A GAME OF CHANCE. "THE *FASTEST EVER BUILT.*"
SO YOU SUPPLY THE POD AND THE ENTRY FEE; I SUPPLY THE BOY. WE SPLIT THE WINNINGS FIFTY-FIFTY, I THINK.
IF IT'S *GOING* TO BE FIFTY-FIFTY, I SUGGEST ***YOU*** PUT UP THE CASH FOR THE ENTRY. IF WE WIN, YOU KEEP ***ALL*** THE WINNINGS, MINUS THE COST OF THE PARTS I NEED...
... IF WE LOSE, YOU KEEP MY SHIP. EITHER WAY, YOU WIN.
DEAL!
YOUR FRIEND IS A FOOLISH ONE, METHINKS.

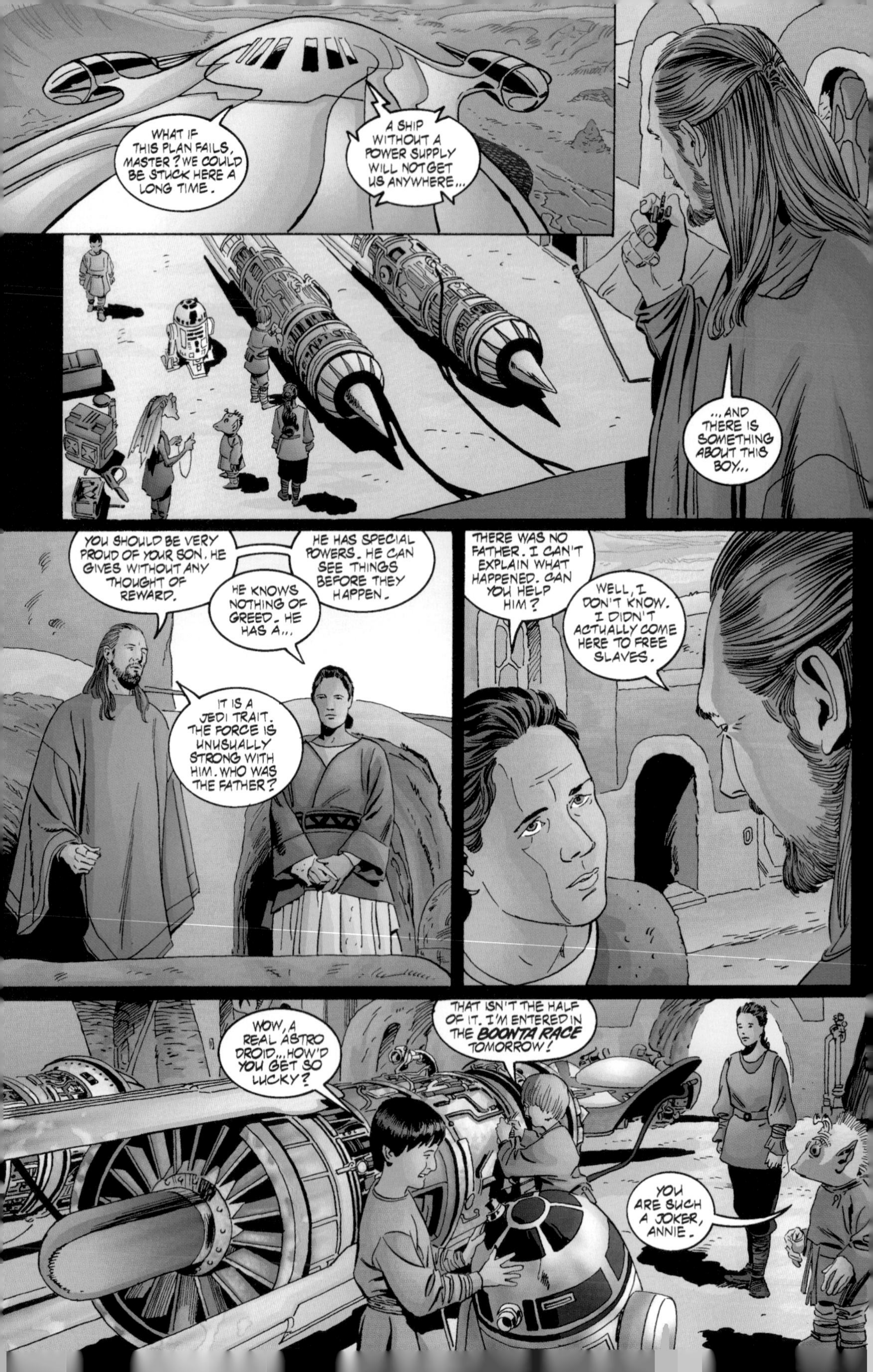
WHAT IF THIS PLAN FAILS, MASTER? WE COULD BE STUCK HERE A LONG TIME.
A SHIP WITHOUT A POWER SUPPLY WILL NOT GET US ANYWHERE...
...AND THERE IS SOMETHING ABOUT THIS BOY...
YOU SHOULD BE VERY PROUD OF YOUR SON. HE GIVES WITHOUT ANY THOUGHT OF REWARD.
HE KNOWS NOTHING OF GREED. HE HAS A...
HE HAS SPECIAL POWERS. HE CAN SEE THINGS BEFORE THEY HAPPEN.
IT IS A JEDI TRAIT. THE FORCE IS UNUSUALLY STRONG WITH HIM. WHO WAS THE FATHER?
THERE WAS NO FATHER. I CAN'T EXPLAIN WHAT HAPPENED. CAN YOU HELP HIM?
WELL, I DON'T KNOW. I DIDN'T ACTUALLY COME HERE TO FREE SLAVES.
WOW, A REAL ASTRO DROID...HOW'D YOU GET SO LUCKY?
THAT ISN'T THE HALF OF IT. I'M ENTERED IN THE BOONTA RACE TOMORROW!
YOU ARE SUCH A JOKER, ANNIE.

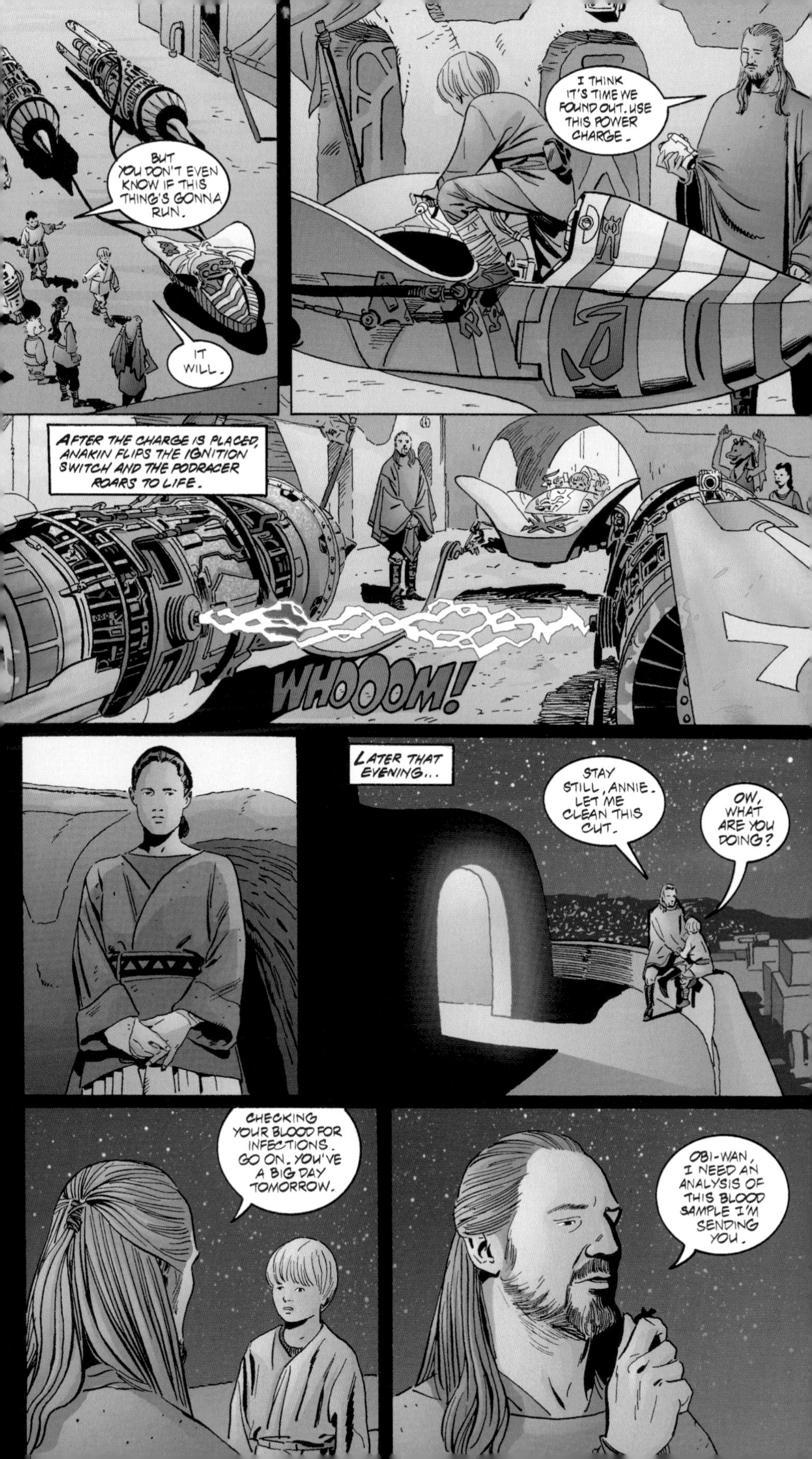
BUT YOU DON'T EVEN KNOW IF THIS THING'S GONNA RUN.
IT WILL.
I THINK IT'S TIME WE FOUND OUT. USE THIS POWER CHARGE.
AFTER THE CHARGE IS PLACED, ANAKIN FLIPS THE IGNITION SWITCH AND THE PODRACER ROARS TO LIFE.
WHOOOM!
LATER THAT EVENING...
STAY STILL, ANNIE. LET ME CLEAN THIS CUT.
OW, WHAT ARE YOU DOING?
CHECKING YOUR BLOOD FOR INFECTIONS. GO ON. YOU'VE A BIG DAY TOMORROW.
OBI-WAN, I NEED AN ANALYSIS OF THIS BLOOD SAMPLE I'M SENDING YOU.

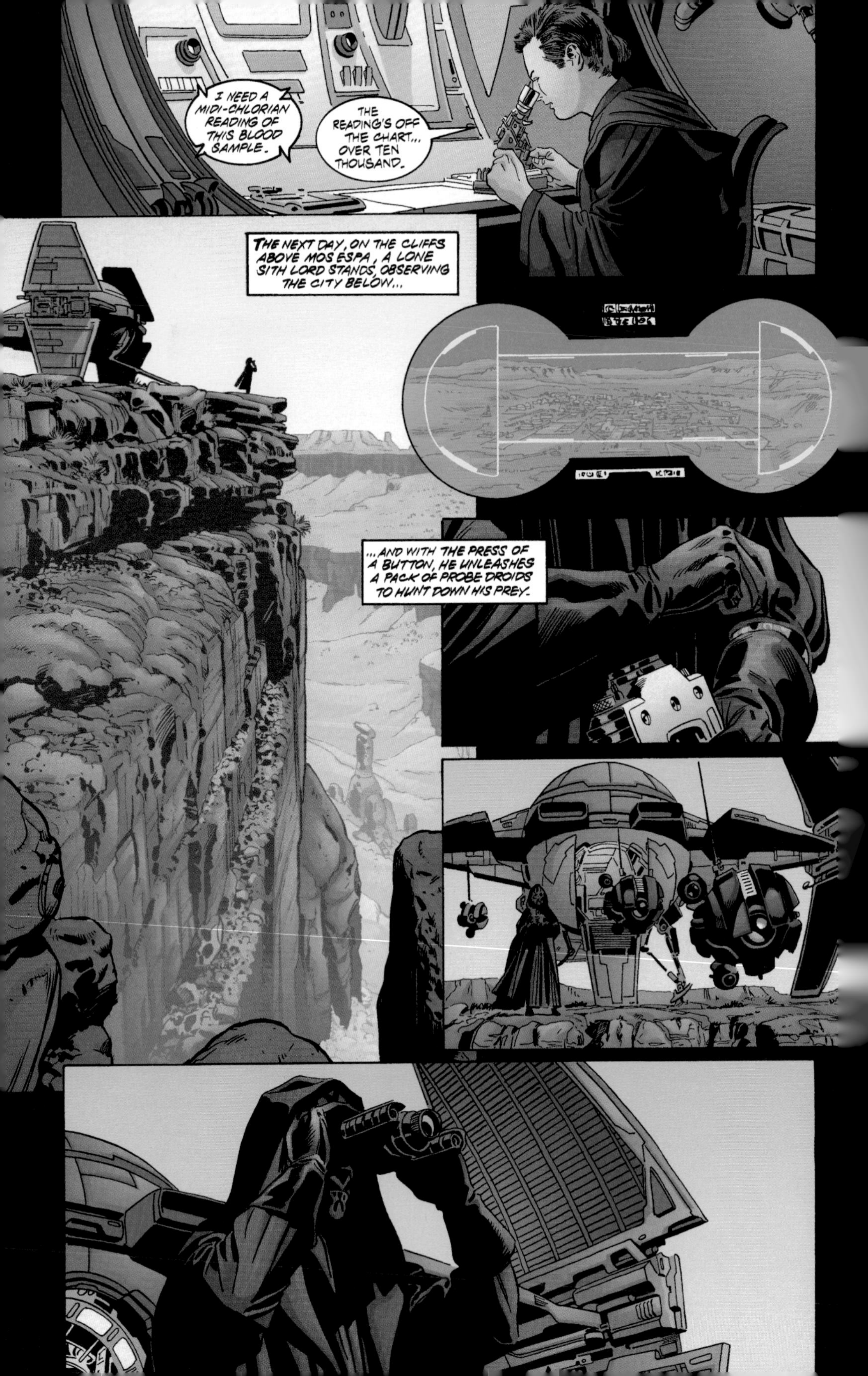
I NEED A MIDI-CHLORIAN READING OF THIS BLOOD SAMPLE.
THE READING'S OFF THE CHART... OVER TEN THOUSAND.
THE NEXT DAY, ON THE CLIFFS ABOVE MOS ESPA, A LONE SITH LORD STANDS, OBSERVING THE CITY BELOW...
...AND WITH THE PRESS OF A BUTTON, HE UNLEASHES A PACK OF PROBE DROIDS TO HUNT DOWN HIS PREY.

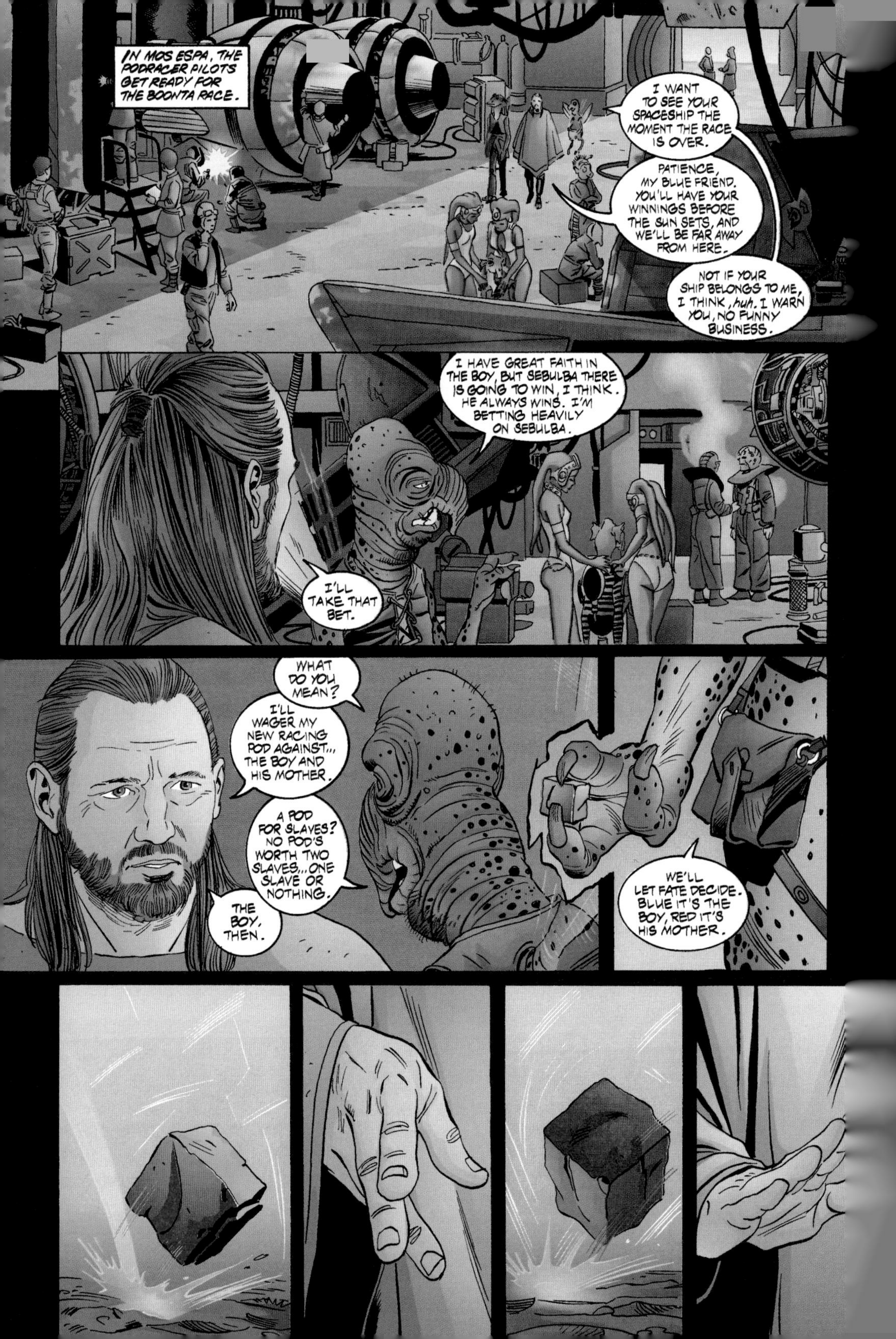
IN MOS ESPA, THE PODRACER PILOTS GET READY FOR THE BOONTA RACE.
I WANT TO SEE YOUR SPACESHIP THE MOMENT THE RACE IS OVER.
PATIENCE, MY BLUE FRIEND. YOU'LL HAVE YOUR WINNINGS BEFORE THE SUN SETS, AND WE'LL BE FAR AWAY FROM HERE.
NOT IF YOUR SHIP BELONGS TO ME, I THINK, huh. I WARN YOU, NO FUNNY BUSINESS.
I HAVE GREAT FAITH IN THE BOY, BUT SEBULBA THERE IS GOING TO WIN, I THINK. HE ALWAYS WINS. I'M BETTING HEAVILY ON SEBULBA.
I'LL TAKE THAT BET.
WHAT DO YOU MEAN?
I'LL WAGER MY NEW RACING POD AGAINST... THE BOY AND HIS MOTHER.
A POD FOR SLAVES? NO POD'S WORTH TWO SLAVES... ONE SLAVE OR NOTHING.
THE BOY, THEN.
WE'LL LET FATE DECIDE. BLUE IT'S THE BOY, RED IT'S HIS MOTHER.

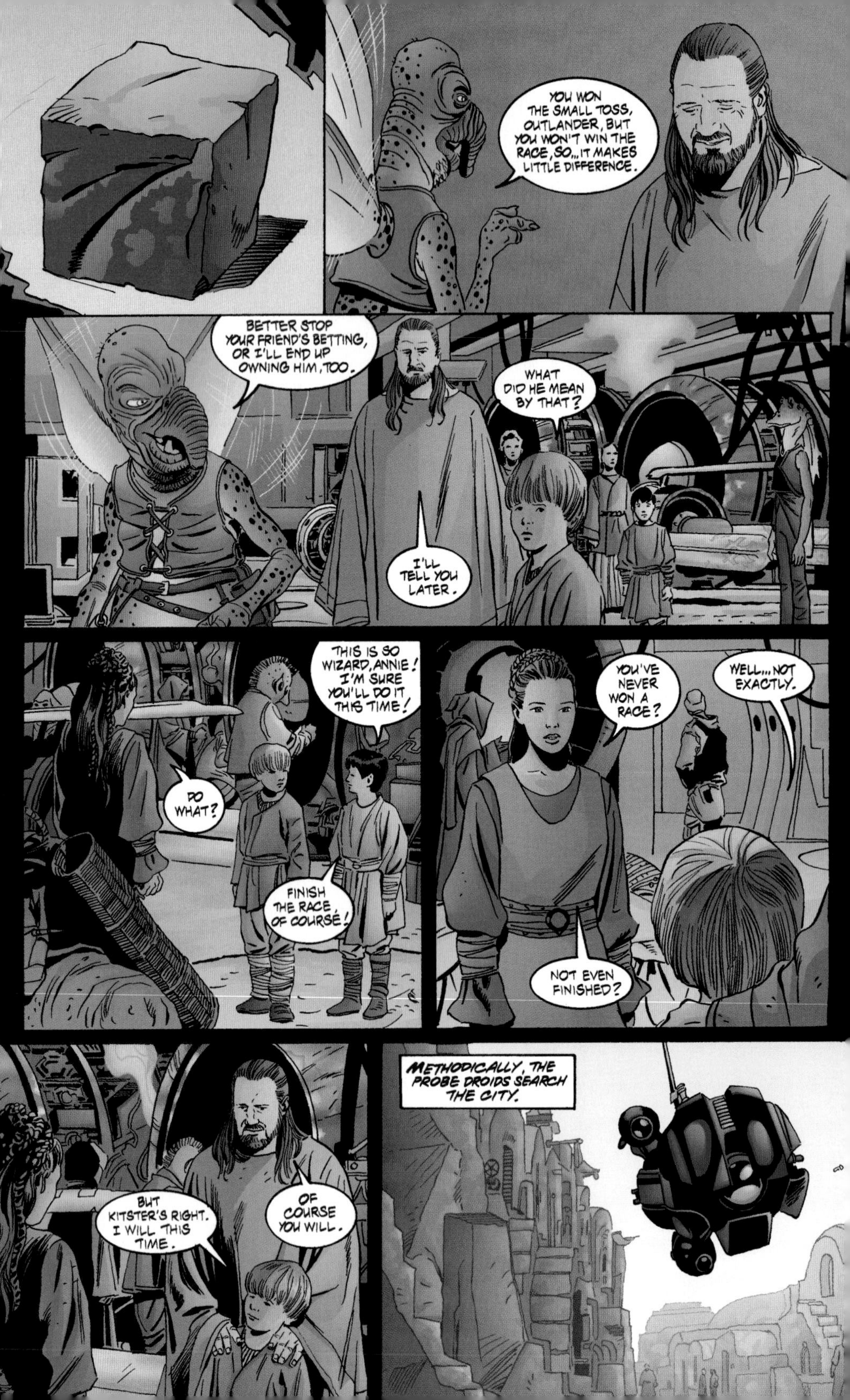
YOU WON THE SMALL TOSS, OUTLANDER, BUT YOU WON'T WIN THE RACE, SO... IT MAKES LITTLE DIFFERENCE.
BETTER STOP YOUR FRIEND'S BETTING, OR I'LL END UP OWNING HIM, TOO.
WHAT DID HE MEAN BY THAT?
I'LL TELL YOU LATER.
THIS IS SO WIZARD, ANNIE! I'M SURE YOU'LL DO IT THIS TIME!
DO WHAT?
FINISH THE RACE, OF COURSE!
YOU'VE NEVER WON A RACE?
WELL... NOT EXACTLY.
NOT EVEN FINISHED?
BUT KITSTER'S RIGHT. I WILL THIS TIME.
OF COURSE YOU WILL.
METHODICALLY, THE PROBE DROIDS SEARCH THE CITY.

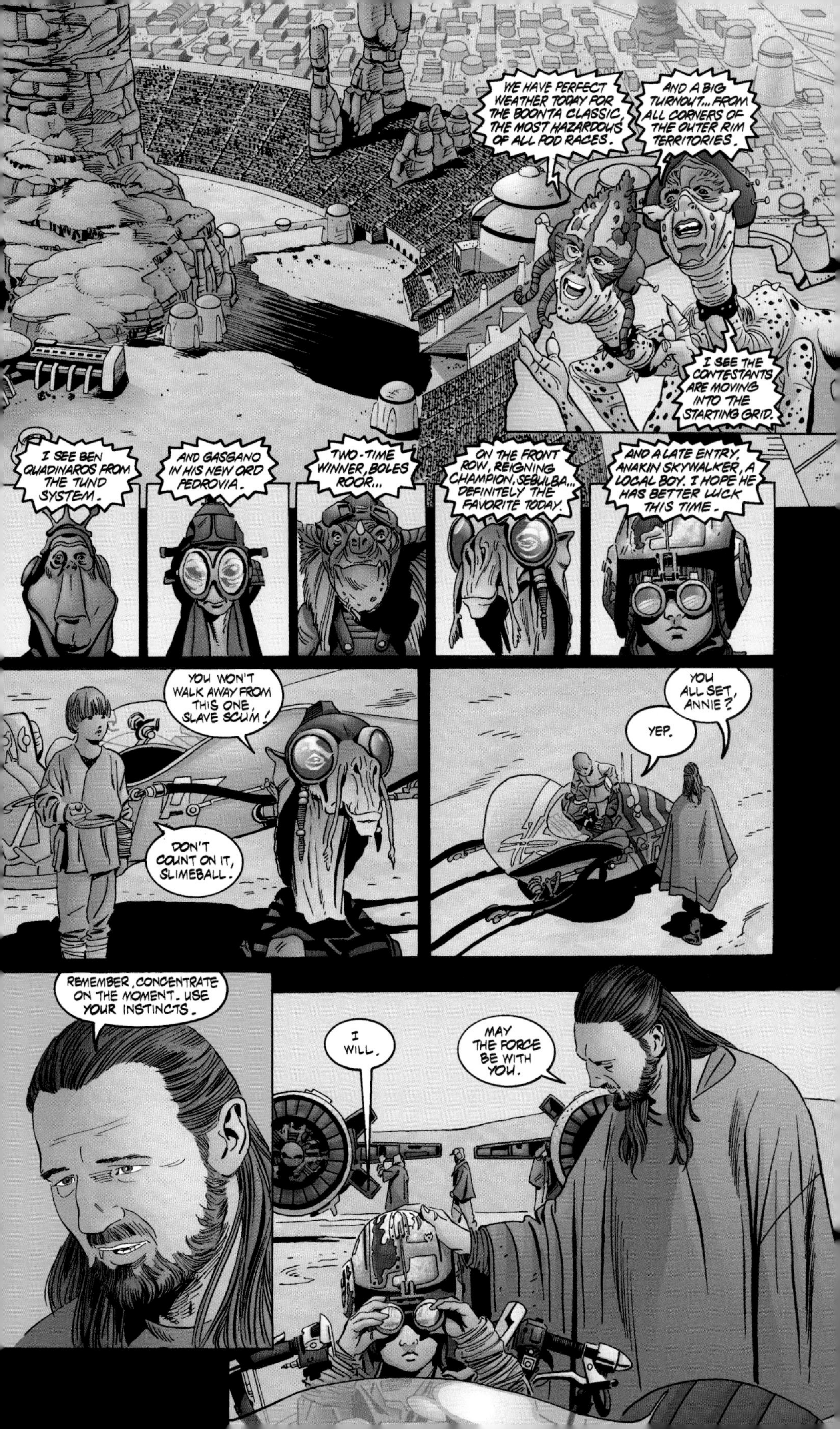
WE HAVE PERFECT WEATHER TODAY FOR THE BOONTA CLASSIC, THE MOST HAZARDOUS OF ALL POD RACES.
AND A BIG TURNOUT... FROM ALL CORNERS OF THE OUTER RIM TERRITORIES.
I SEE THE CONTESTANTS ARE MOVING INTO THE STARTING GRID.
I SEE BEN QUADINAROS FROM THE TUND SYSTEM.
AND GASGANO IN HIS NEW ORD PEDROVIA.
TWO-TIME WINNER, BOLES ROOR...
ON THE FRONT ROW, REIGNING CHAMPION, SEBULBA... DEFINITELY THE FAVORITE TODAY.
AND A LATE ENTRY, ANAKIN SKYWALKER, A LOCAL BOY. I HOPE HE HAS BETTER LUCK THIS TIME.
YOU WON'T WALK AWAY FROM THIS ONE, SLAVE SCUM!
DON'T COUNT ON IT, SLIMEBALL.
YOU ALL SET, ANNIE?
YEP.
REMEMBER, CONCENTRATE ON THE MOMENT. USE YOUR INSTINCTS.
I WILL.
MAY THE FORCE BE WITH YOU.

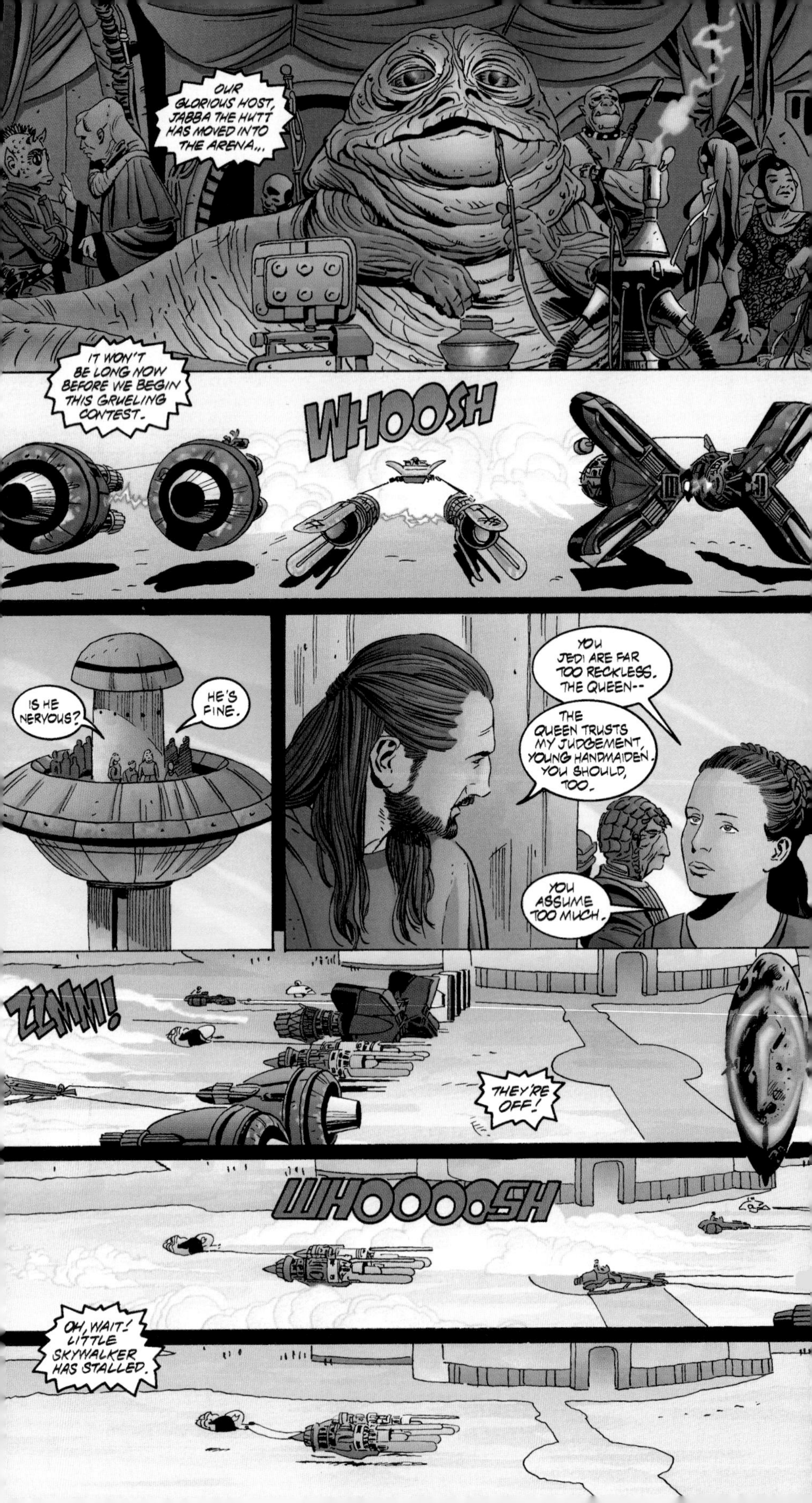
OUR GLORIOUS HOST, JABBA THE HUTT HAS MOVED INTO THE ARENA...
IT WON'T BE LONG NOW BEFORE WE BEGIN THIS GRUELING CONTEST.
WHOOSH
IS HE NERVOUS?
HE'S FINE.
YOU JEDI ARE FAR TOO RECKLESS. THE QUEEN--
THE QUEEN TRUSTS MY JUDGEMENT, YOUNG HANDMAIDEN. YOU SHOULD, TOO.
YOU ASSUME TOO MUCH.
ZZMMM!
THEY'RE OFF!
WHOOOOOSH
OH, WAIT! LITTLE SKYWALKER HAS STALLED.

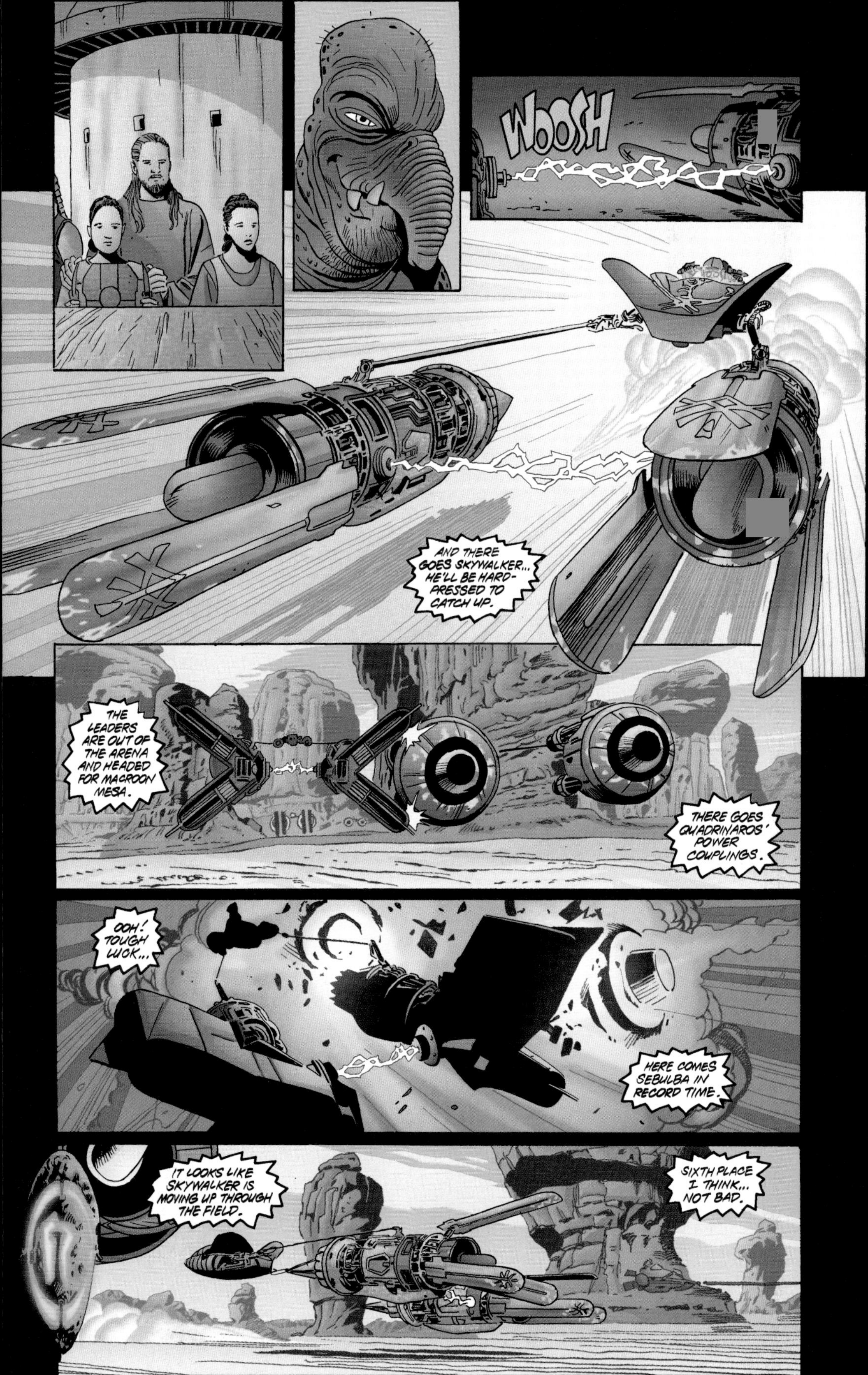
WOOSH
AND THERE GOES SKYWALKER... HE'LL BE HARD-PRESSED TO CATCH UP.
THE LEADERS ARE OUT OF THE ARENA AND HEADED FOR MACROON MESA.
THERE GOES QUADRINAROS' POWER COUPLINGS.
OOH! TOUGH LUCK...
HERE COMES SEBULBA IN RECORD TIME.
IT LOOKS LIKE SKYWALKER IS MOVING UP THROUGH THE FIELD.
SIXTH PLACE I THINK... NOT BAD.

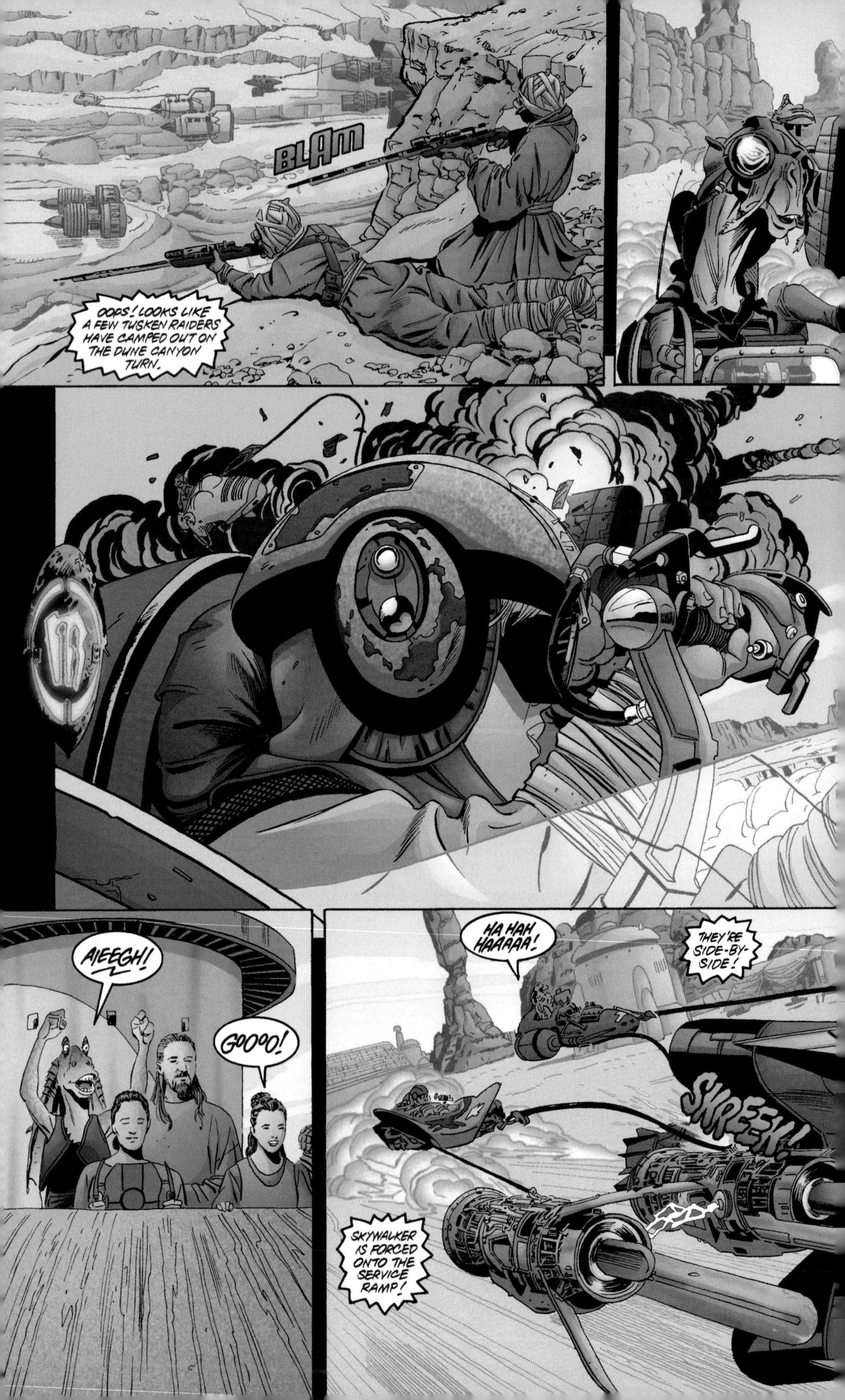
BLAM
OOPS! LOOKS LIKE A FEW TUSKEN RAIDERS HAVE CAMPED OUT ON THE DUNE CANYON TURN.
AIEEGH!
GOOOO!
HA HAH HAAAAA!
THEY'RE SIDE-BY-SIDE!
SKREEEK!
SKYWALKER IS FORCED ONTO THE SERVICE RAMP!

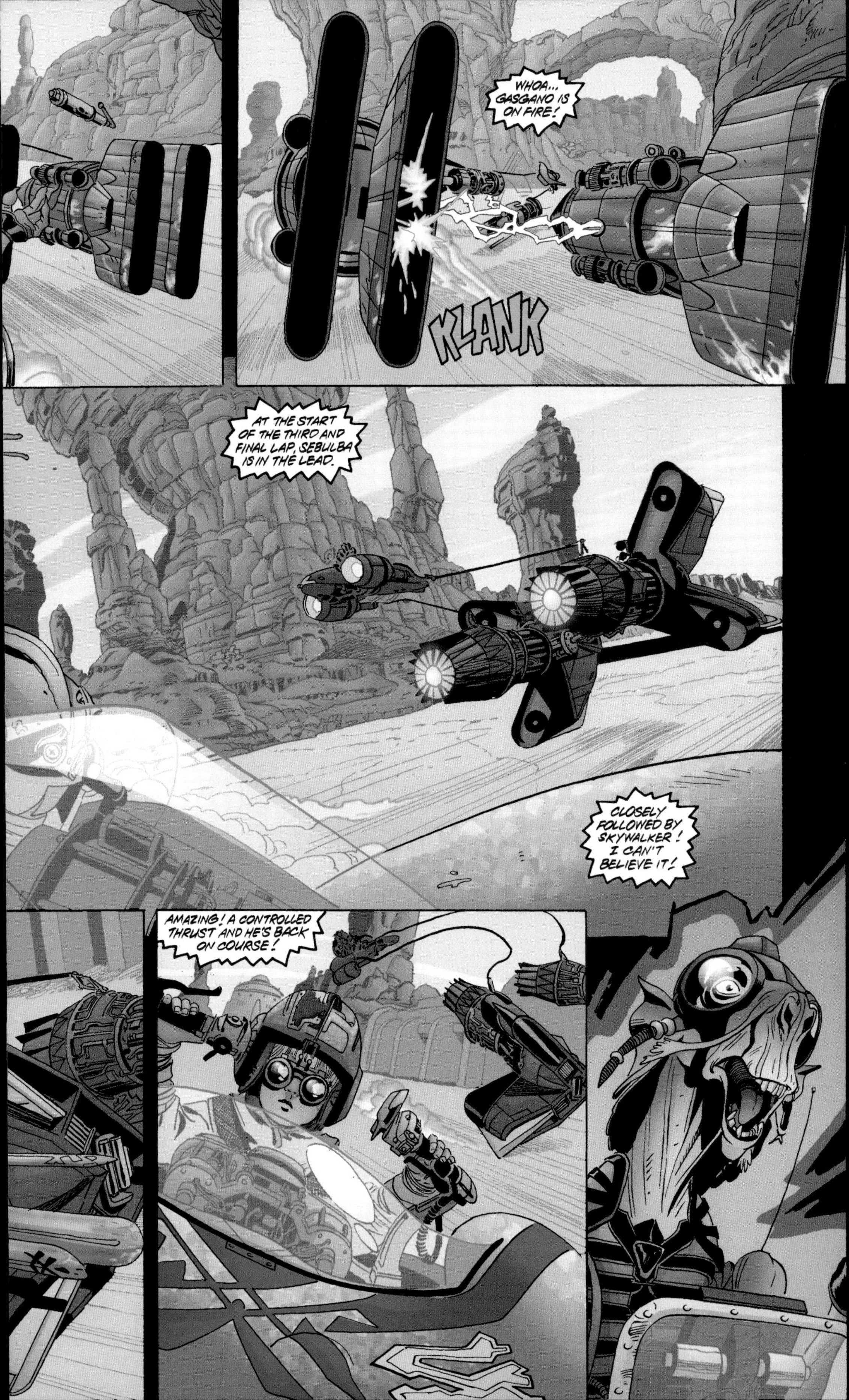
WHOA... GASGANO IS ON FIRE!
KLANK
AT THE START OF THE THIRD AND FINAL LAP, SEBULBA IS IN THE LEAD.
CLOSELY FOLLOWED BY SKYWALKER! I CAN'T BELIEVE IT!
AMAZING! A CONTROLLED THRUST AND HE'S BACK ON COURSE!

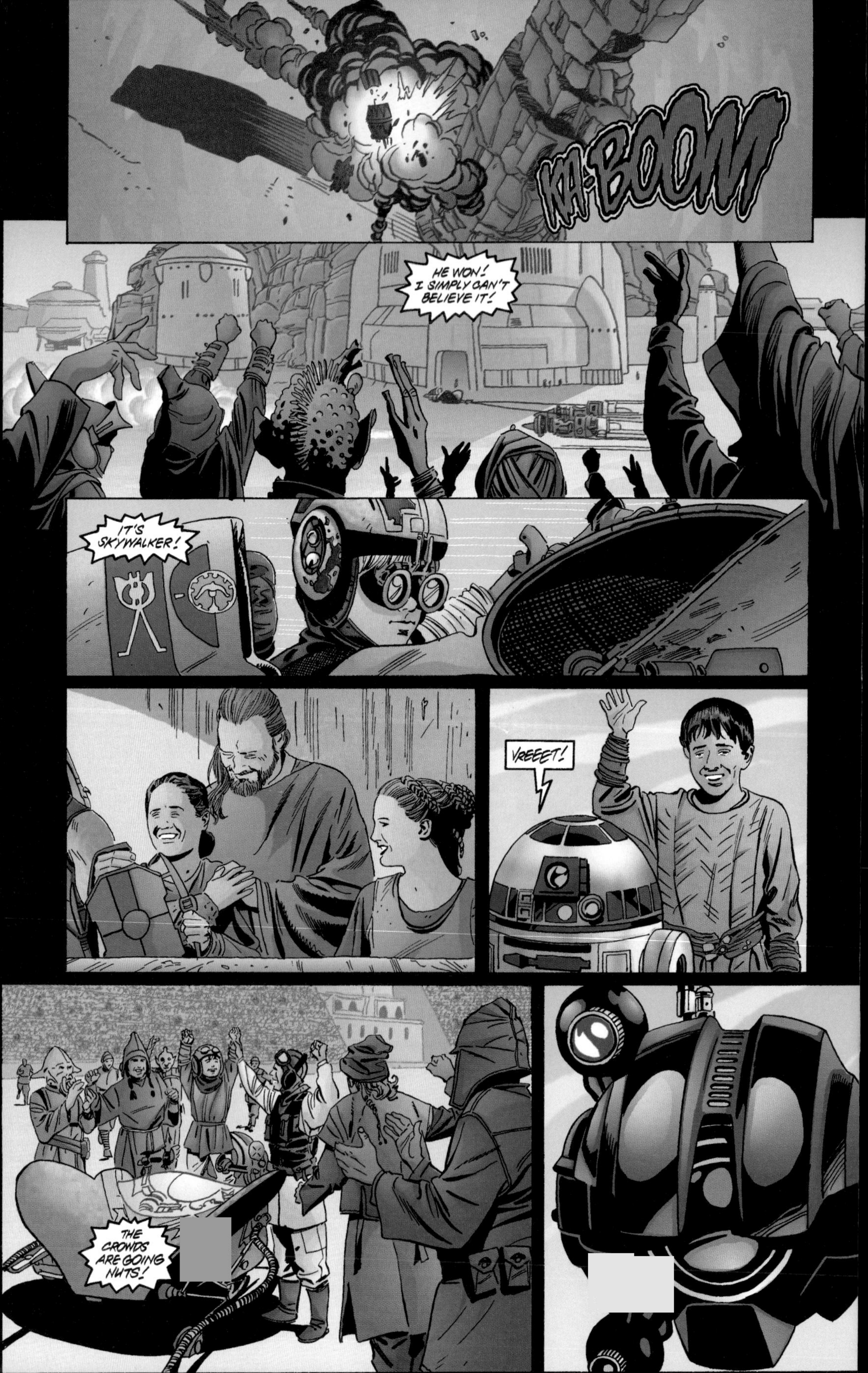
KA-BOOM
HE WON! I SIMPLY CAN'T BELIEVE IT!
IT'S SKYWALKER!
VREEET!
THE CROWDS ARE GOING NUTS!

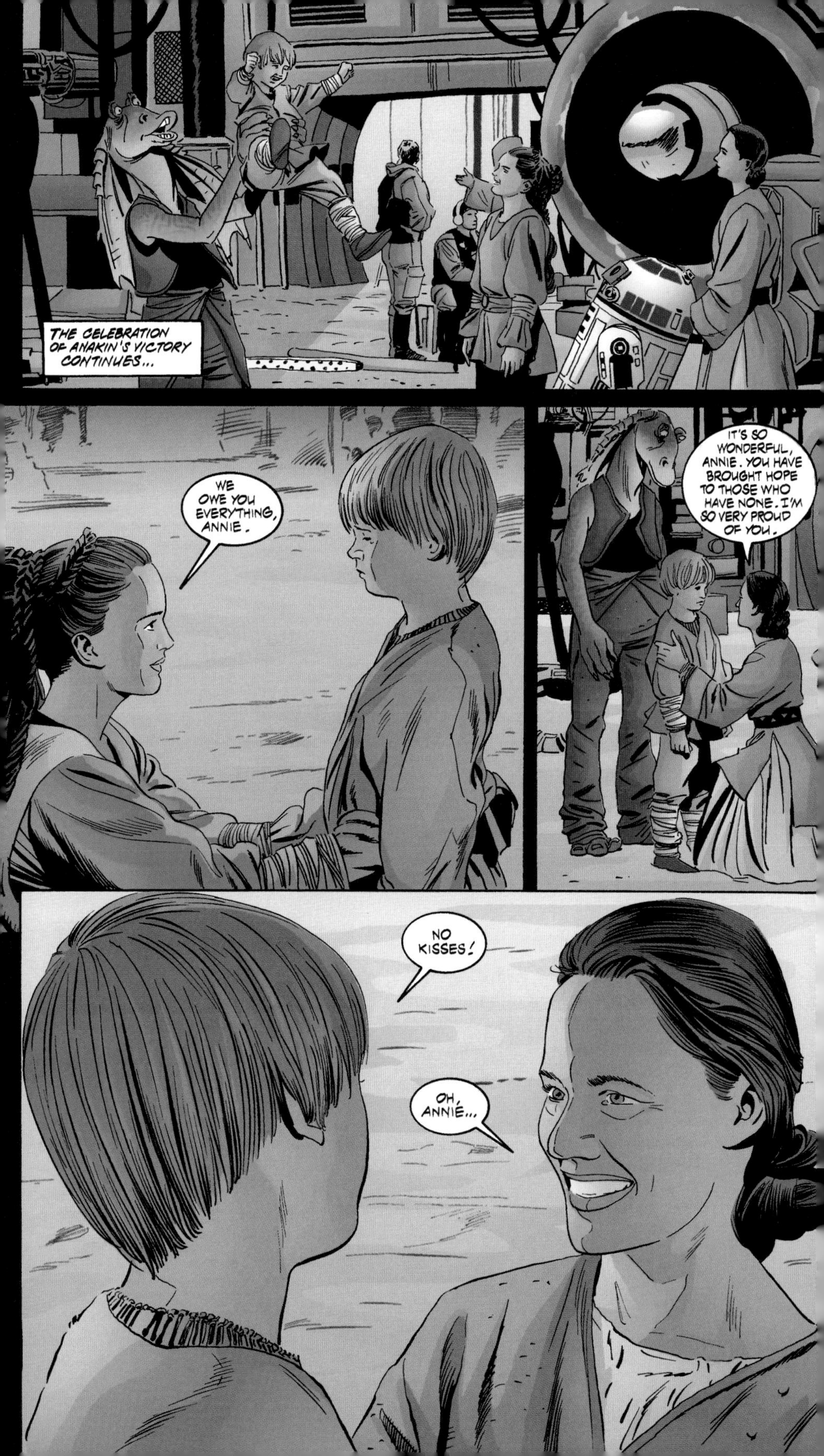
THE CELEBRATION OF ANAKIN'S VICTORY CONTINUES...
WE OWE YOU EVERYTHING, ANNIE.
IT'S SO WONDERFUL, ANNIE. YOU HAVE BROUGHT HOPE TO THOSE WHO HAVE NONE. I'M SO VERY PROUD OF YOU.
NO KISSES!
OH, ANNIE...

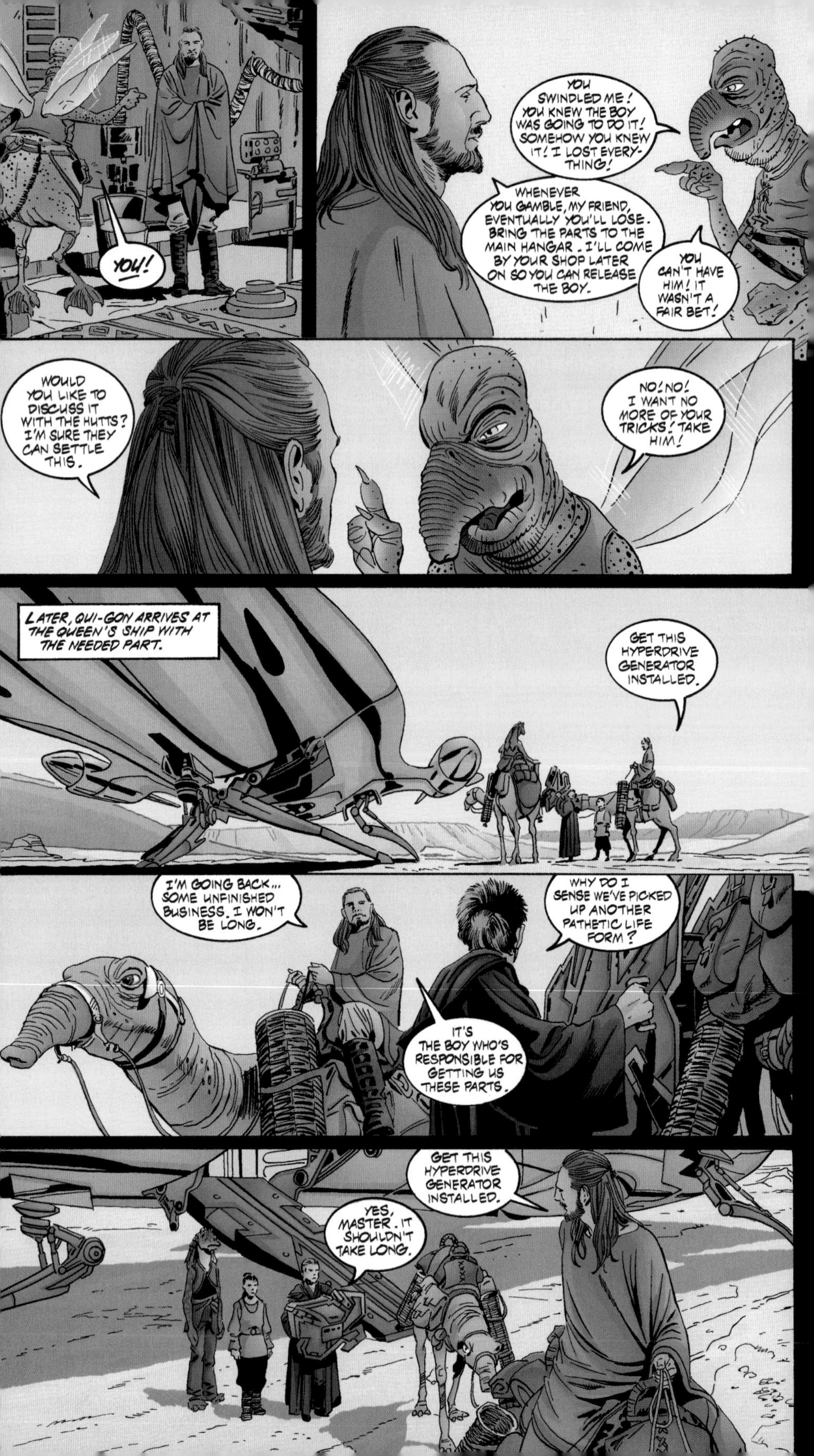
YOU!
YOU SWINDLED ME! YOU KNEW THE BOY WAS GOING TO DO IT! SOMEHOW YOU KNEW IT! I LOST EVERYTHING!
WHENEVER YOU GAMBLE, MY FRIEND, EVENTUALLY YOU'LL LOSE. BRING THE PARTS TO THE MAIN HANGAR. I'LL COME BY YOUR SHOP LATER ON SO YOU CAN RELEASE THE BOY.
YOU CAN'T HAVE HIM! IT WASN'T A FAIR BET!
WOULD YOU LIKE TO DISCUSS IT WITH THE HUTTS? I'M SURE THEY CAN SETTLE THIS.
NO! NO! I WANT NO MORE OF YOUR TRICKS! TAKE HIM!
LATER, QUI-GON ARRIVES AT THE QUEEN'S SHIP WITH THE NEEDED PART.
GET THIS HYPERDRIVE GENERATOR INSTALLED.
I'M GOING BACK... SOME UNFINISHED BUSINESS. I WON'T BE LONG.
WHY DO I SENSE WE'VE PICKED UP ANOTHER PATHETIC LIFE FORM?
IT'S THE BOY WHO'S RESPONSIBLE FOR GETTING US THESE PARTS.
GET THIS HYPERDRIVE GENERATOR INSTALLED.
YES, MASTER. IT SHOULDN'T TAKE LONG.

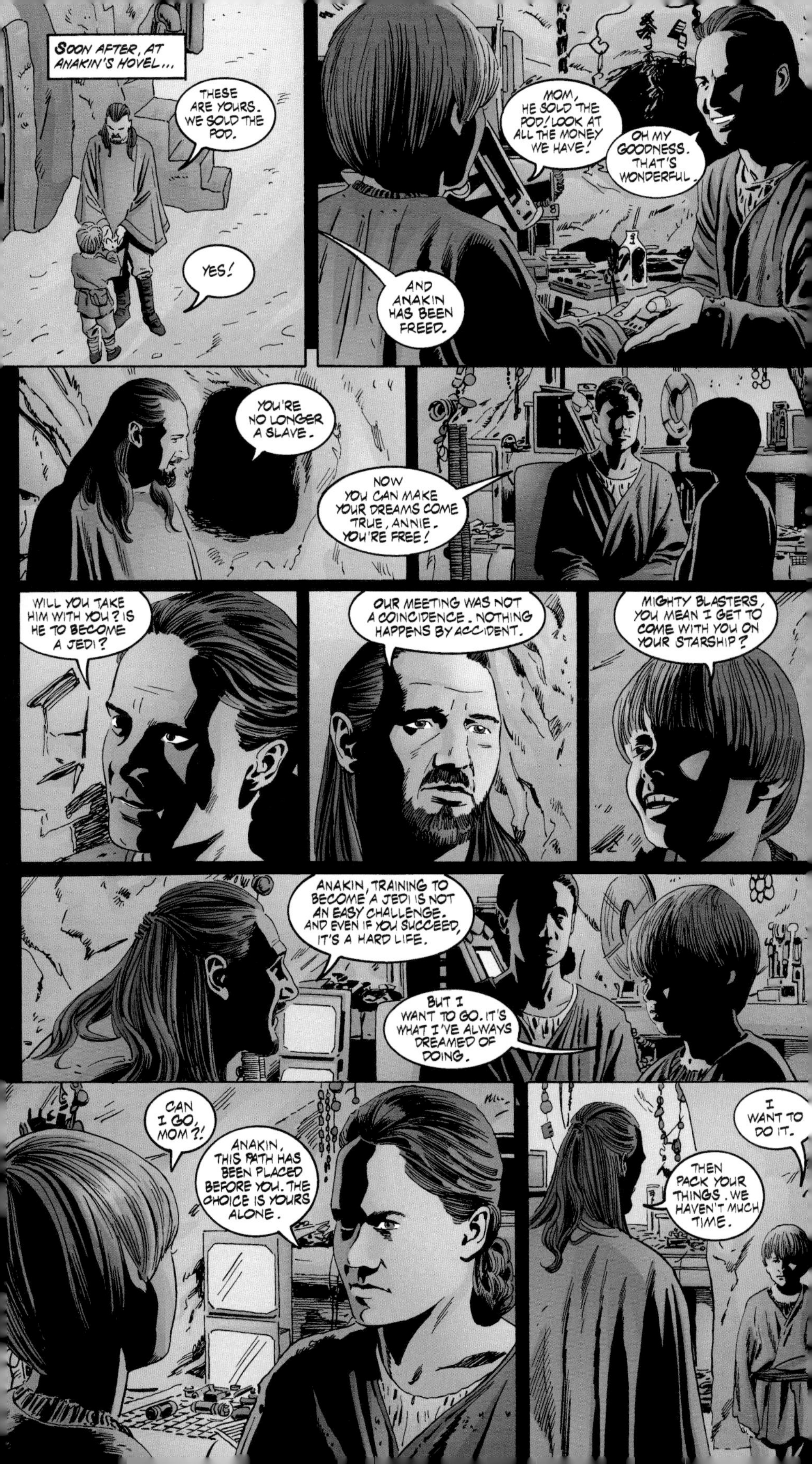
SOON AFTER, AT ANAKIN'S HOVEL...
THESE ARE YOURS. WE SOLD THE POD.
YES!
MOM, HE SOLD THE POD! LOOK AT ALL THE MONEY WE HAVE!
OH MY GOODNESS. THAT'S WONDERFUL.
AND ANAKIN HAS BEEN FREED.
YOU'RE NO LONGER A SLAVE.
NOW YOU CAN MAKE YOUR DREAMS COME TRUE, ANNIE. YOU'RE FREE!
WILL YOU TAKE HIM WITH YOU? IS HE TO BECOME A JEDI?
OUR MEETING WAS NOT A COINCIDENCE. NOTHING HAPPENS BY ACCIDENT.
MIGHTY BLASTERS, YOU MEAN I GET TO COME WITH YOU ON YOUR STARSHIP?
ANAKIN, TRAINING TO BECOME A JEDI IS NOT AN EASY CHALLENGE. AND EVEN IF YOU SUCCEED, IT'S A HARD LIFE.
BUT I WANT TO GO. IT'S WHAT I'VE ALWAYS DREAMED OF DOING.
CAN I GO, MOM?!
ANAKIN, THIS PATH HAS BEEN PLACED BEFORE YOU. THE CHOICE IS YOURS ALONE.
I WANT TO DO IT.
THEN PACK YOUR THINGS. WE HAVEN'T MUCH TIME.

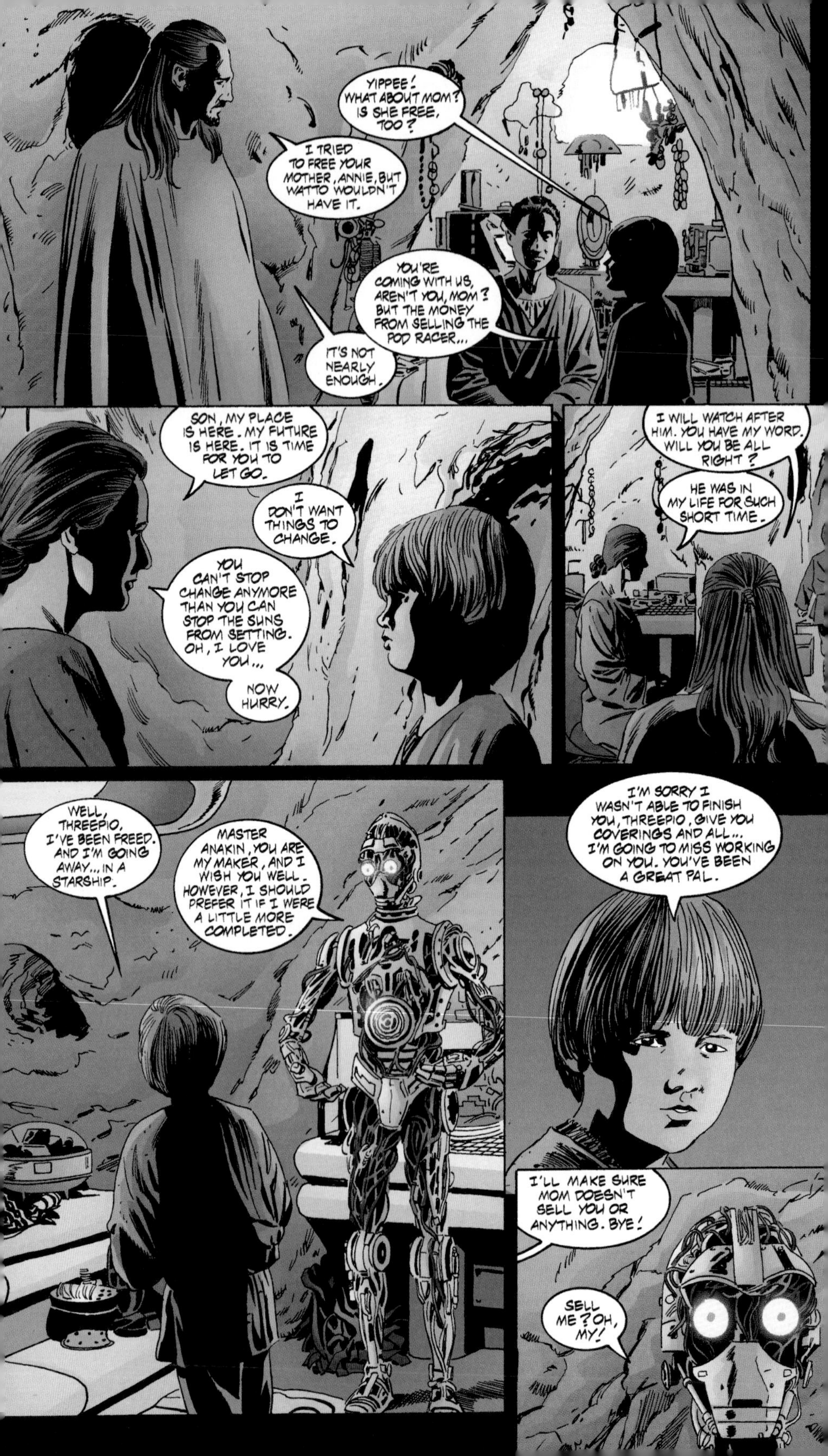
YIPPEE! WHAT ABOUT MOM? IS SHE FREE, TOO?
I TRIED TO FREE YOUR MOTHER, ANNIE, BUT WATTO WOULDN'T HAVE IT.
YOU'RE COMING WITH US, AREN'T YOU, MOM? BUT THE MONEY FROM SELLING THE POD RACER...
IT'S NOT NEARLY ENOUGH.
SON, MY PLACE IS HERE. MY FUTURE IS HERE. IT IS TIME FOR YOU TO LET GO.
I DON'T WANT THINGS TO CHANGE.
YOU CAN'T STOP CHANGE ANYMORE THAN YOU CAN STOP THE SUNS FROM SETTING. OH, I LOVE YOU...
NOW HURRY.
I WILL WATCH AFTER HIM. YOU HAVE MY WORD. WILL YOU BE ALL RIGHT?
HE WAS IN MY LIFE FOR SUCH SHORT TIME.
WELL, THREEPIO, I'VE BEEN FREED. AND I'M GOING AWAY... IN A STARSHIP.
MASTER ANAKIN, YOU ARE MY MAKER, AND I WISH YOU WELL. HOWEVER, I SHOULD PREFER IT IF I WERE A LITTLE MORE COMPLETED.
I'M SORRY I WASN'T ABLE TO FINISH YOU, THREEPIO, GIVE YOU COVERINGS AND ALL... I'M GOING TO MISS WORKING ON YOU. YOU'VE BEEN A GREAT PAL.
I'LL MAKE SURE MOM DOESN'T SELL YOU OR ANYTHING. BYE!
SELL ME? OH, MY!

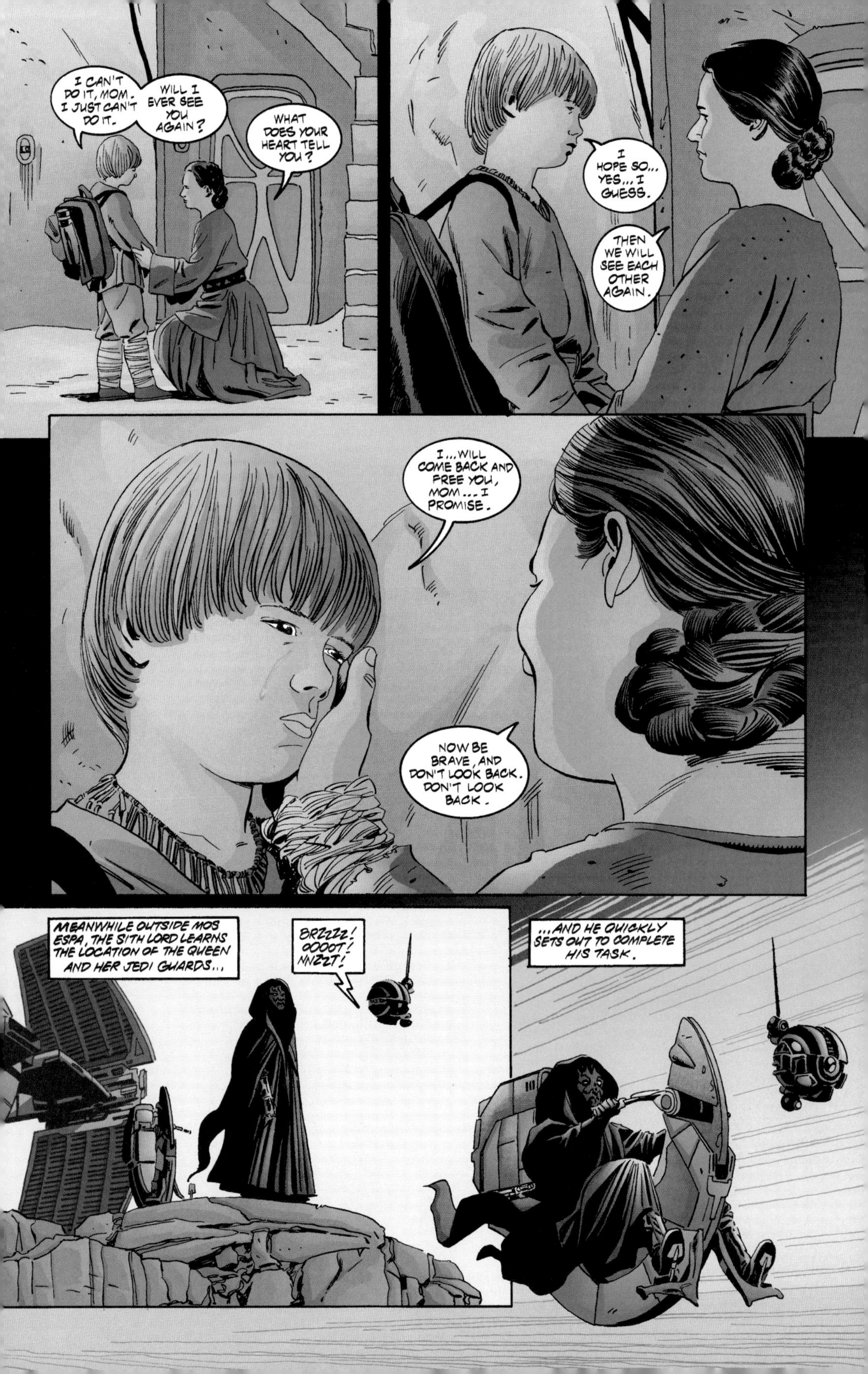
I CAN'T DO IT, MOM. I JUST CAN'T DO IT.
WILL I EVER SEE YOU AGAIN?
WHAT DOES YOUR HEART TELL YOU?
I HOPE SO... YES... I GUESS.
THEN WE WILL SEE EACH OTHER AGAIN.
I...WILL COME BACK AND FREE YOU, MOM... I PROMISE.
NOW BE BRAVE, AND DON'T LOOK BACK. DON'T LOOK BACK.
MEANWHILE OUTSIDE MOS ESPA, THE SITH LORD LEARNS THE LOCATION OF THE QUEEN AND HER JEDI GUARDS...
BRZZZZ! OOOOT! NNZZZT!
...AND HE QUICKLY SETS OUT TO COMPLETE HIS TASK.

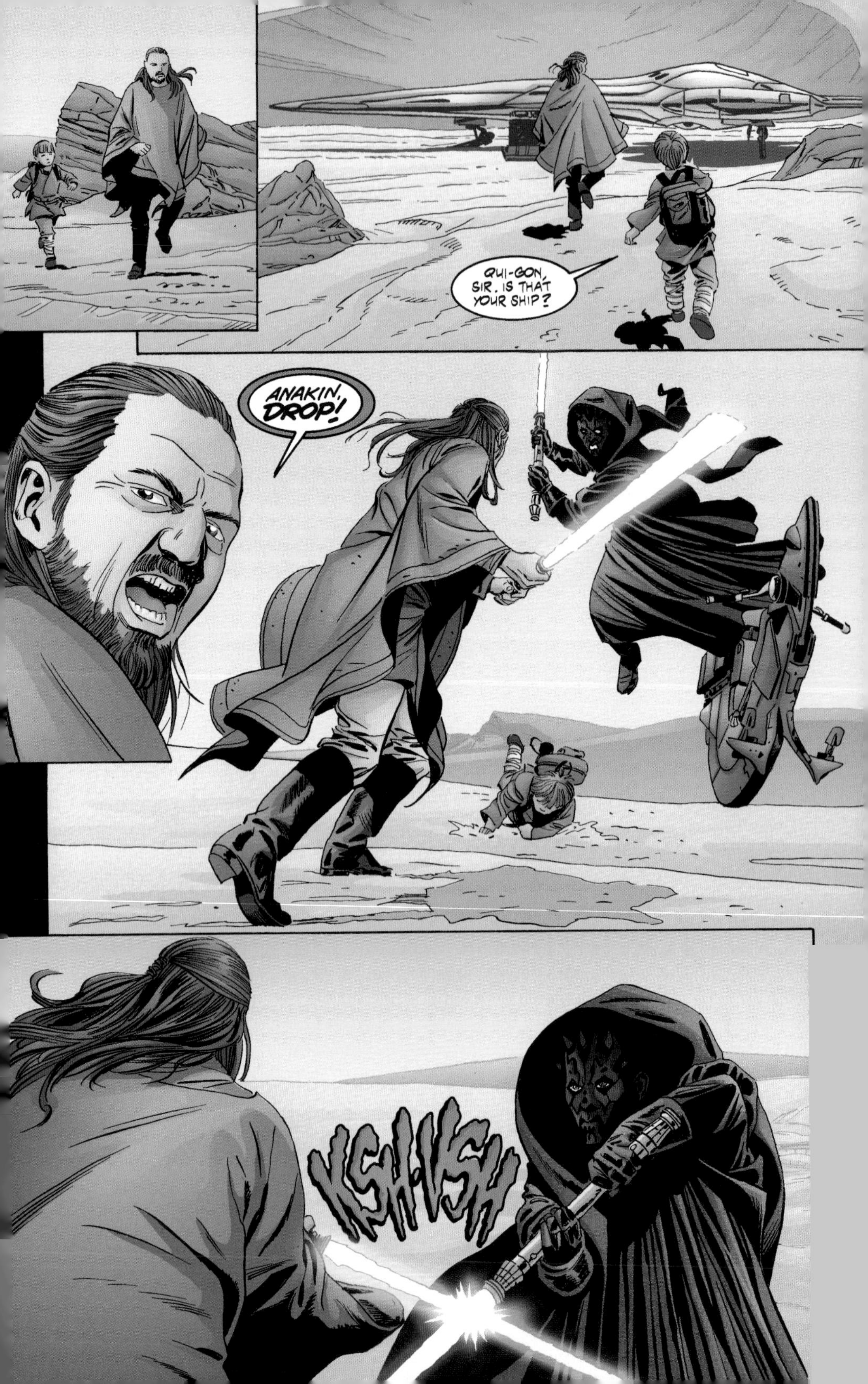
QUI-GON, SIR. IS THAT YOUR SHIP?
ANAKIN, DROP!
KSH-VSH

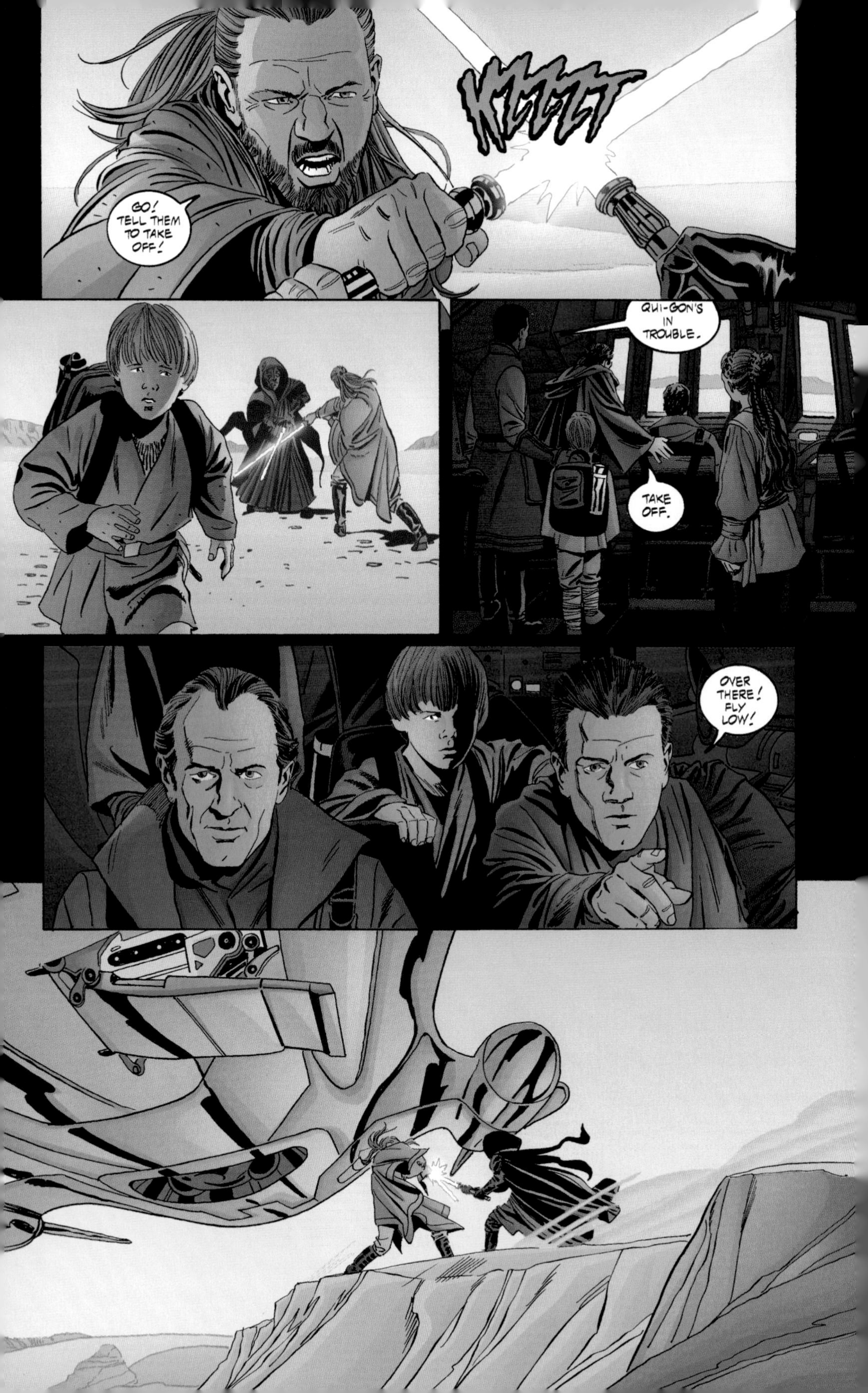
KZZZT
GO! TELL THEM TO TAKE OFF!
QUI-GON'S IN TROUBLE.
TAKE OFF.
OVER THERE! FLY LOW!

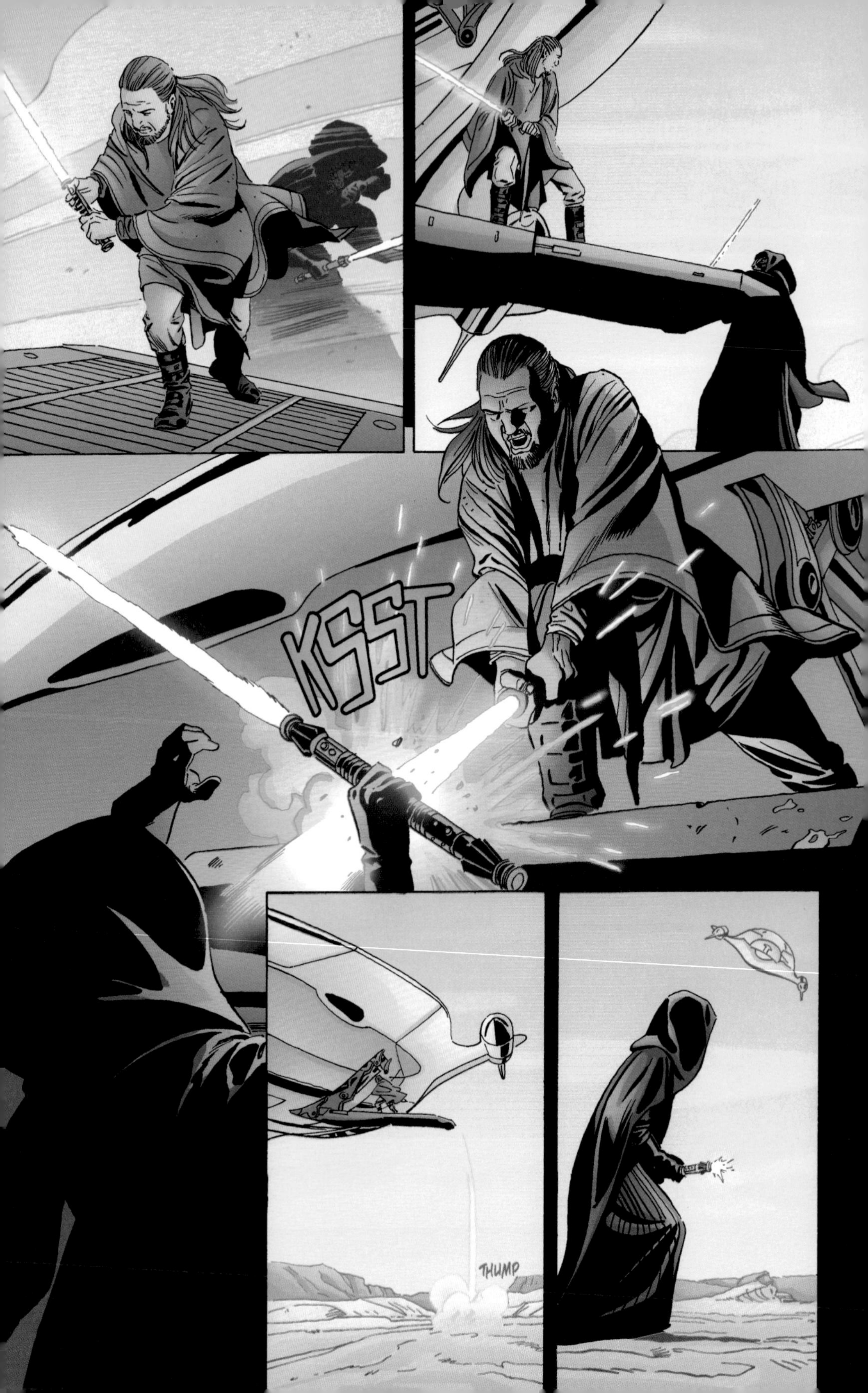
KSST
THUMP

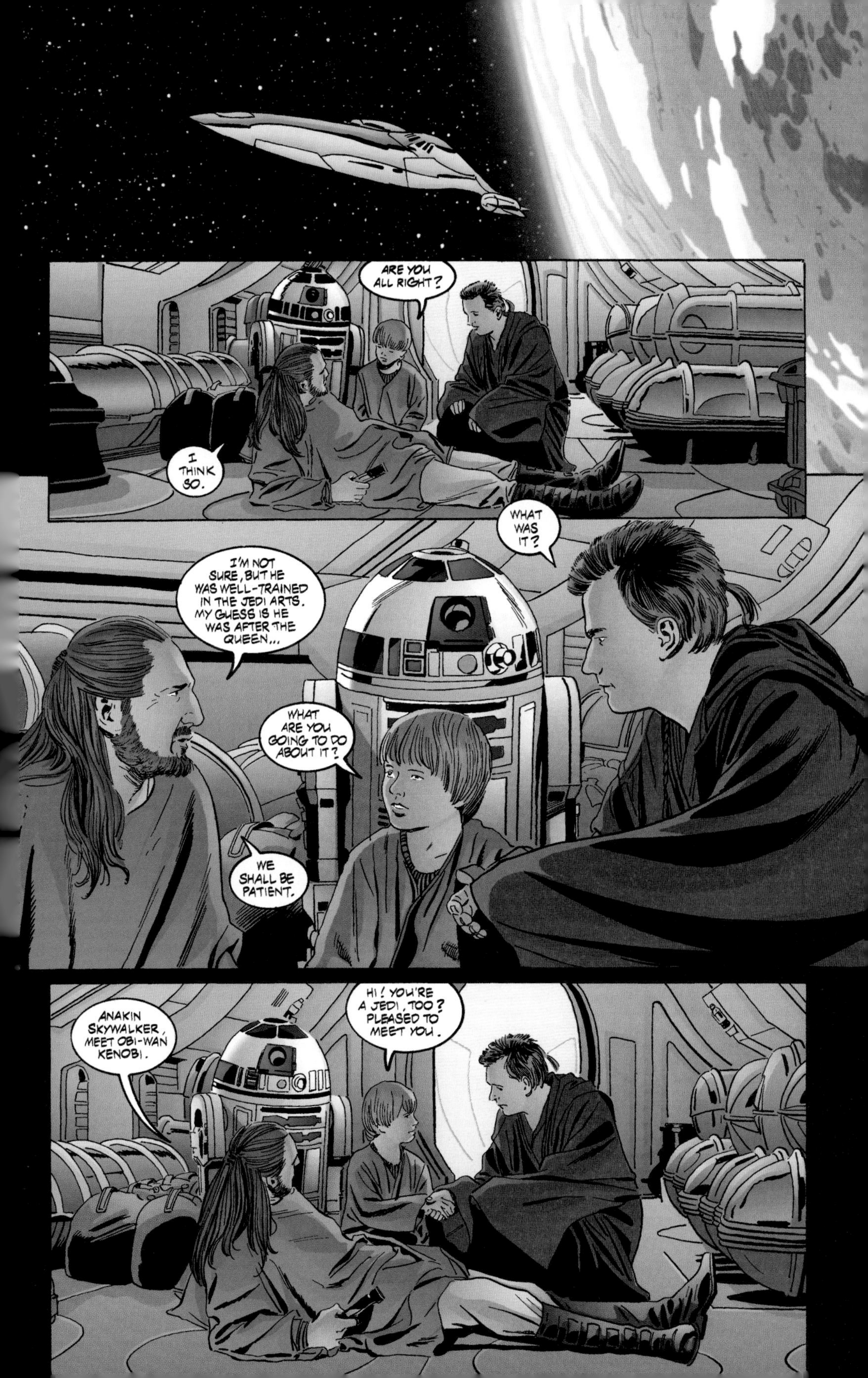
ARE YOU ALL RIGHT?
I THINK SO.
WHAT WAS IT?
I'M NOT SURE, BUT HE WAS WELL-TRAINED IN THE JEDI ARTS. MY GUESS IS HE WAS AFTER THE QUEEN...
WHAT ARE YOU GOING TO DO ABOUT IT?
WE SHALL BE PATIENT.
ANAKIN SKYWALKER, MEET OBI-WAN KENOBI.
HI! YOU'RE A JEDI, TOO? PLEASED TO MEET YOU.

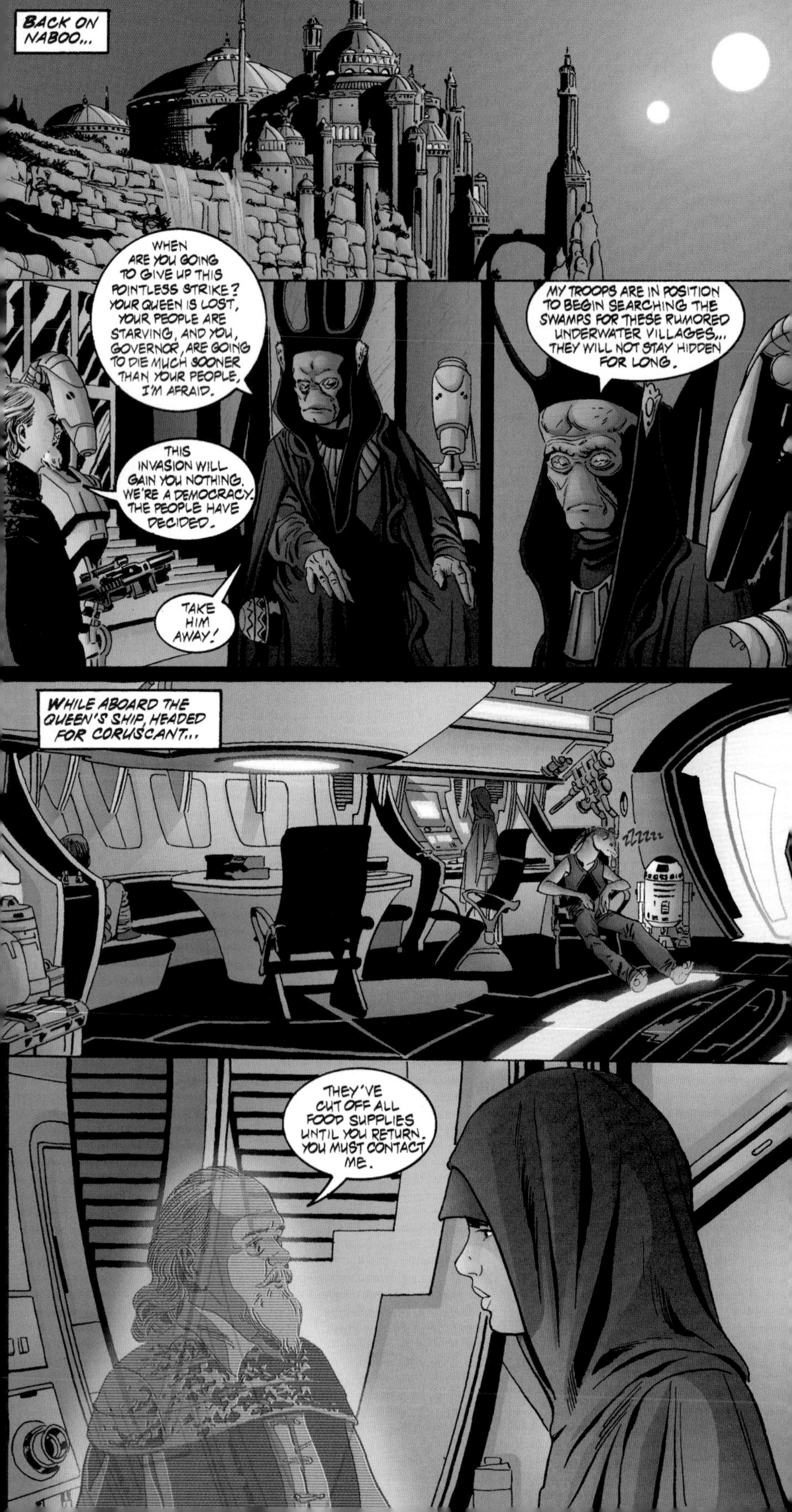
BACK ON NABOO...
WHEN ARE YOU GOING TO GIVE UP THIS POINTLESS STRIKE? YOUR QUEEN IS LOST, YOUR PEOPLE ARE STARVING, AND YOU, GOVERNOR, ARE GOING TO DIE MUCH SOONER THAN YOUR PEOPLE, I'M AFRAID.
THIS INVASION WILL GAIN YOU NOTHING. WE'RE A DEMOCRACY. THE PEOPLE HAVE DECIDED.
TAKE HIM AWAY!
MY TROOPS ARE IN POSITION TO BEGIN SEARCHING THE SWAMPS FOR THESE RUMORED UNDERWATER VILLAGES... THEY WILL NOT STAY HIDDEN FOR LONG.
WHILE ABOARD THE QUEEN'S SHIP, HEADED FOR CORUSCANT...
ZZZZZ
THEY'VE CUT OFF ALL FOOD SUPPLIES UNTIL YOU RETURN. YOU MUST CONTACT ME.

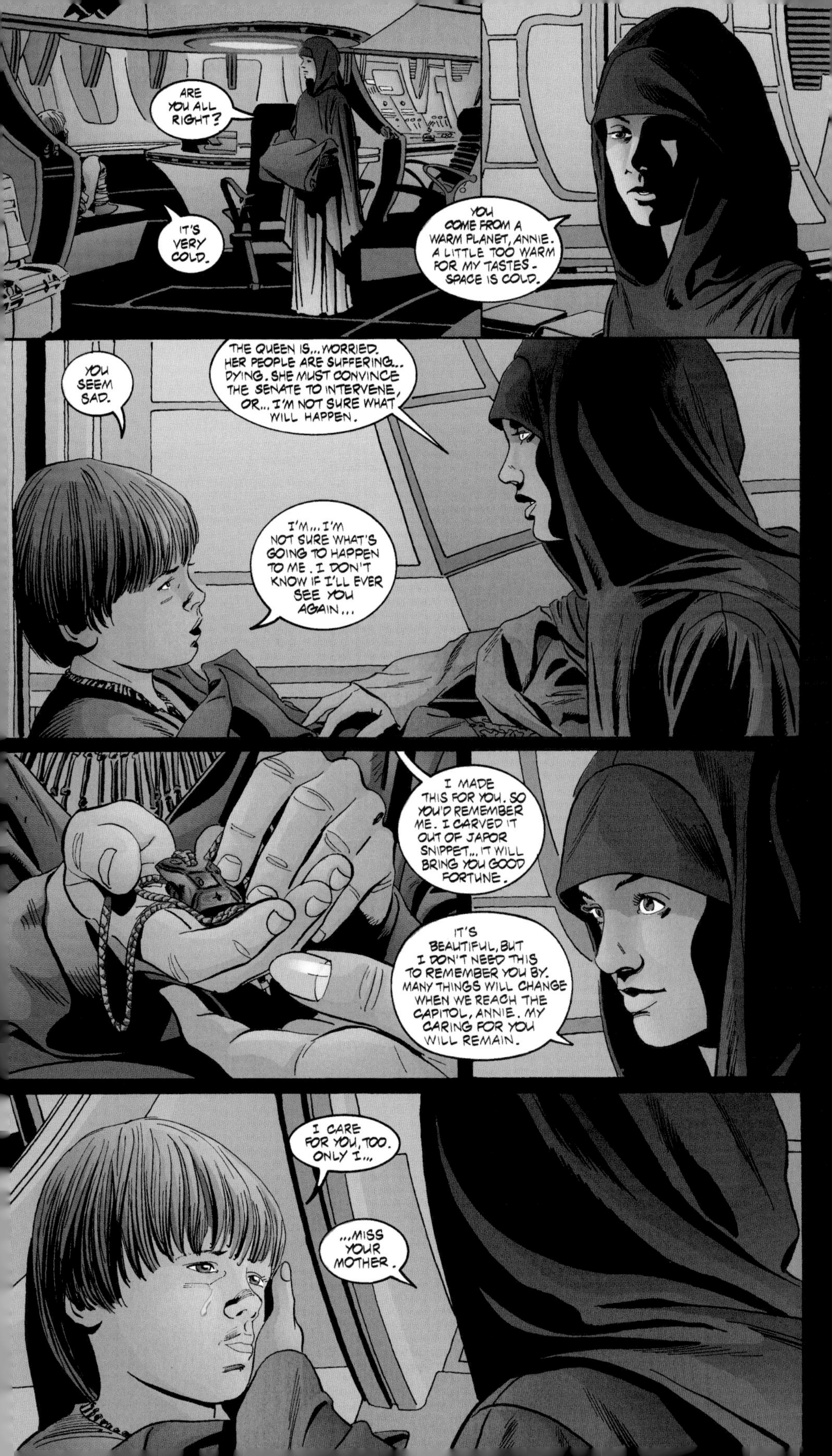
ARE YOU ALL RIGHT?
IT'S VERY COLD.
YOU COME FROM A WARM PLANET, ANNIE. A LITTLE TOO WARM FOR MY TASTES. SPACE IS COLD.
YOU SEEM SAD.
THE QUEEN IS... WORRIED. HER PEOPLE ARE SUFFERING... DYING. SHE MUST CONVINCE THE SENATE TO INTERVENE, OR... I'M NOT SURE WHAT WILL HAPPEN.
I'M... I'M NOT SURE WHAT'S GOING TO HAPPEN TO ME. I DON'T KNOW IF I'LL EVER SEE YOU AGAIN...
I MADE THIS FOR YOU. SO YOU'D REMEMBER ME. I CARVED IT OUT OF JAPOR SNIPPET... IT WILL BRING YOU GOOD FORTUNE.
IT'S BEAUTIFUL, BUT I DON'T NEED THIS TO REMEMBER YOU BY. MANY THINGS WILL CHANGE WHEN WE REACH THE CAPITOL, ANNIE. MY CARING FOR YOU WILL REMAIN.
I CARE FOR YOU, TOO. ONLY I...
...MISS YOUR MOTHER.

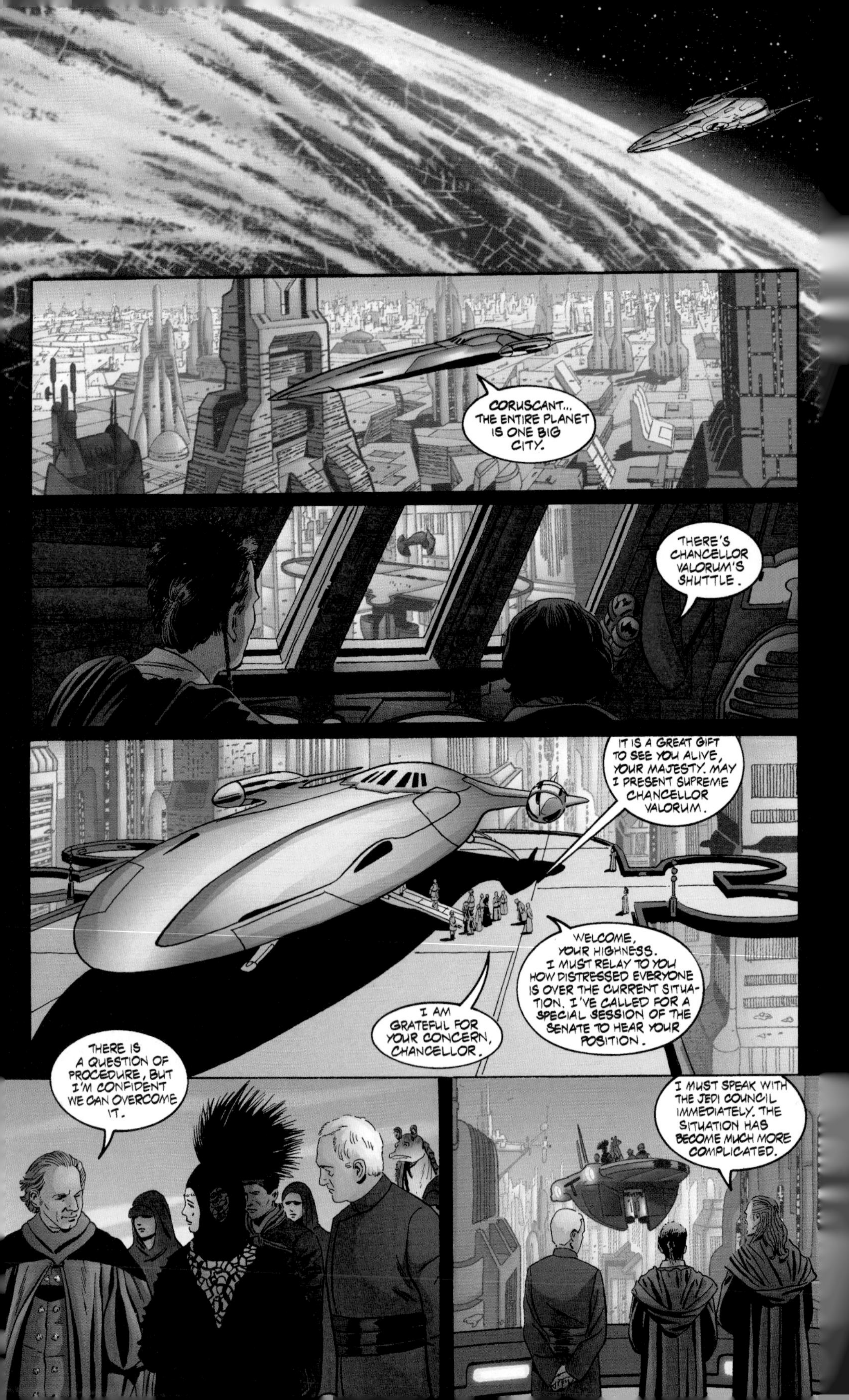
CORUSCANT... THE ENTIRE PLANET IS ONE BIG CITY.
THERE'S CHANCELLOR VALORUM'S SHUTTLE.
IT IS A GREAT GIFT TO SEE YOU ALIVE, YOUR MAJESTY. MAY I PRESENT SUPREME CHANCELLOR VALORUM.
WELCOME, YOUR HIGHNESS. I MUST RELAY TO YOU HOW DISTRESSED EVERYONE IS OVER THE CURRENT SITUATION. I'VE CALLED FOR A SPECIAL SESSION OF THE SENATE TO HEAR YOUR POSITION.
I AM GRATEFUL FOR YOUR CONCERN, CHANCELLOR.
THERE IS A QUESTION OF PROCEDURE, BUT I'M CONFIDENT WE CAN OVERCOME IT.
I MUST SPEAK WITH THE JEDI COUNCIL IMMEDIATELY. THE SITUATION HAS BECOME MUCH MORE COMPLICATED.

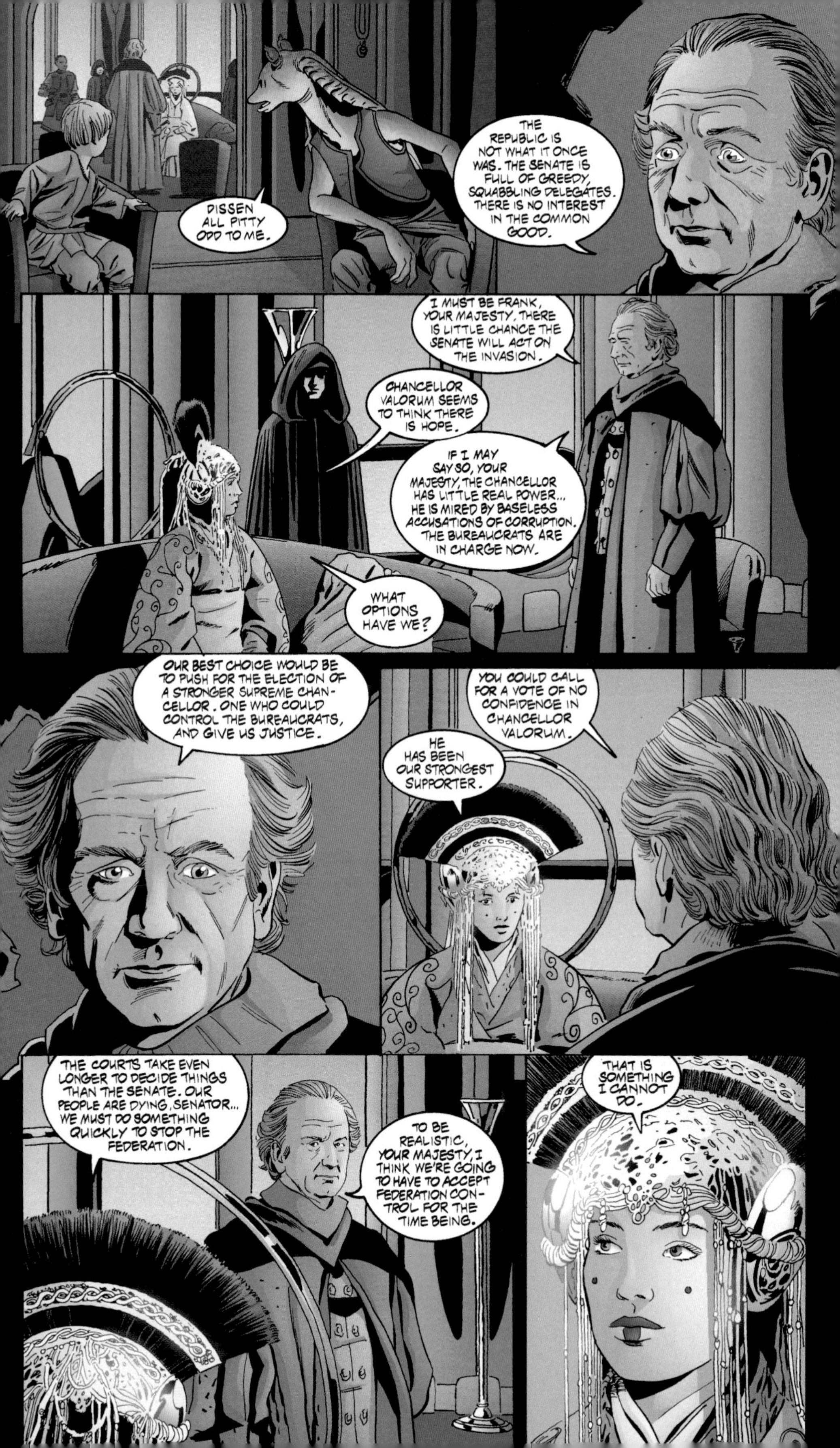
DISSEN ALL PITTY ODD TO ME.
THE REPUBLIC IS NOT WHAT IT ONCE WAS. THE SENATE IS FULL OF GREEDY, SQUABBLING DELEGATES. THERE IS NO INTEREST IN THE COMMON GOOD.
I MUST BE FRANK, YOUR MAJESTY. THERE IS LITTLE CHANCE THE SENATE WILL ACT ON THE INVASION.
CHANCELLOR VALORUM SEEMS TO THINK THERE IS HOPE.
IF I MAY SAY SO, YOUR MAJESTY, THE CHANCELLOR HAS LITTLE REAL POWER... HE IS MIRED BY BASELESS ACCUSATIONS OF CORRUPTION. THE BUREAUCRATS ARE IN CHARGE NOW.
WHAT OPTIONS HAVE WE?
OUR BEST CHOICE WOULD BE TO PUSH FOR THE ELECTION OF A STRONGER SUPREME CHAN-CELLOR. ONE WHO COULD CONTROL THE BUREAUCRATS, AND GIVE US JUSTICE.
YOU COULD CALL FOR A VOTE OF NO CONFIDENCE IN CHANCELLOR VALORUM.
HE HAS BEEN OUR STRONGEST SUPPORTER.
THE COURTS TAKE EVEN LONGER TO DECIDE THINGS THAN THE SENATE. OUR PEOPLE ARE DYING, SENATOR... WE MUST DO SOMETHING QUICKLY TO STOP THE FEDERATION.
TO BE REALISTIC, YOUR MAJESTY, I THINK WE'RE GOING TO HAVE TO ACCEPT FEDERATION CON-TROL FOR THE TIME BEING.
THAT IS SOMETHING I CANNOT DO.

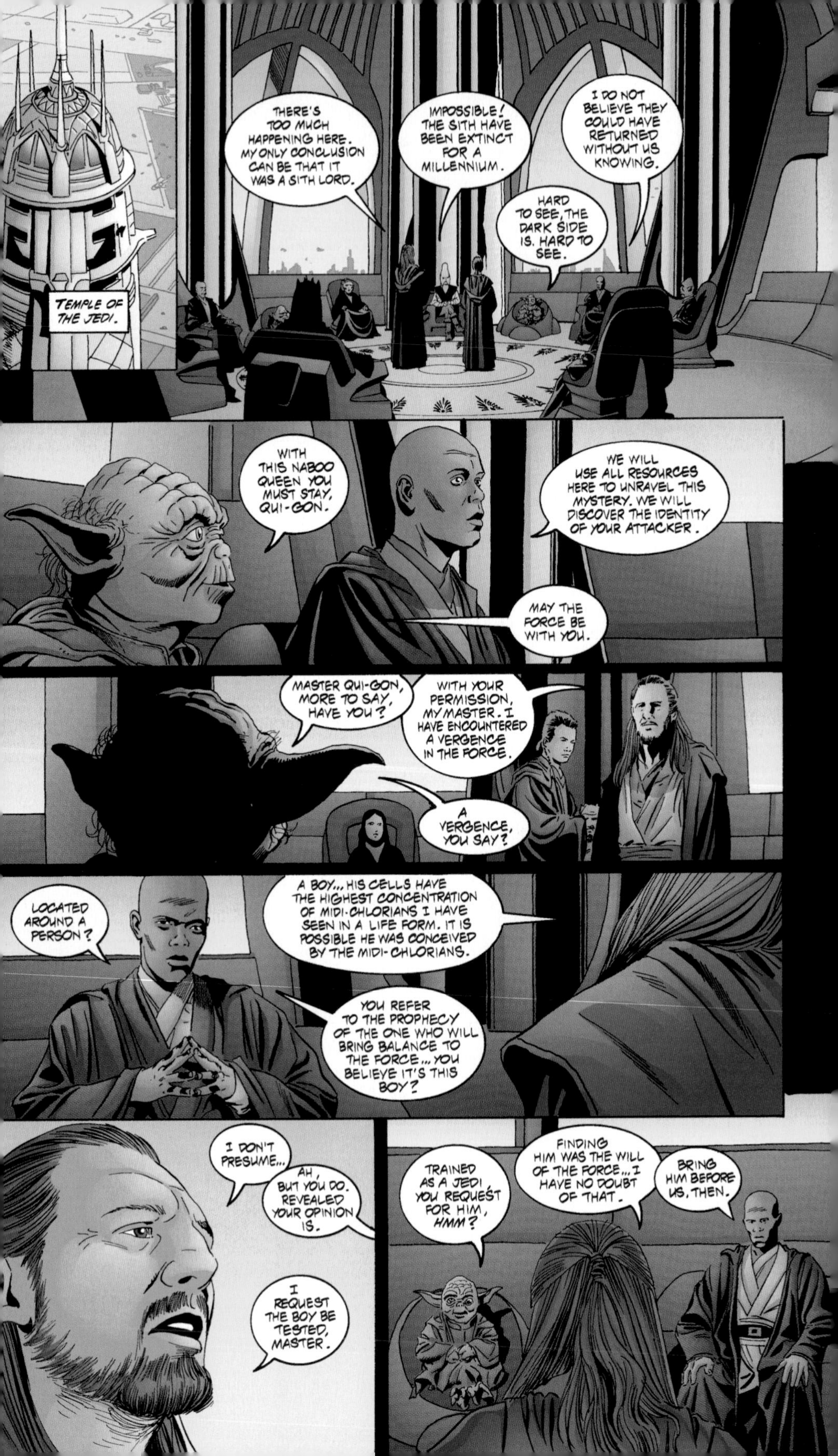

TEMPLE OF THE JEDI.
THERE'S TOO MUCH HAPPENING HERE. MY ONLY CONCLUSION CAN BE THAT IT WAS A SITH LORD.
IMPOSSIBLE! THE SITH HAVE BEEN EXTINCT FOR A MILLENNIUM.
I DO NOT BELIEVE THEY COULD HAVE RETURNED WITHOUT US KNOWING.
HARD TO SEE, THE DARK SIDE IS. HARD TO SEE.
WITH THIS NABOO QUEEN YOU MUST STAY, QUI-GON.
WE WILL USE ALL RESOURCES HERE TO UNRAVEL THIS MYSTERY. WE WILL DISCOVER THE IDENTITY OF YOUR ATTACKER.
MAY THE FORCE BE WITH YOU.
MASTER QUI-GON, MORE TO SAY, HAVE YOU?
WITH YOUR PERMISSION, MY MASTER. I HAVE ENCOUNTERED A VERGENCE IN THE FORCE.
A VERGENCE, YOU SAY?
LOCATED AROUND A PERSON?
A BOY... HIS CELLS HAVE THE HIGHEST CONCENTRATION OF MIDI-CHLORIANS I HAVE SEEN IN A LIFE FORM. IT IS POSSIBLE HE WAS CONCEIVED BY THE MIDI-CHLORIANS.
YOU REFER TO THE PROPHECY OF THE ONE WHO WILL BRING BALANCE TO THE FORCE... YOU BELIEVE IT'S THIS BOY?
I DON'T PRESUME...
AH, BUT YOU DO. REVEALED YOUR OPINION IS.
I REQUEST THE BOY BE TESTED, MASTER.
TRAINED AS A JEDI, YOU REQUEST FOR HIM, HMM?
FINDING HIM WAS THE WILL OF THE FORCE... I HAVE NO DOUBT OF THAT.
BRING HIM BEFORE US, THEN.

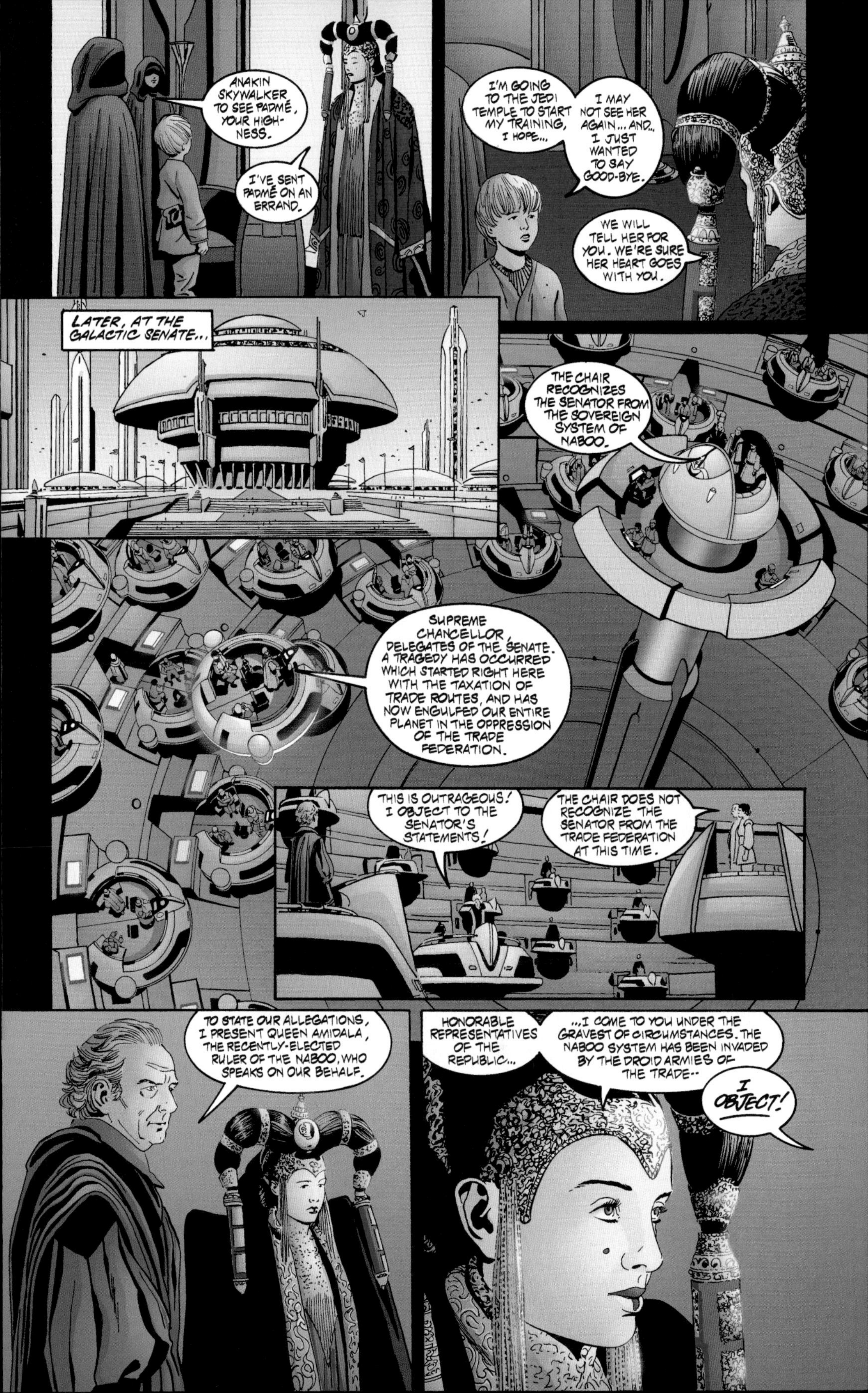
ANAKIN SKYWALKER TO SEE PADMÉ, YOUR HIGH-NESS.
I'VE SENT PADMÉ ON AN ERRAND.
I'M GOING TO THE JEDI TEMPLE TO START MY TRAINING, I HOPE...
I MAY NOT SEE HER AGAIN... AND.. I JUST WANTED TO SAY GOOD-BYE.
WE WILL TELL HER FOR YOU. WE'RE SURE HER HEART GOES WITH YOU.
LATER, AT THE GALACTIC SENATE...
THE CHAIR RECOGNIZES THE SENATOR FROM THE SOVEREIGN SYSTEM OF NABOO.
SUPREME CHANCELLOR, DELEGATES OF THE SENATE. A TRAGEDY HAS OCCURRED WHICH STARTED RIGHT HERE WITH THE TAXATION OF TRADE ROUTES, AND HAS NOW ENGULFED OUR ENTIRE PLANET IN THE OPPRESSION OF THE TRADE FEDERATION.
THIS IS OUTRAGEOUS! I OBJECT TO THE SENATOR'S STATEMENTS!
THE CHAIR DOES NOT RECOGNIZE THE SENATOR FROM THE TRADE FEDERATION AT THIS TIME.
TO STATE OUR ALLEGATIONS, I PRESENT QUEEN AMIDALA, THE RECENTLY-ELECTED RULER OF THE NABOO, WHO SPEAKS ON OUR BEHALF.
HONORABLE REPRESENTATIVES OF THE REPUBLIC...
...I COME TO YOU UNDER THE GRAVEST OF CIRCUMSTANCES. THE NABOO SYSTEM HAS BEEN INVADED BY THE DROID ARMIES OF THE TRADE--
I OBJECT!

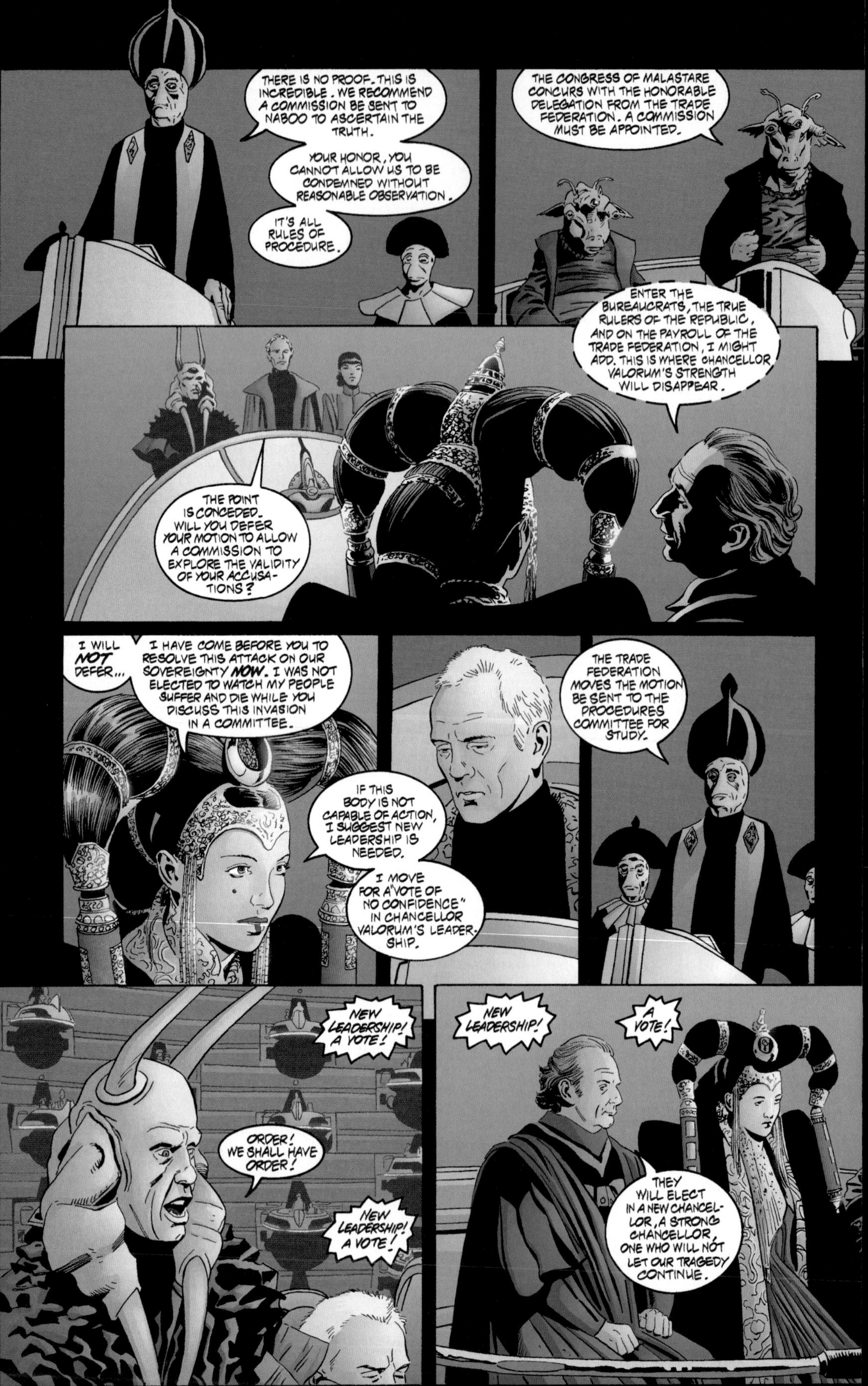
THERE IS NO PROOF. THIS IS INCREDIBLE. WE RECOMMEND A COMMISSION BE SENT TO NABOO TO ASCERTAIN THE TRUTH.
YOUR HONOR, YOU CANNOT ALLOW US TO BE CONDEMNED WITHOUT REASONABLE OBSERVATION.
IT'S ALL RULES OF PROCEDURE.
THE CONGRESS OF MALASTARE CONCURS WITH THE HONORABLE DELEGATION FROM THE TRADE FEDERATION. A COMMISSION MUST BE APPOINTED.
ENTER THE BUREAUCRATS, THE TRUE RULERS OF THE REPUBLIC, AND ON THE PAYROLL OF THE TRADE FEDERATION, I MIGHT ADD. THIS IS WHERE CHANCELLOR VALORUM'S STRENGTH WILL DISAPPEAR.
THE POINT IS CONCEDED. WILL YOU DEFER YOUR MOTION TO ALLOW A COMMISSION TO EXPLORE THE VALIDITY OF YOUR ACCUSATIONS?
I WILL NOT DEFER...
I HAVE COME BEFORE YOU TO RESOLVE THIS ATTACK ON OUR SOVEREIGNTY NOW. I WAS NOT ELECTED TO WATCH MY PEOPLE SUFFER AND DIE WHILE YOU DISCUSS THIS INVASION IN A COMMITTEE.
IF THIS BODY IS NOT CAPABLE OF ACTION, I SUGGEST NEW LEADERSHIP IS NEEDED.
I MOVE FOR A "VOTE OF NO CONFIDENCE" IN CHANCELLOR VALORUM'S LEADERSHIP.
THE TRADE FEDERATION MOVES THE MOTION BE SENT TO THE PROCEDURES COMMITTEE FOR STUDY.
NEW LEADERSHIP! A VOTE!
ORDER! WE SHALL HAVE ORDER!
NEW LEADERSHIP! A VOTE!
NEW LEADERSHIP!
A VOTE!
THEY WILL ELECT IN A NEW CHANCELLOR, A STRONG CHANCELLOR, ONE WHO WILL NOT LET OUR TRAGEDY CONTINUE.

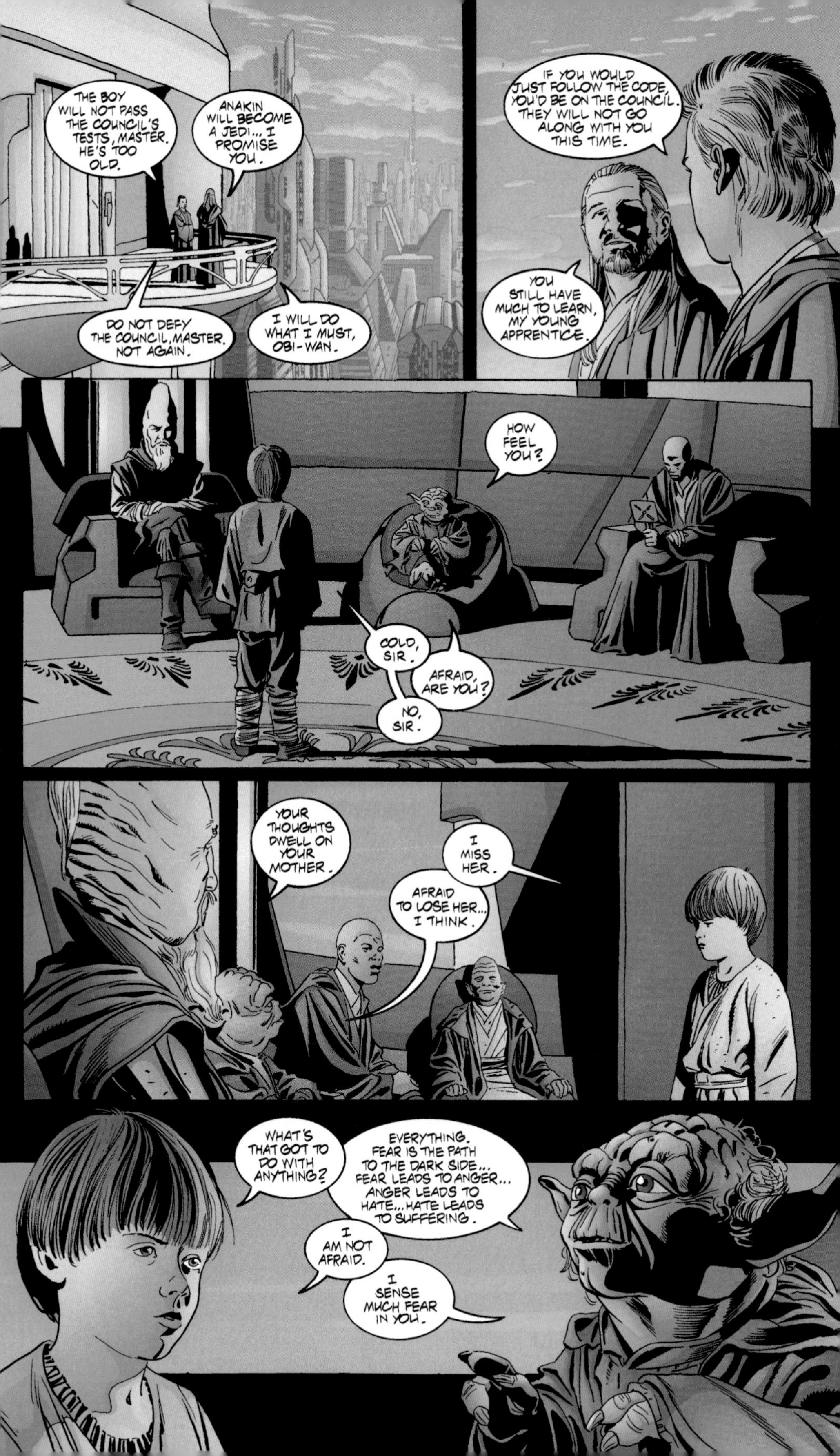
THE BOY WILL NOT PASS THE COUNCIL'S TESTS, MASTER. HE'S TOO OLD.
ANAKIN WILL BECOME A JEDI... I PROMISE YOU.
DO NOT DEFY THE COUNCIL, MASTER. NOT AGAIN.
I WILL DO WHAT I MUST, OBI-WAN.
IF YOU WOULD JUST FOLLOW THE CODE, YOU'D BE ON THE COUNCIL. THEY WILL NOT GO ALONG WITH YOU THIS TIME.
YOU STILL HAVE MUCH TO LEARN, MY YOUNG APPRENTICE.
HOW FEEL YOU?
COLD, SIR.
AFRAID, ARE YOU?
NO, SIR.
YOUR THOUGHTS DWELL ON YOUR MOTHER.
I MISS HER.
AFRAID TO LOSE HER... I THINK.
WHAT'S THAT GOT TO DO WITH ANYTHING?
EVERYTHING. FEAR IS THE PATH TO THE DARK SIDE... FEAR LEADS TO ANGER... ANGER LEADS TO HATE... HATE LEADS TO SUFFERING.
I AM NOT AFRAID.
I SENSE MUCH FEAR IN YOU.

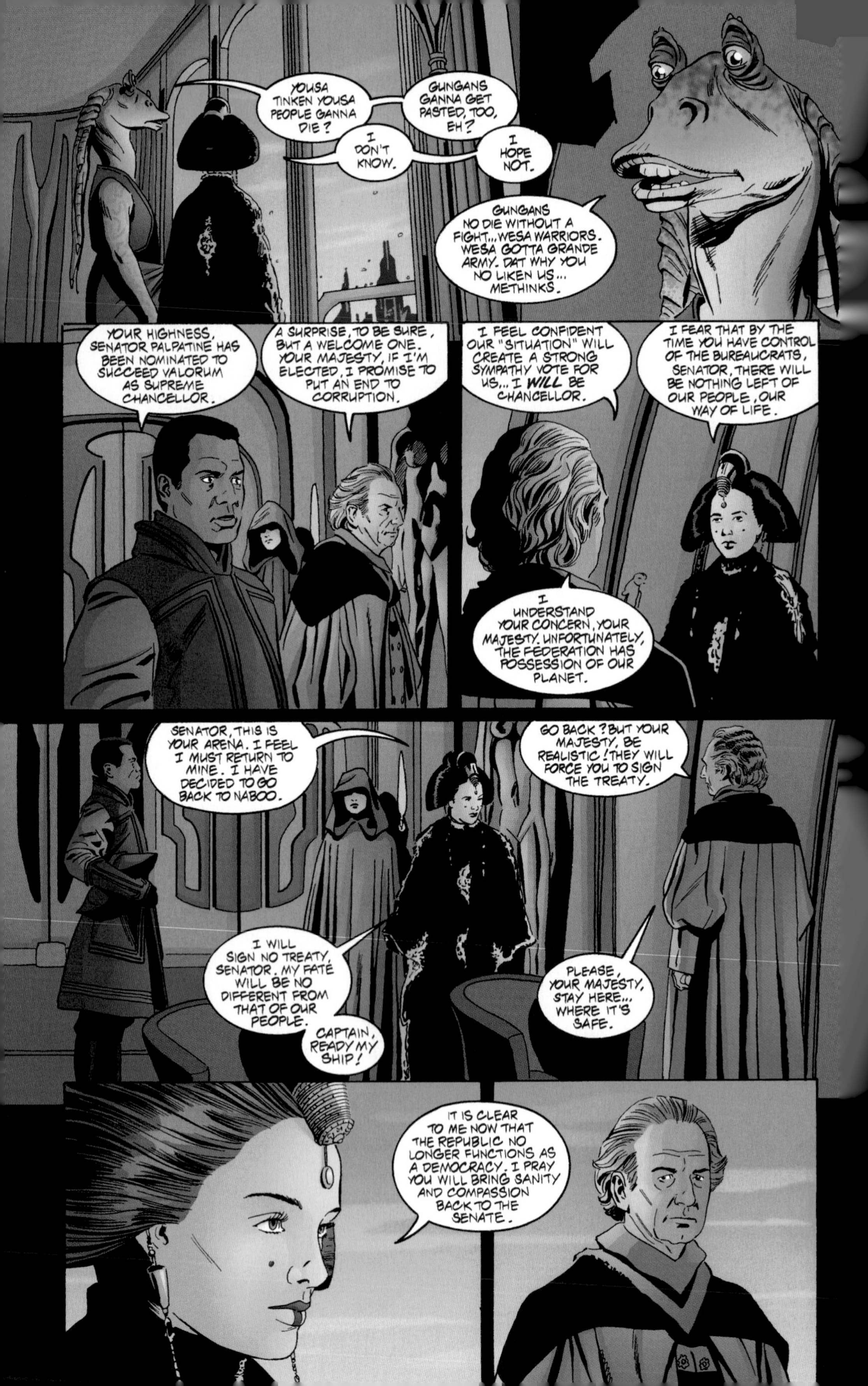
YOUSA TINKEN YOUSA PEOPLE GANNA DIE?
I DON'T KNOW.
GUNGANS GANNA GET PASTED, TOO, EH?
I HOPE NOT.
GUNGANS NO DIE WITHOUT A FIGHT... WESA WARRIORS. WESA GOTTA GRANDE ARMY. DAT WHY YOU NO LIKEN US... METHINKS.
YOUR HIGHNESS, SENATOR PALPATINE HAS BEEN NOMINATED TO SUCCEED VALORUM AS SUPREME CHANCELLOR.
A SURPRISE, TO BE SURE, BUT A WELCOME ONE. YOUR MAJESTY, IF I'M ELECTED, I PROMISE TO PUT AN END TO CORRUPTION.
I FEEL CONFIDENT OUR "SITUATION" WILL CREATE A STRONG SYMPATHY VOTE FOR US... I WILL BE CHANCELLOR.
I FEAR THAT BY THE TIME YOU HAVE CONTROL OF THE BUREAUCRATS, SENATOR, THERE WILL BE NOTHING LEFT OF OUR PEOPLE, OUR WAY OF LIFE.
I UNDERSTAND YOUR CONCERN, YOUR MAJESTY. UNFORTUNATELY, THE FEDERATION HAS POSSESSION OF OUR PLANET.
SENATOR, THIS IS YOUR ARENA. I FEEL I MUST RETURN TO MINE. I HAVE DECIDED TO GO BACK TO NABOO.
GO BACK? BUT YOUR MAJESTY, BE REALISTIC! THEY WILL FORCE YOU TO SIGN THE TREATY.
I WILL SIGN NO TREATY, SENATOR. MY FATE WILL BE NO DIFFERENT FROM THAT OF OUR PEOPLE.
CAPTAIN, READY MY SHIP!
PLEASE, YOUR MAJESTY, STAY HERE... WHERE IT'S SAFE.
IT IS CLEAR TO ME NOW THAT THE REPUBLIC NO LONGER FUNCTIONS AS A DEMOCRACY. I PRAY YOU WILL BRING SANITY AND COMPASSION BACK TO THE SENATE.

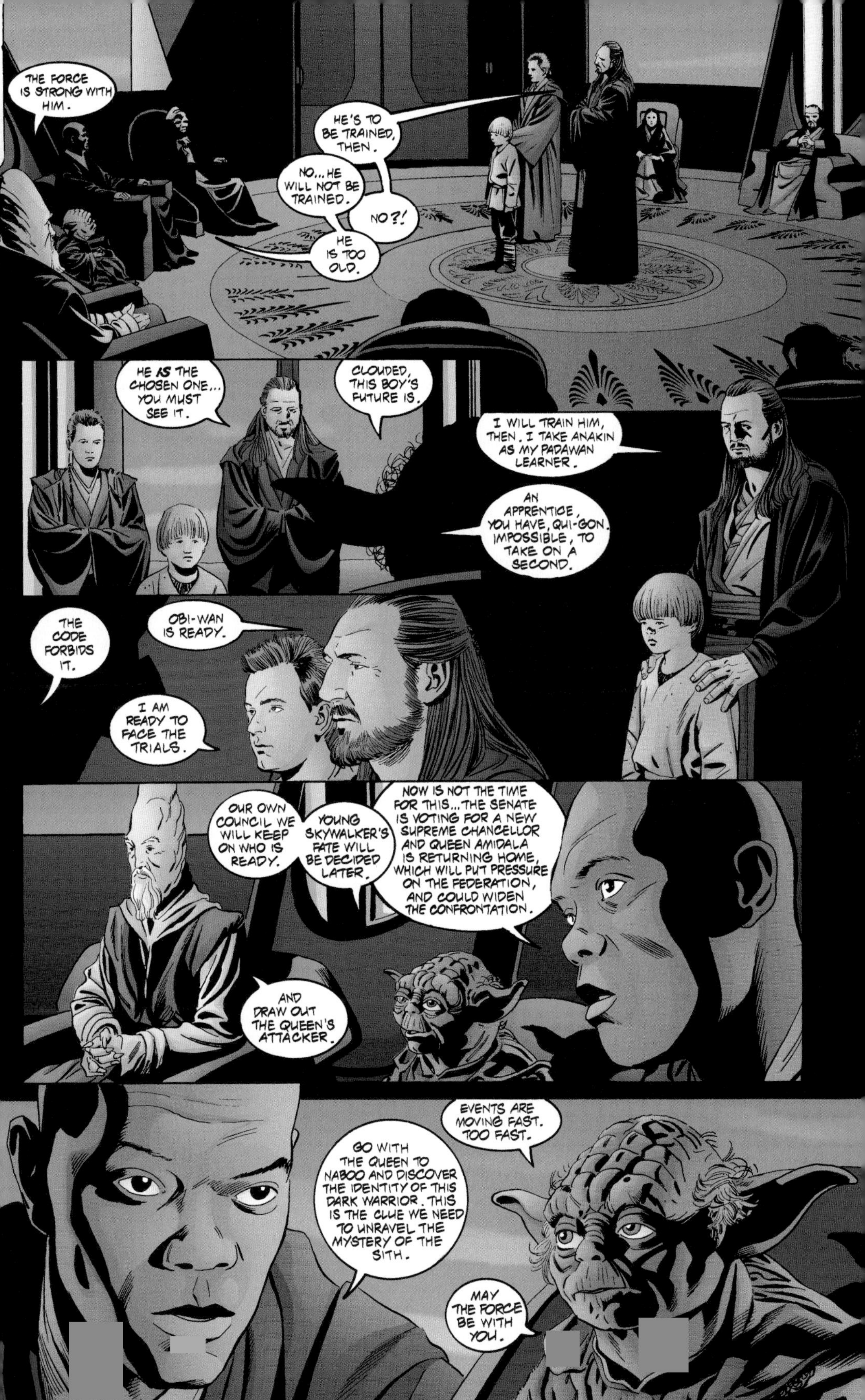
THE FORCE IS STRONG WITH HIM.
HE'S TO BE TRAINED, THEN.
NO... HE WILL NOT BE TRAINED.
NO?!
HE IS TOO OLD.
HE IS THE CHOSEN ONE... YOU MUST SEE IT.
CLOUDED, THIS BOY'S FUTURE IS.
I WILL TRAIN HIM, THEN. I TAKE ANAKIN AS MY PADAWAN LEARNER.
AN APPRENTICE, YOU HAVE, QUI-GON. IMPOSSIBLE, TO TAKE ON A SECOND.
THE CODE FORBIDS IT.
OBI-WAN IS READY.
I AM READY TO FACE THE TRIALS.
OUR OWN COUNCIL WE WILL KEEP ON WHO IS READY.
YOUNG SKYWALKER'S FATE WILL BE DECIDED LATER.
NOW IS NOT THE TIME FOR THIS... THE SENATE IS VOTING FOR A NEW SUPREME CHANCELLOR AND QUEEN AMIDALA IS RETURNING HOME, WHICH WILL PUT PRESSURE ON THE FEDERATION, AND COULD WIDEN THE CONFRONTATION.
AND DRAW OUT THE QUEEN'S ATTACKER.
EVENTS ARE MOVING FAST. TOO FAST.
GO WITH THE QUEEN TO NABOO AND DISCOVER THE IDENTITY OF THIS DARK WARRIOR. THIS IS THE CLUE WE NEED TO UNRAVEL THE MYSTERY OF THE SITH.
MAY THE FORCE BE WITH YOU.

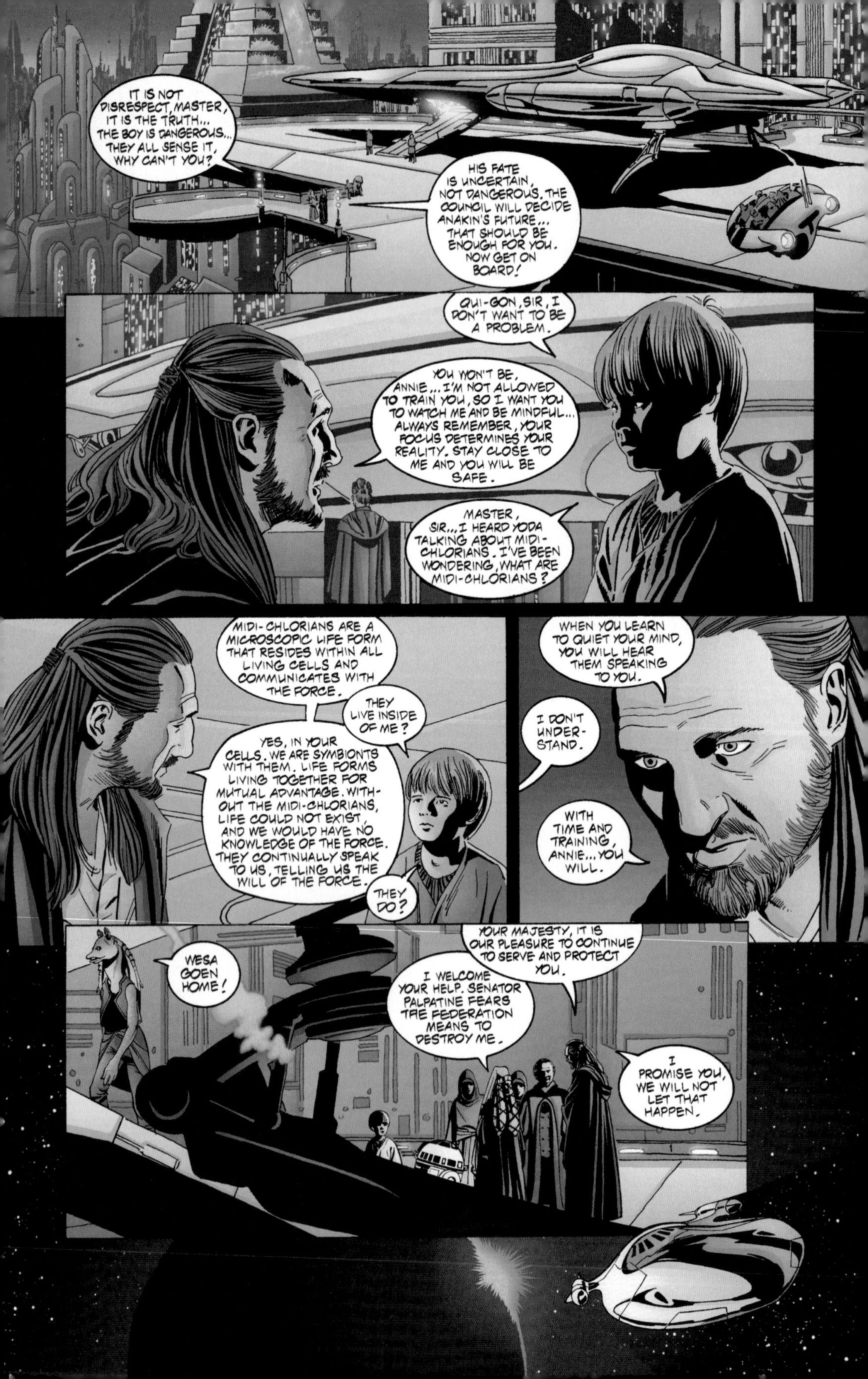
IT IS NOT DISRESPECT, MASTER, IT IS THE TRUTH... THE BOY IS DANGEROUS... THEY ALL SENSE IT, WHY CAN'T YOU?
HIS FATE IS UNCERTAIN, NOT DANGEROUS. THE COUNCIL WILL DECIDE ANAKIN'S FUTURE... THAT SHOULD BE ENOUGH FOR YOU. NOW GET ON BOARD!
QUI-GON, SIR, I DON'T WANT TO BE A PROBLEM.
YOU WON'T BE, ANNIE... I'M NOT ALLOWED TO TRAIN YOU, SO I WANT YOU TO WATCH ME AND BE MINDFUL... ALWAYS REMEMBER, YOUR FOCUS DETERMINES YOUR REALITY. STAY CLOSE TO ME AND YOU WILL BE SAFE.
MASTER, SIR... I HEARD YODA TALKING ABOUT MIDI-CHLORIANS. I'VE BEEN WONDERING, WHAT ARE MIDI-CHLORIANS?
MIDI-CHLORIANS ARE A MICROSCOPIC LIFE FORM THAT RESIDES WITHIN ALL LIVING CELLS AND COMMUNICATES WITH THE FORCE.
THEY LIVE INSIDE OF ME?
YES, IN YOUR CELLS. WE ARE SYMBIONTS WITH THEM. LIFE FORMS LIVING TOGETHER FOR MUTUAL ADVANTAGE. WITHOUT THE MIDI-CHLORIANS, LIFE COULD NOT EXIST, AND WE WOULD HAVE NO KNOWLEDGE OF THE FORCE. THEY CONTINUALLY SPEAK TO US, TELLING US THE WILL OF THE FORCE.
THEY DO?
WHEN YOU LEARN TO QUIET YOUR MIND, YOU WILL HEAR THEM SPEAKING TO YOU.
I DON'T UNDERSTAND.
WITH TIME AND TRAINING, ANNIE... YOU WILL.
WESA GOEN HOME!
YOUR MAJESTY, IT IS OUR PLEASURE TO CONTINUE TO SERVE AND PROTECT YOU.
I WELCOME YOUR HELP. SENATOR PALPATINE FEARS THE FEDERATION MEANS TO DESTROY ME.
I PROMISE YOU, WE WILL NOT LET THAT HAPPEN.

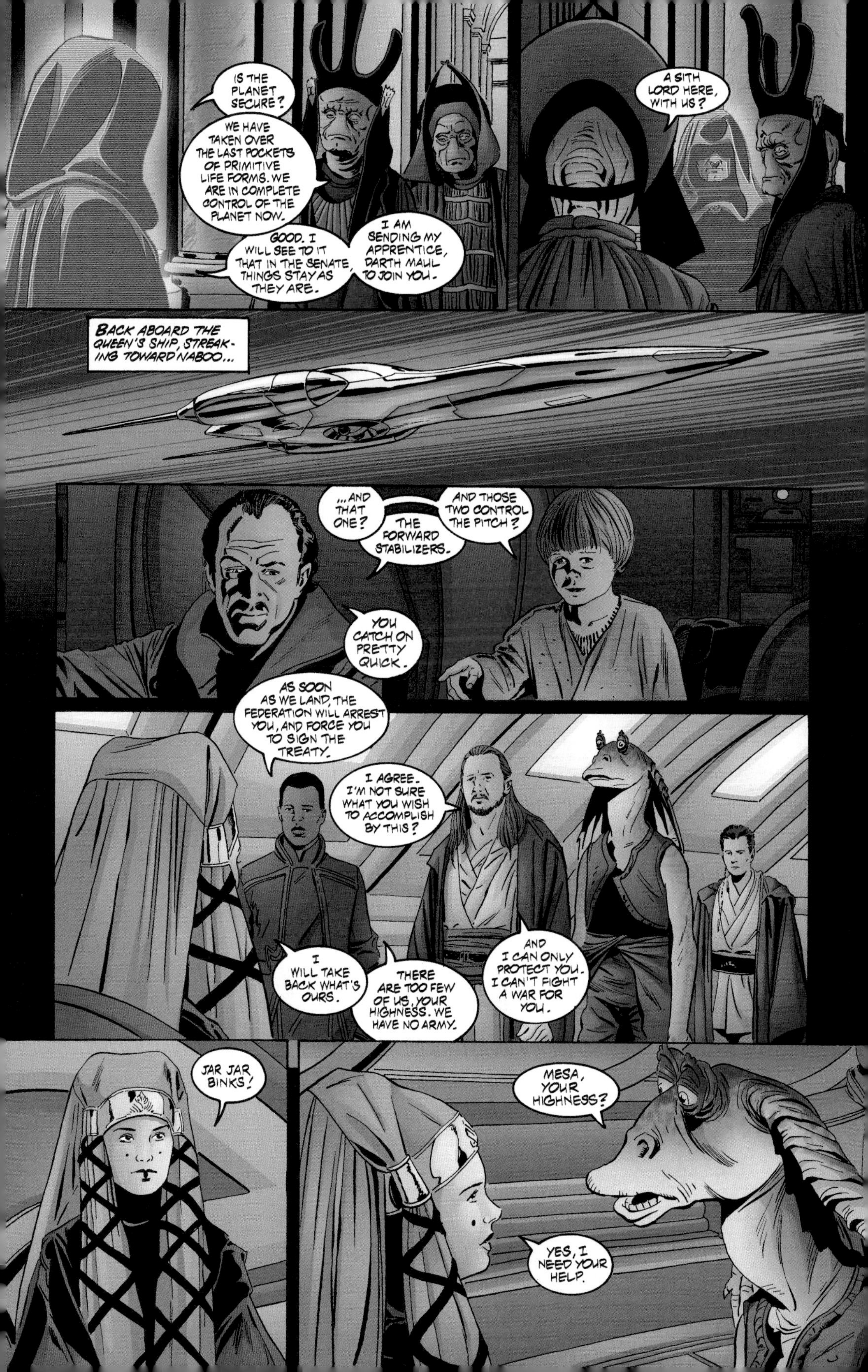
IS THE PLANET SECURE?
WE HAVE TAKEN OVER THE LAST POCKETS OF PRIMITIVE LIFE FORMS. WE ARE IN COMPLETE CONTROL OF THE PLANET NOW.
GOOD. I WILL SEE TO IT THAT IN THE SENATE, THINGS STAY AS THEY ARE.
I AM SENDING MY APPRENTICE, DARTH MAUL TO JOIN YOU.
A SITH LORD HERE, WITH US?
BACK ABOARD THE QUEEN'S SHIP, STREAKING TOWARD NABOO...
...AND THAT ONE?
THE FORWARD STABILIZERS.
AND THOSE TWO CONTROL THE PITCH?
YOU CATCH ON PRETTY QUICK.
AS SOON AS WE LAND, THE FEDERATION WILL ARREST YOU, AND FORCE YOU TO SIGN THE TREATY.
I AGREE. I'M NOT SURE WHAT YOU WISH TO ACCOMPLISH BY THIS?
I WILL TAKE BACK WHAT'S OURS.
THERE ARE TOO FEW OF US, YOUR HIGHNESS. WE HAVE NO ARMY.
AND I CAN ONLY PROTECT YOU. I CAN'T FIGHT A WAR FOR YOU.
JAR JAR BINKS!
MESA, YOUR HIGHNESS?
YES, I NEED YOUR HELP.

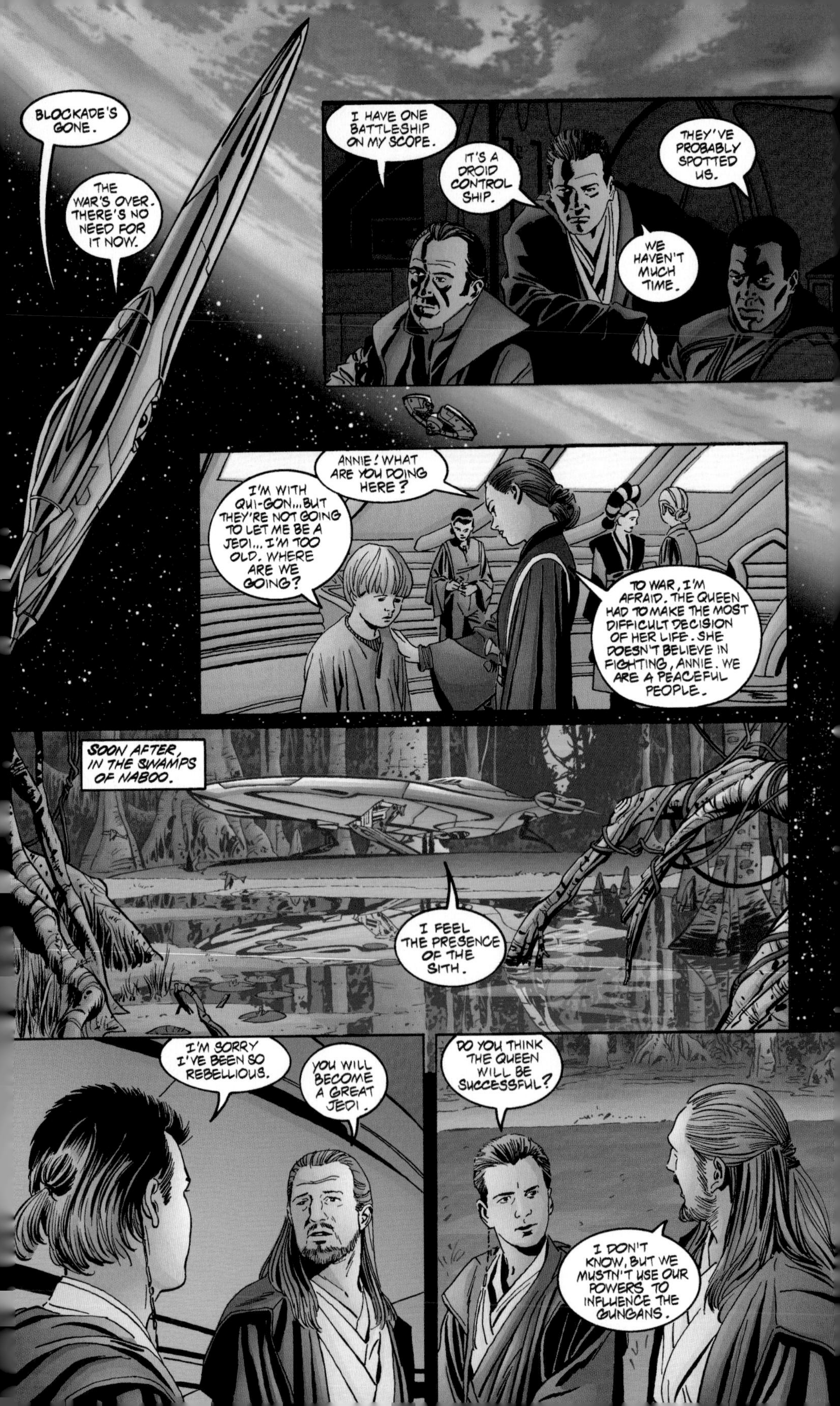
BLOCKADE'S GONE.
THE WAR'S OVER. THERE'S NO NEED FOR IT NOW.
I HAVE ONE BATTLESHIP ON MY SCOPE.
IT'S A DROID CONTROL SHIP.
THEY'VE PROBABLY SPOTTED US.
WE HAVEN'T MUCH TIME.
ANNIE! WHAT ARE YOU DOING HERE?
I'M WITH QUI-GON... BUT THEY'RE NOT GOING TO LET ME BE A JEDI... I'M TOO OLD. WHERE ARE WE GOING?
TO WAR, I'M AFRAID. THE QUEEN HAD TO MAKE THE MOST DIFFICULT DECISION OF HER LIFE. SHE DOESN'T BELIEVE IN FIGHTING, ANNIE. WE ARE A PEACEFUL PEOPLE.
SOON AFTER, IN THE SWAMPS OF NABOO.
I FEEL THE PRESENCE OF THE SITH.
I'M SORRY I'VE BEEN SO REBELLIOUS.
YOU WILL BECOME A GREAT JEDI.
DO YOU THINK THE QUEEN WILL BE SUCCESSFUL?
I DON'T KNOW, BUT WE MUSTN'T USE OUR POWERS TO INFLUENCE THE GUNGANS.

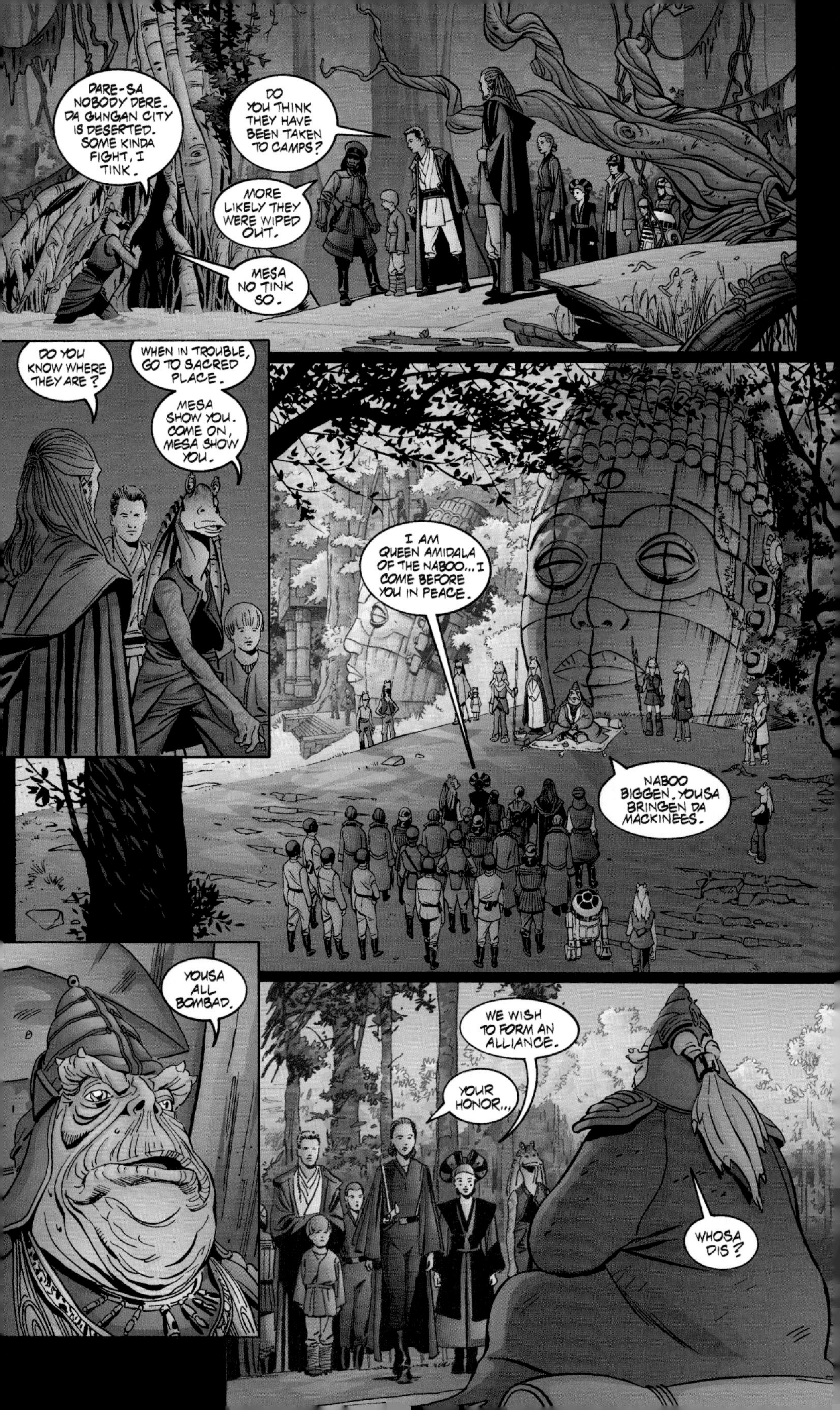
DARE-SA NOBODY DERE. DA GUNGAN CITY IS DESERTED. SOME KINDA FIGHT, I TINK.
DO YOU THINK THEY HAVE BEEN TAKEN TO CAMPS?
MORE LIKELY THEY WERE WIPED OUT.
MESA NO TINK SO.
DO YOU KNOW WHERE THEY ARE?
WHEN IN TROUBLE, GO TO SACRED PLACE.
MESA SHOW YOU. COME ON, MESA SHOW YOU.
I AM QUEEN AMIDALA OF THE NABOO... I COME BEFORE YOU IN PEACE.
NABOO BIGGEN. YOUSA BRINGEN DA MACKINEES.
YOUSA ALL BOMBAD.
WE WISH TO FORM AN ALLIANCE.
YOUR HONOR...
WHOSA DIS?

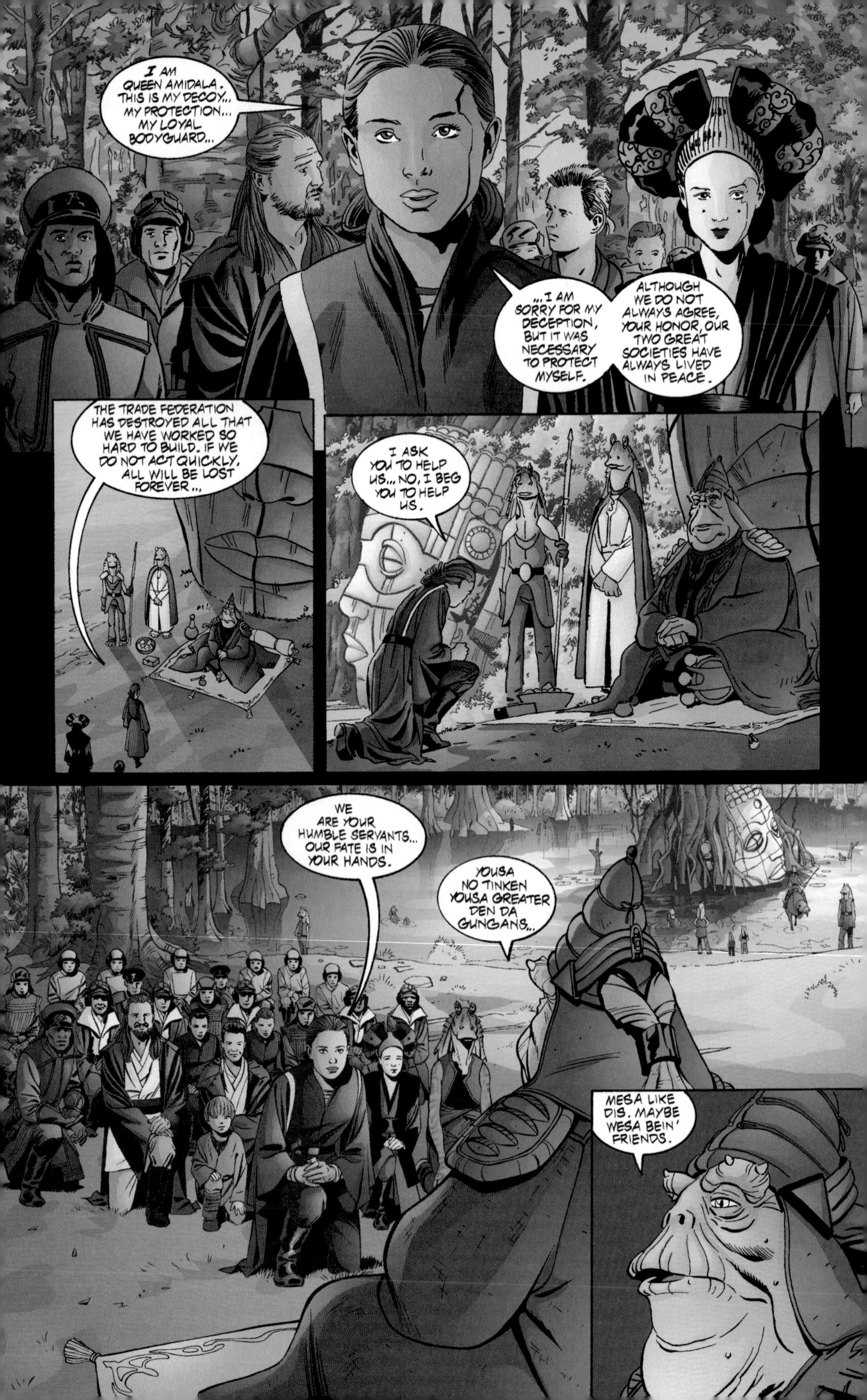
I AM QUEEN AMIDALA. THIS IS MY DECOY... MY PROTECTION... MY LOYAL BODYGUARD...
...I AM SORRY FOR MY DECEPTION, BUT IT WAS NECESSARY TO PROTECT MYSELF.
ALTHOUGH WE DO NOT ALWAYS AGREE, YOUR HONOR, OUR TWO GREAT SOCIETIES HAVE ALWAYS LIVED IN PEACE.
THE TRADE FEDERATION HAS DESTROYED ALL THAT WE HAVE WORKED SO HARD TO BUILD. IF WE DO NOT ACT QUICKLY, ALL WILL BE LOST FOREVER...
I ASK YOU TO HELP US... NO, I BEG YOU TO HELP US.
WE ARE YOUR HUMBLE SERVANTS... OUR FATE IS IN YOUR HANDS.
YOUSA NO TINKEN YOUSA GREATER DEN DA GUNGANS...
MESA LIKE DIS. MAYBE WESA BEIN' FRIENDS.

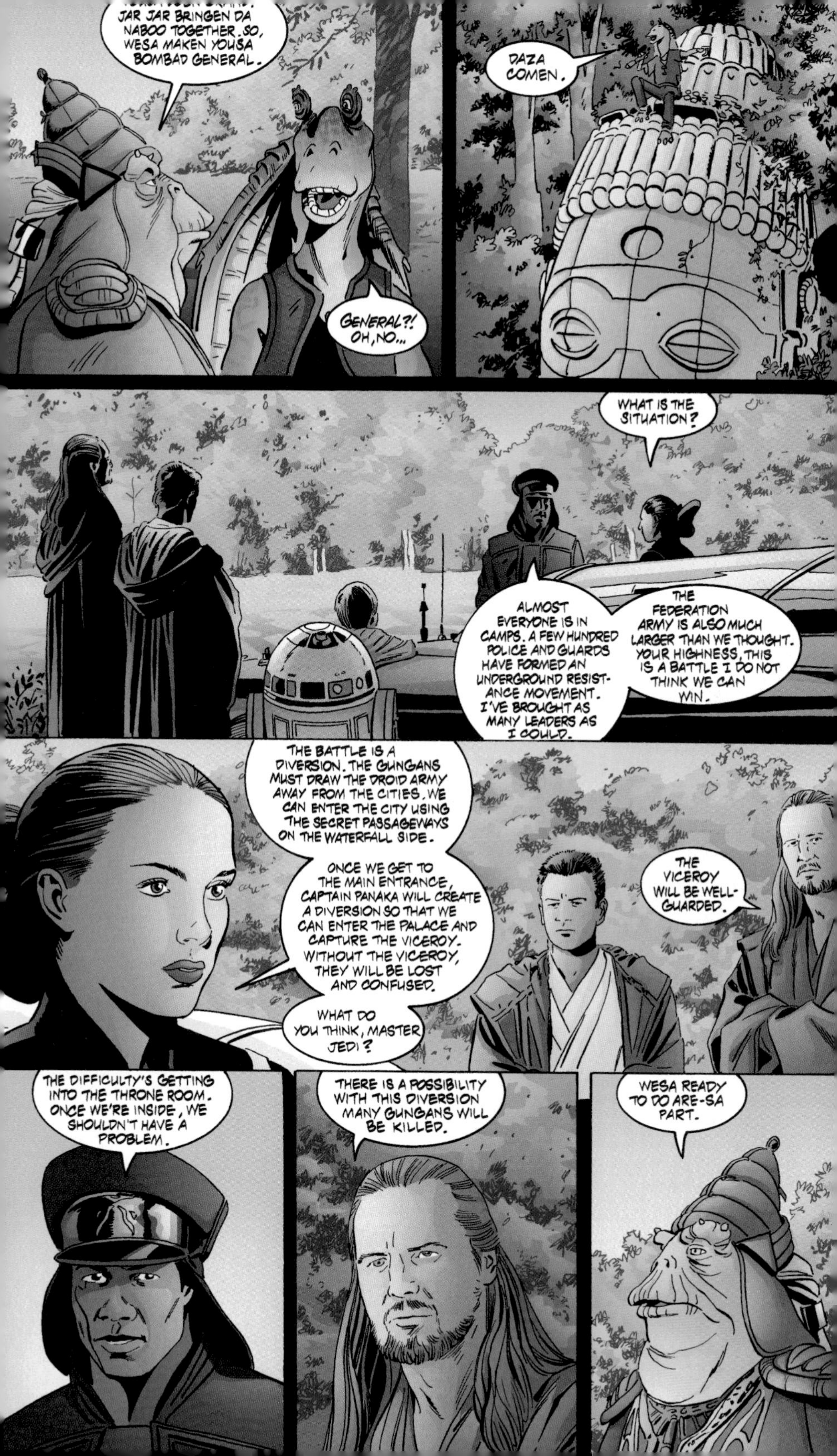

JAR JAR BRINGEN DA NABOO TOGETHER. SO, WESA MAKEN YOUSA BOMBAD GENERAL.
GENERAL?! OH, NO...
DAZA COMEN.
WHAT IS THE SITUATION?
ALMOST EVERYONE IS IN CAMPS. A FEW HUNDRED POLICE AND GUARDS HAVE FORMED AN UNDERGROUND RESIST-ANCE MOVEMENT. I'VE BROUGHT AS MANY LEADERS AS I COULD.
THE FEDERATION ARMY IS ALSO MUCH LARGER THAN WE THOUGHT. YOUR HIGHNESS, THIS IS A BATTLE I DO NOT THINK WE CAN WIN.
THE BATTLE IS A DIVERSION. THE GUNGANS MUST DRAW THE DROID ARMY AWAY FROM THE CITIES. WE CAN ENTER THE CITY USING THE SECRET PASSAGEWAYS ON THE WATERFALL SIDE.
ONCE WE GET TO THE MAIN ENTRANCE, CAPTAIN PANAKA WILL CREATE A DIVERSION SO THAT WE CAN ENTER THE PALACE AND CAPTURE THE VICEROY. WITHOUT THE VICEROY, THEY WILL BE LOST AND CONFUSED.
WHAT DO YOU THINK, MASTER JEDI?
THE VICEROY WILL BE WELL-GUARDED.
THE DIFFICULTY'S GETTING INTO THE THRONE ROOM. ONCE WE'RE INSIDE, WE SHOULDN'T HAVE A PROBLEM.
THERE IS A POSSIBILITY WITH THIS DIVERSION MANY GUNGANS WILL BE KILLED.
WESA READY TO DO ARE-SA PART.

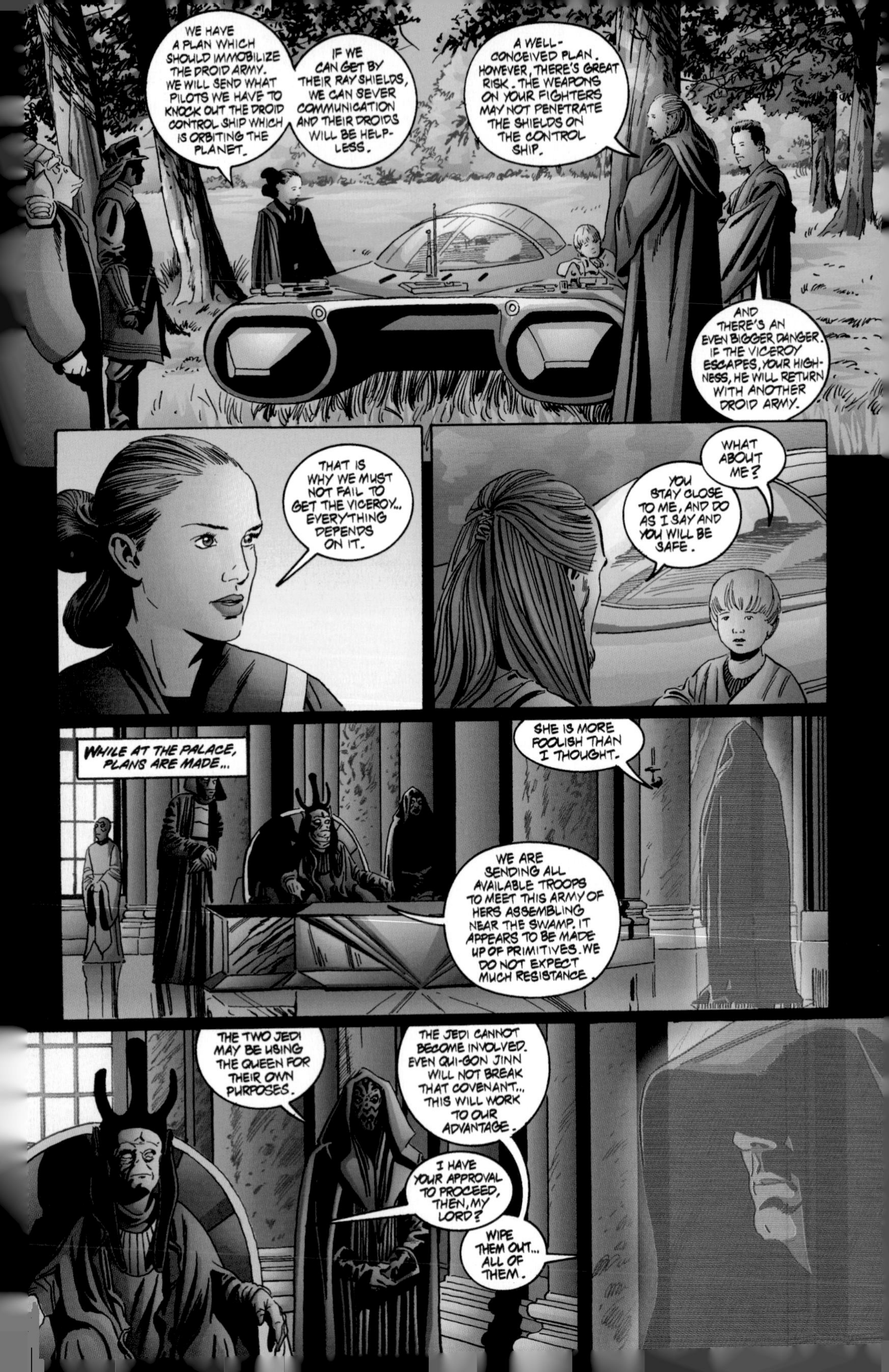
WE HAVE A PLAN WHICH SHOULD IMMOBILIZE THE DROID ARMY. WE WILL SEND WHAT PILOTS WE HAVE TO KNOCK OUT THE DROID CONTROL SHIP WHICH IS ORBITING THE PLANET.
IF WE CAN GET BY THEIR RAY SHIELDS, WE CAN SEVER COMMUNICATION AND THEIR DROIDS WILL BE HELP-LESS.
A WELL-CONCEIVED PLAN. HOWEVER, THERE'S GREAT RISK. THE WEAPONS ON YOUR FIGHTERS MAY NOT PENETRATE THE SHIELDS ON THE CONTROL SHIP.
AND THERE'S AN EVEN BIGGER DANGER. IF THE VICEROY ESCAPES, YOUR HIGH-NESS, HE WILL RETURN WITH ANOTHER DROID ARMY.
THAT IS WHY WE MUST NOT FAIL TO GET THE VICEROY... EVERYTHING DEPENDS ON IT.
WHAT ABOUT ME?
YOU STAY CLOSE TO ME, AND DO AS I SAY AND YOU WILL BE SAFE.
WHILE AT THE PALACE, PLANS ARE MADE...
SHE IS MORE FOOLISH THAN I THOUGHT.
WE ARE SENDING ALL AVAILABLE TROOPS TO MEET THIS ARMY OF HERS ASSEMBLING NEAR THE SWAMP. IT APPEARS TO BE MADE UP OF PRIMITIVES. WE DO NOT EXPECT MUCH RESISTANCE.
THE TWO JEDI MAY BE USING THE QUEEN FOR THEIR OWN PURPOSES.
THE JEDI CANNOT BECOME INVOLVED. EVEN QUI-GON JINN WILL NOT BREAK THAT COVENANT... THIS WILL WORK TO OUR ADVANTAGE.
I HAVE YOUR APPROVAL TO PROCEED, THEN, MY LORD?
WIPE THEM OUT... ALL OF THEM.

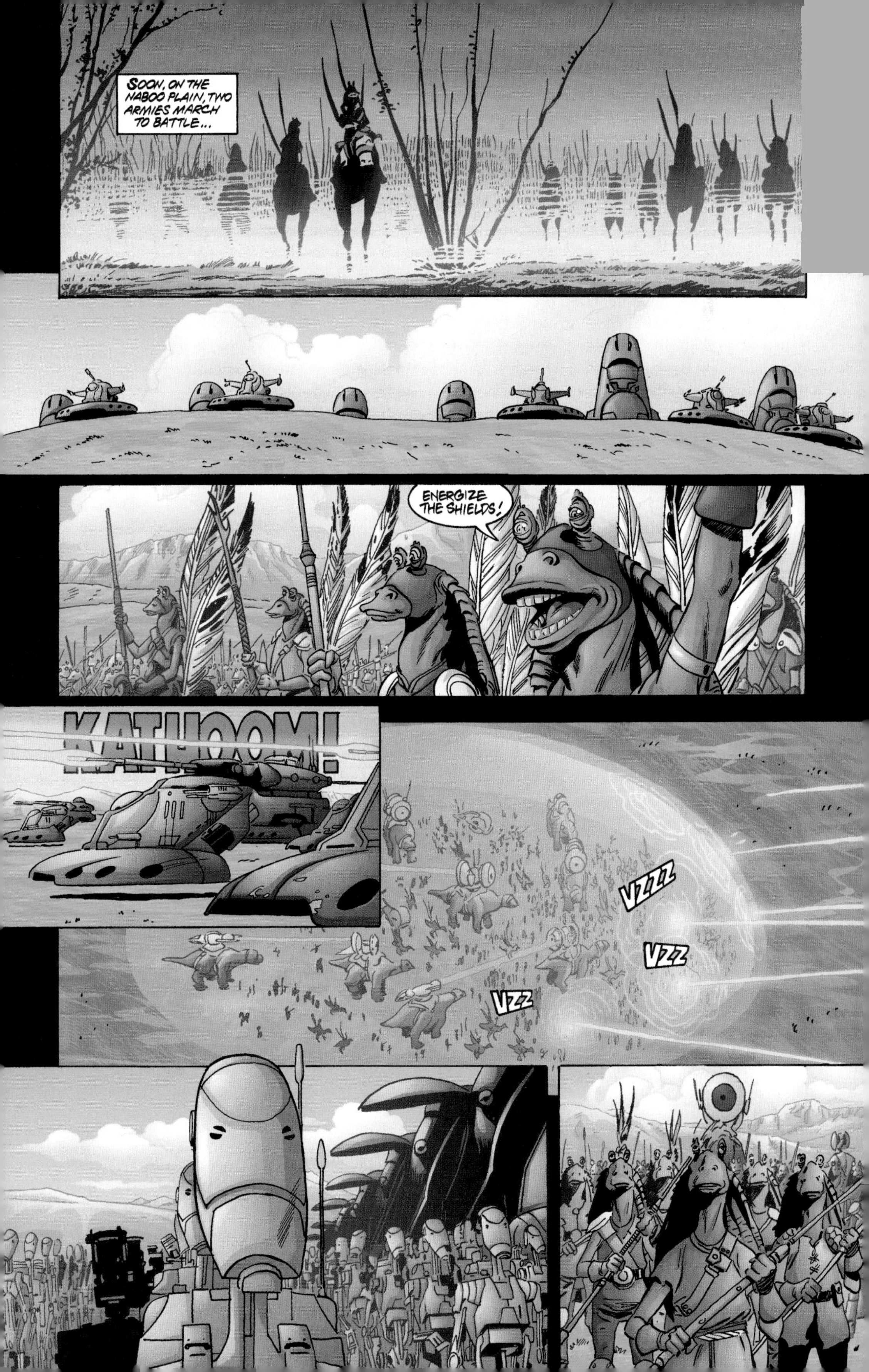
SOON, ON THE NABOO PLAIN, TWO ARMIES MARCH TO BATTLE...
ENERGIZE THE SHIELDS!
KA-THOOM!
VZZZZ
VZZ
VZZ

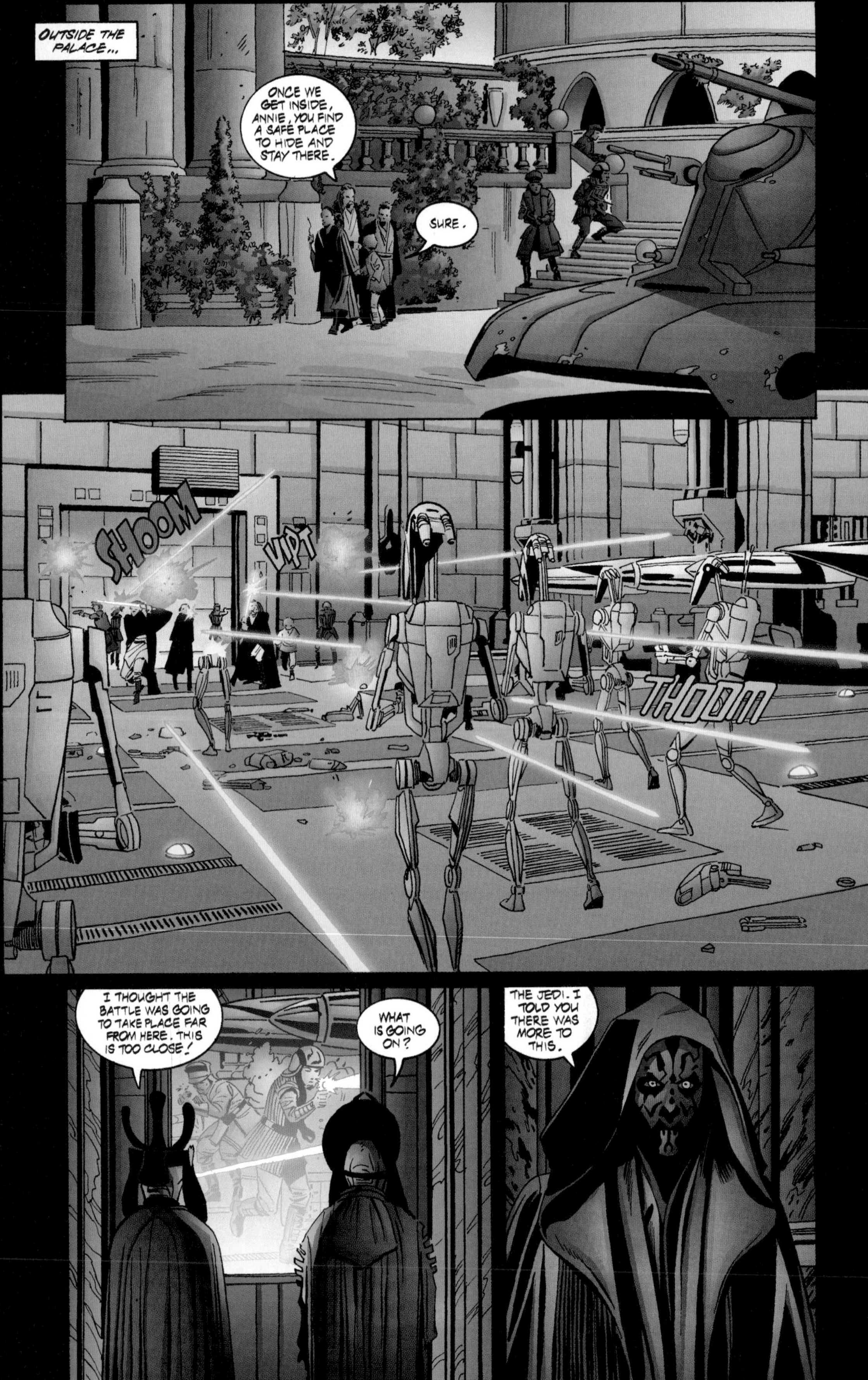
OUTSIDE THE PALACE...
ONCE WE GET INSIDE, ANNIE, YOU FIND A SAFE PLACE TO HIDE AND STAY THERE.
SURE.
SHOOM
VIPT
THOOM
I THOUGHT THE BATTLE WAS GOING TO TAKE PLACE FAR FROM HERE. THIS IS TOO CLOSE!
WHAT IS GOING ON?
THE JEDI. I TOLD YOU THERE WAS MORE TO THIS.

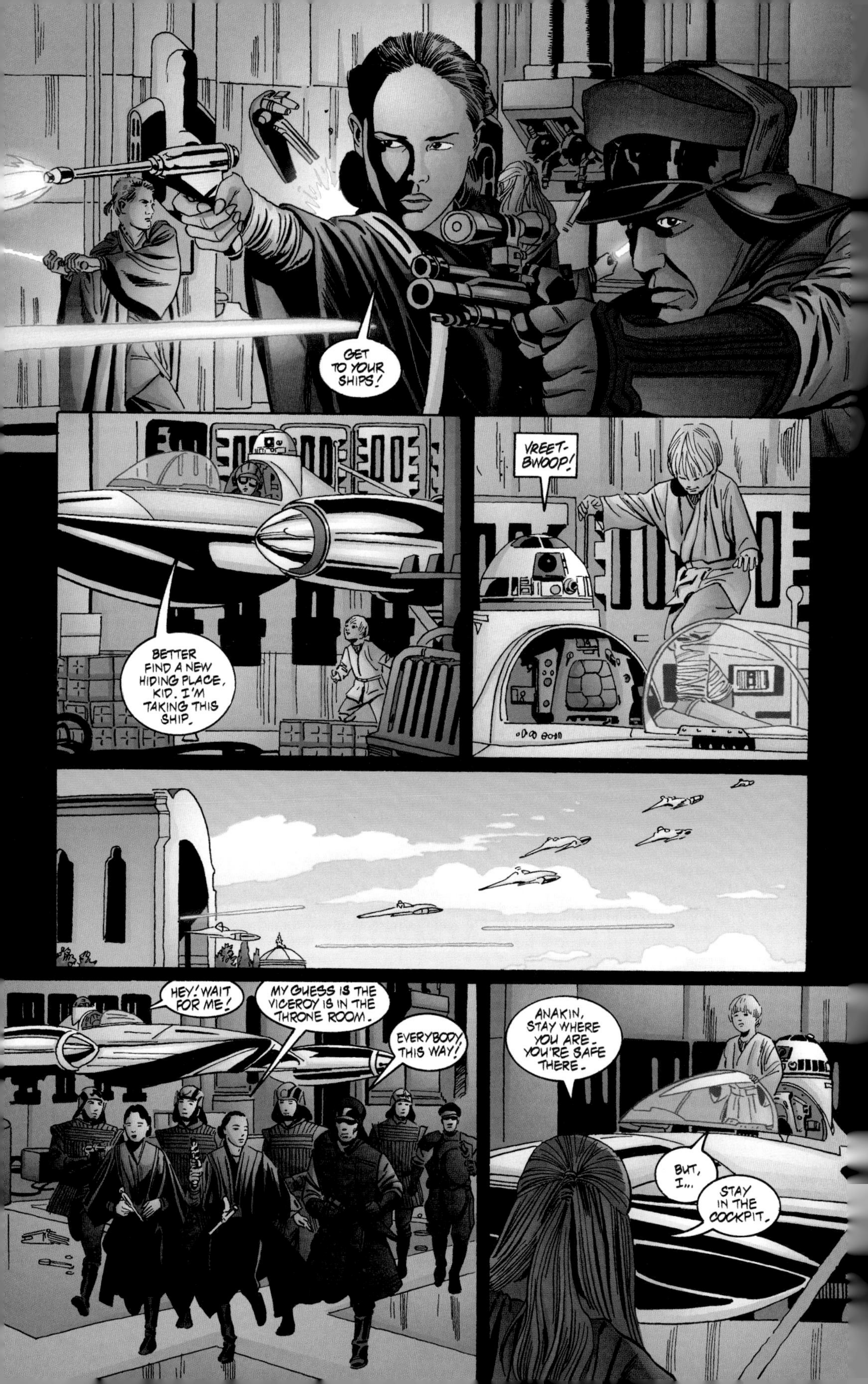

GET TO YOUR SHIPS!
BETTER FIND A NEW HIDING PLACE, KID. I'M TAKING THIS SHIP.
VREET-BWOOP!
HEY! WAIT FOR ME!
MY GUESS IS THE VICEROY IS IN THE THRONE ROOM.
EVERYBODY, THIS WAY!
ANAKIN, STAY WHERE YOU ARE. YOU'RE SAFE THERE.
BUT, I...
STAY IN THE COCKPIT.

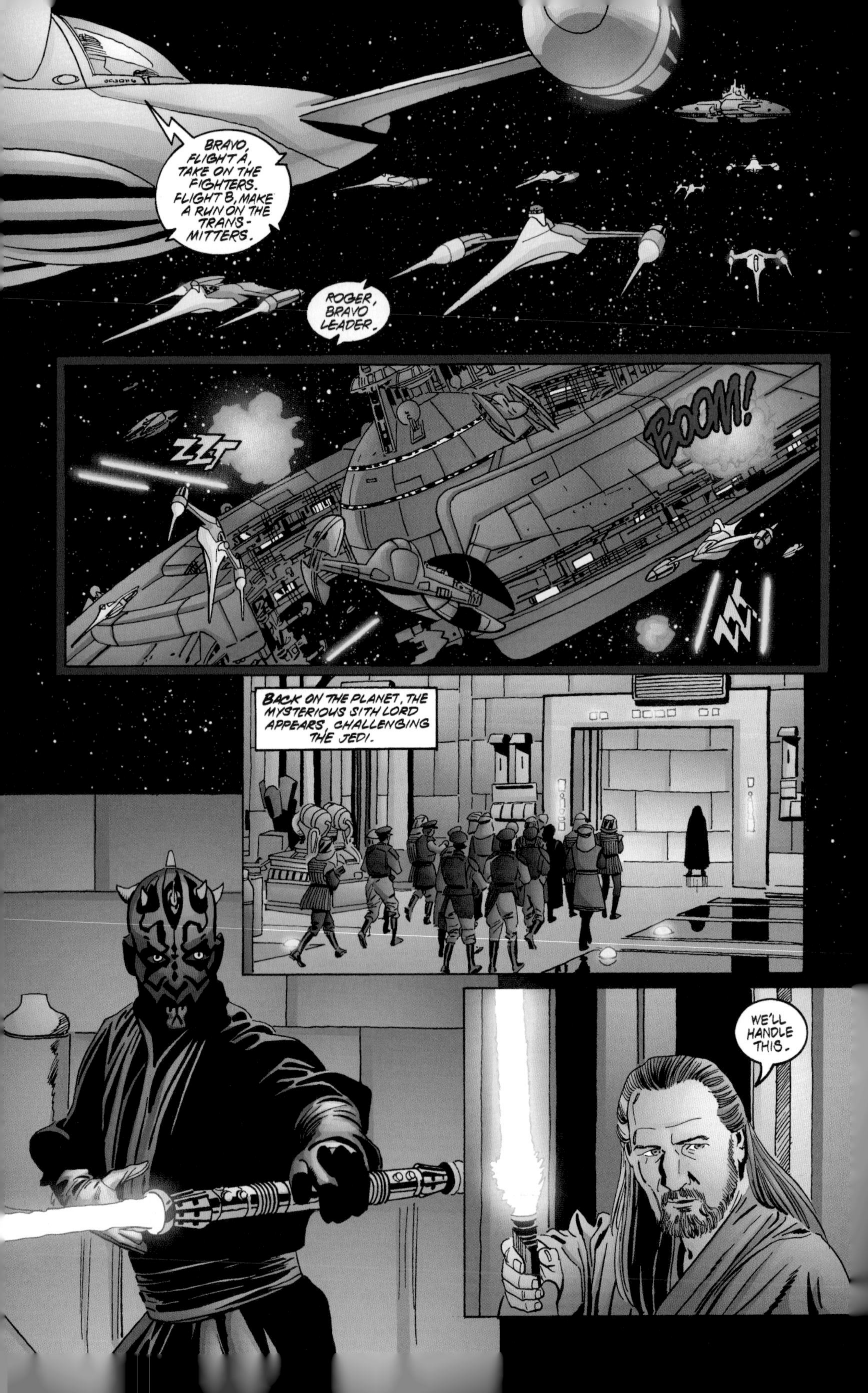
BRAVO, FLIGHT A, TAKE ON THE FIGHTERS. FLIGHT B, MAKE A RUN ON THE TRANS-MITTERS.
ROGER, BRAVO LEADER.
ZZT
BOOM!
ZZT
BACK ON THE PLANET, THE MYSTERIOUS SITH LORD APPEARS, CHALLENGING THE JEDI.
WE'LL HANDLE THIS.

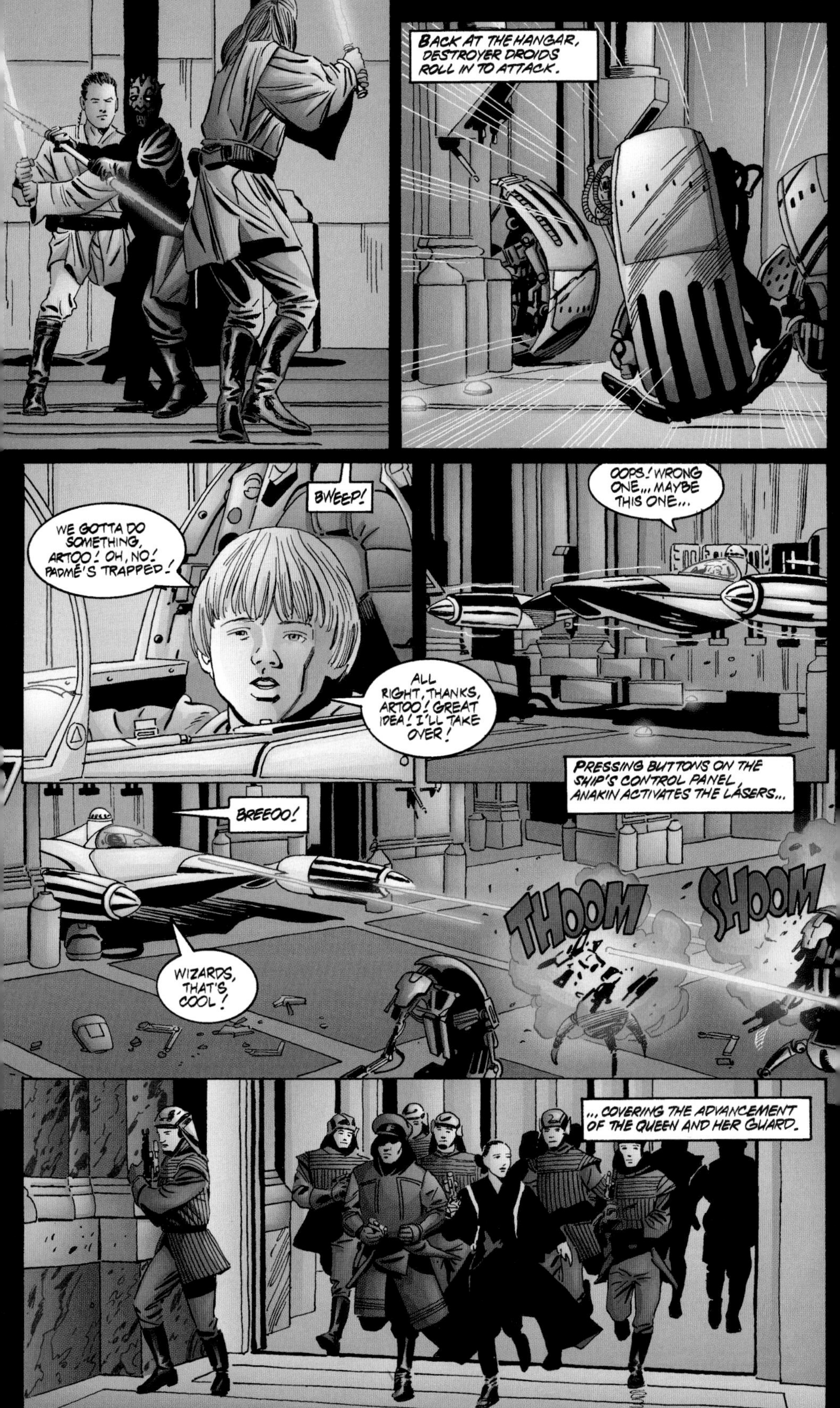
BACK AT THE HANGAR, DESTROYER DROIDS ROLL IN TO ATTACK.
BWEEP!
WE GOTTA DO SOMETHING, ARTOO! OH, NO! PADMÉ'S TRAPPED!
ALL RIGHT, THANKS, ARTOO! GREAT IDEA! I'LL TAKE OVER!
OOPS! WRONG ONE... MAYBE THIS ONE...
PRESSING BUTTONS ON THE SHIP'S CONTROL PANEL, ANAKIN ACTIVATES THE LASERS...
BREEOO!
THOOM
SHOOM
WIZARDS, THAT'S COOL!
...COVERING THE ADVANCEMENT OF THE QUEEN AND HER GUARD.

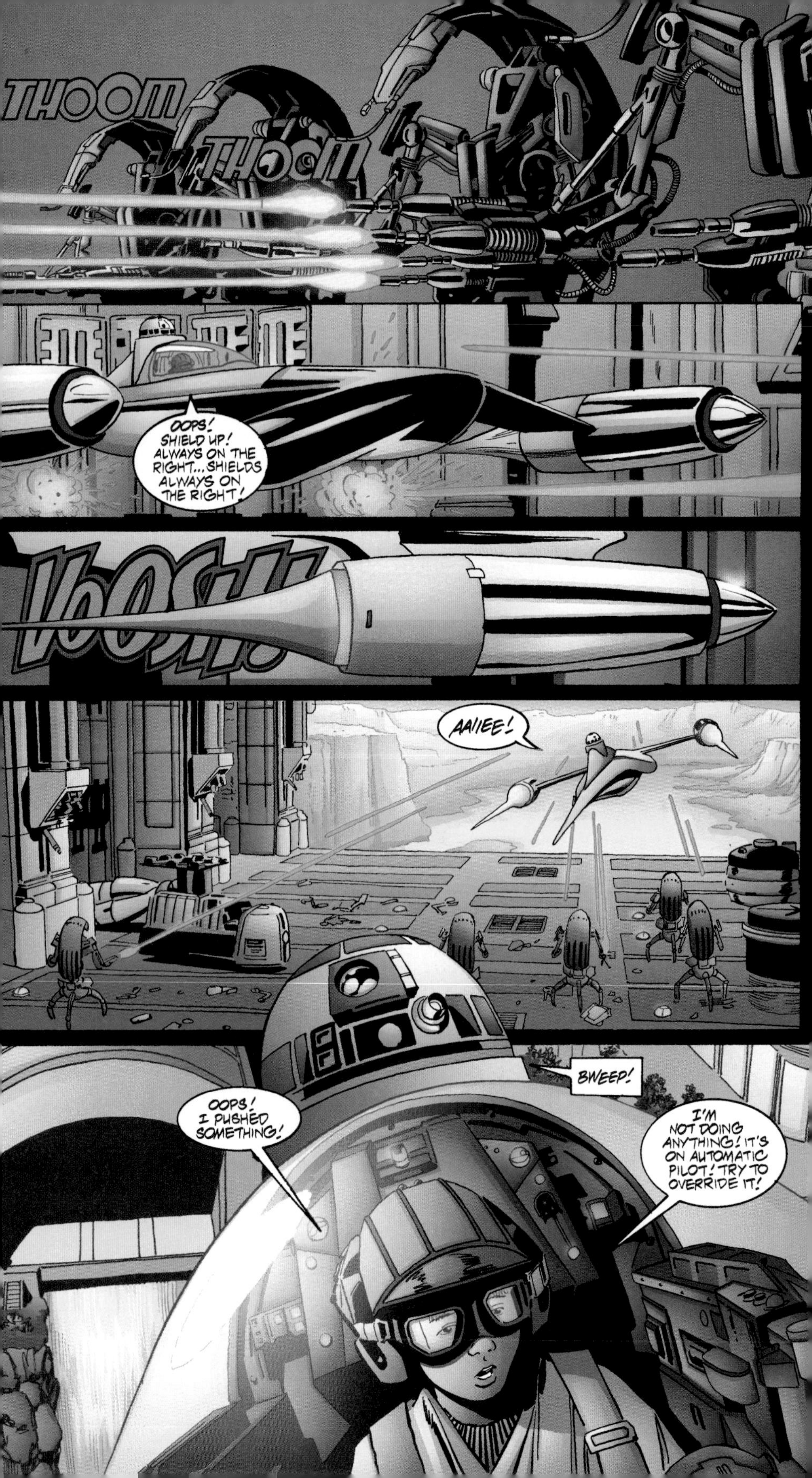
THOOM
THOOM
OOPS! SHIELD UP! ALWAYS ON THE RIGHT... SHIELDS ALWAYS ON THE RIGHT!
VOOSH!
AAIIEE!
BWEEP!
OOPS! I PUSHED SOMETHING!
I'M NOT DOING ANYTHING! IT'S ON AUTOMATIC PILOT! TRY TO OVERRIDE IT!

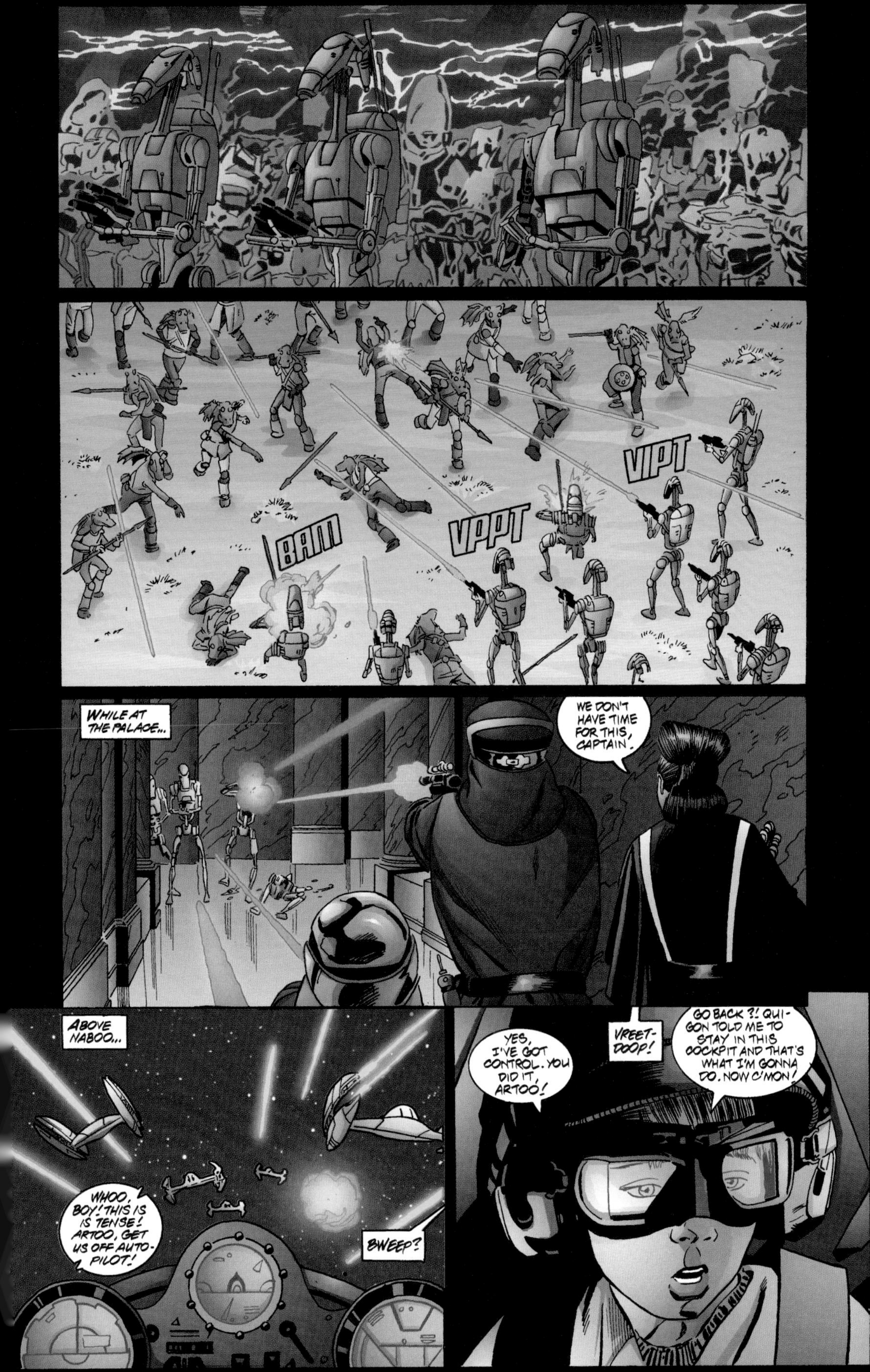
VIPT
VPPT
BAM
WHILE AT THE PALACE...
WE DON'T HAVE TIME FOR THIS, CAPTAIN.
ABOVE NABOO...
WHOO, BOY! THIS IS IS TENSE! ARTOO, GET US OFF AUTO-PILOT!
BWEEP?
YES, I'VE GOT CONTROL. YOU DID IT, ARTOO!
VREET-DOOP!
GO BACK?! QUI-GON TOLD ME TO STAY IN THIS COCKPIT AND THAT'S WHAT I'M GONNA DO. NOW C'MON!

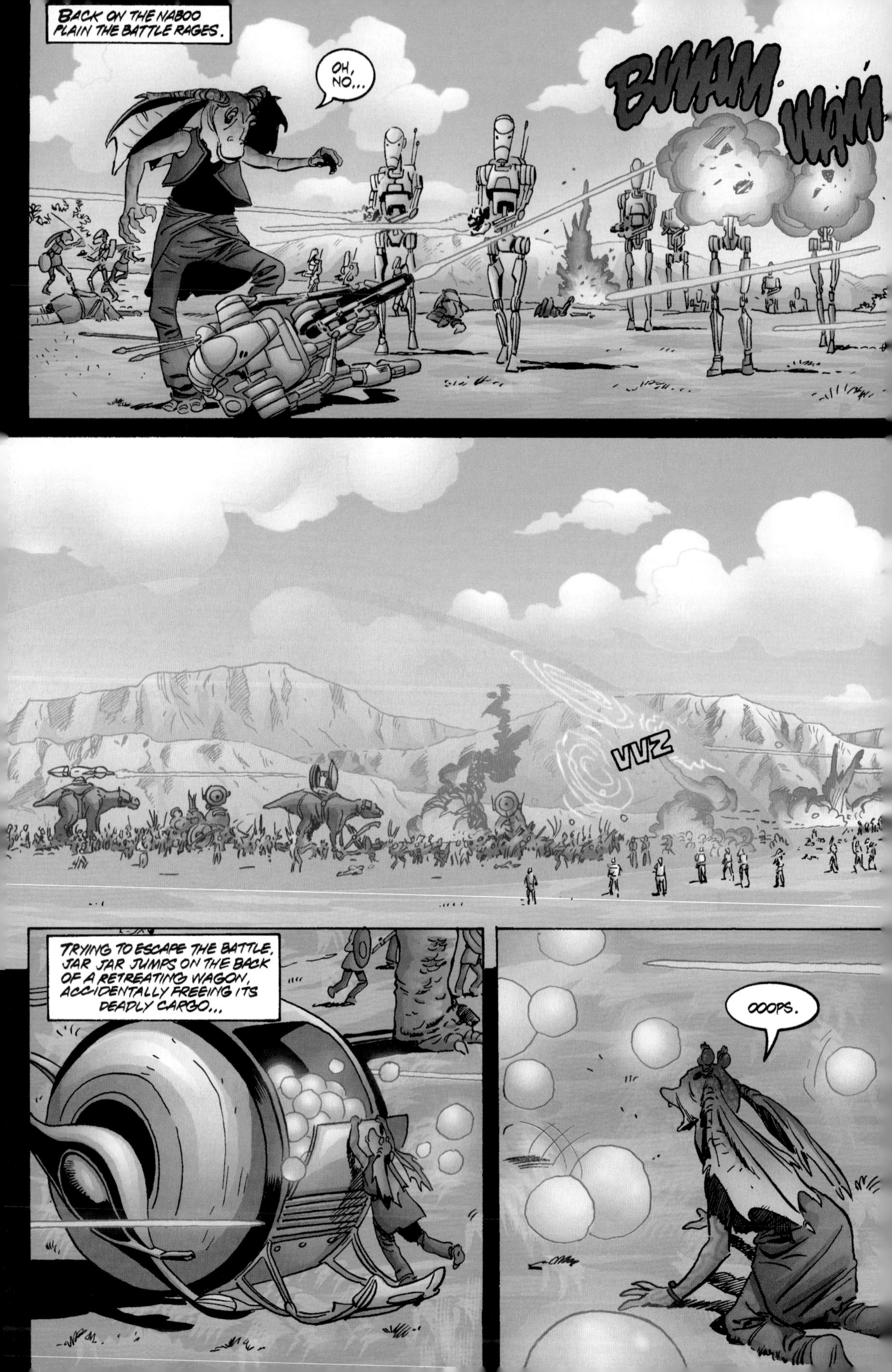
BACK ON THE NABOO PLAIN THE BATTLE RAGES.
OH, NO...
BVVAM
WAM
VVZ
TRYING TO ESCAPE THE BATTLE, JAR JAR JUMPS ON THE BACK OF A RETREATING WAGON, ACCIDENTALLY FREEING ITS DEADLY CARGO...
OOOPS.

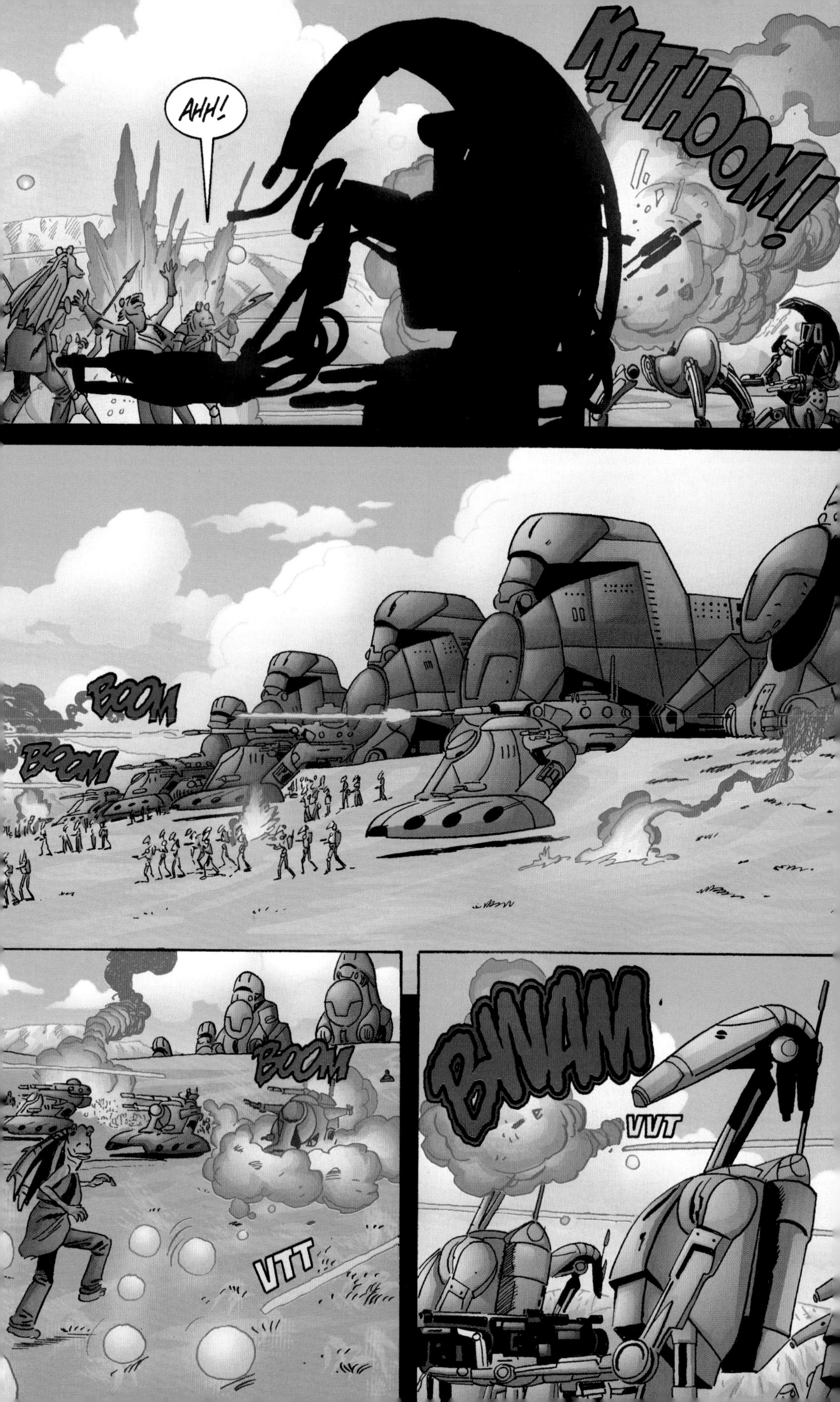
AHH!
KATHOOM!
BOOM
BOOM
BOOM
VTT
BWAM
VVT

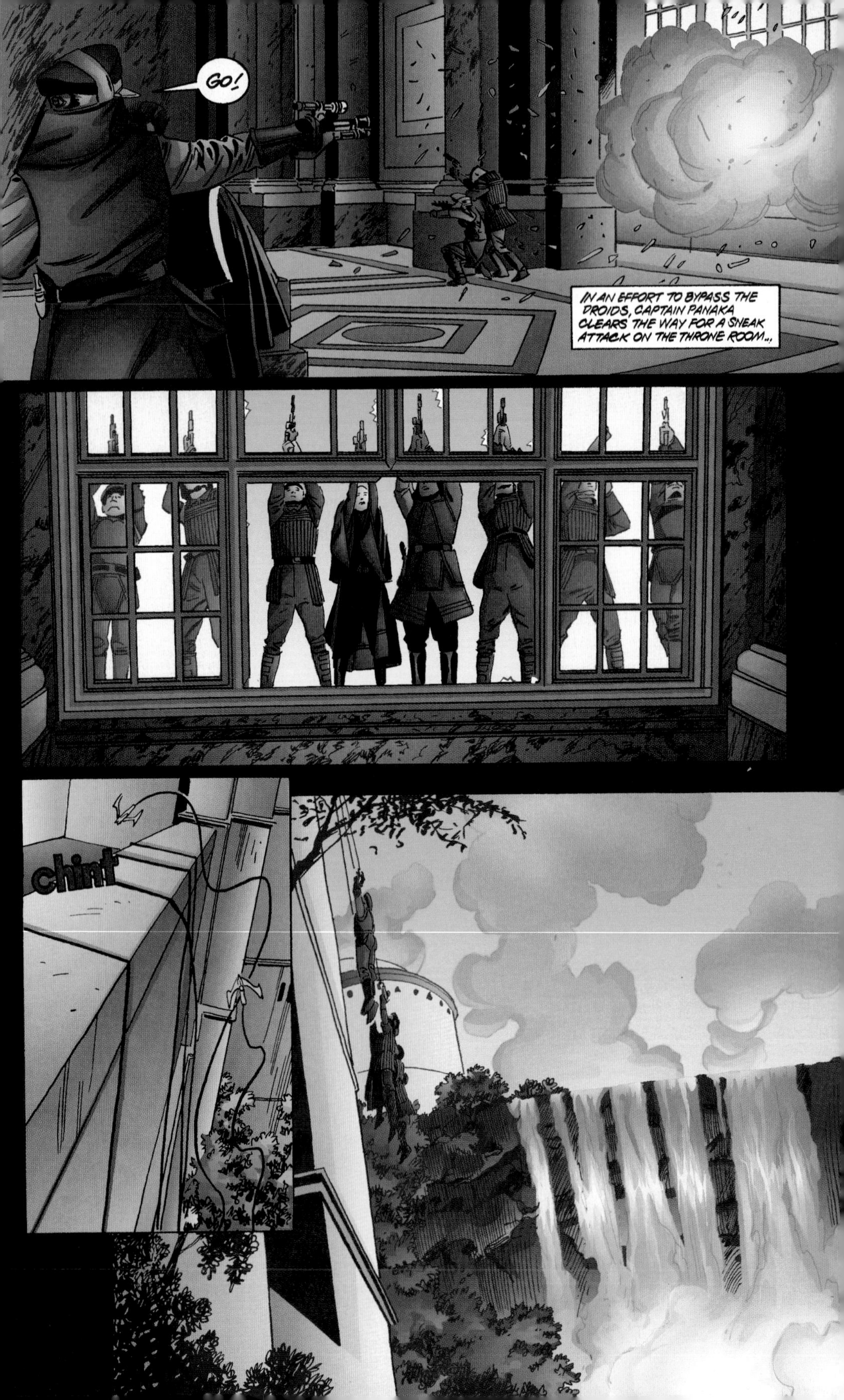
GO!
IN AN EFFORT TO BYPASS THE DROIDS, CAPTAIN PANAKA CLEARS THE WAY FOR A SNEAK ATTACK ON THE THRONE ROOM...
chint

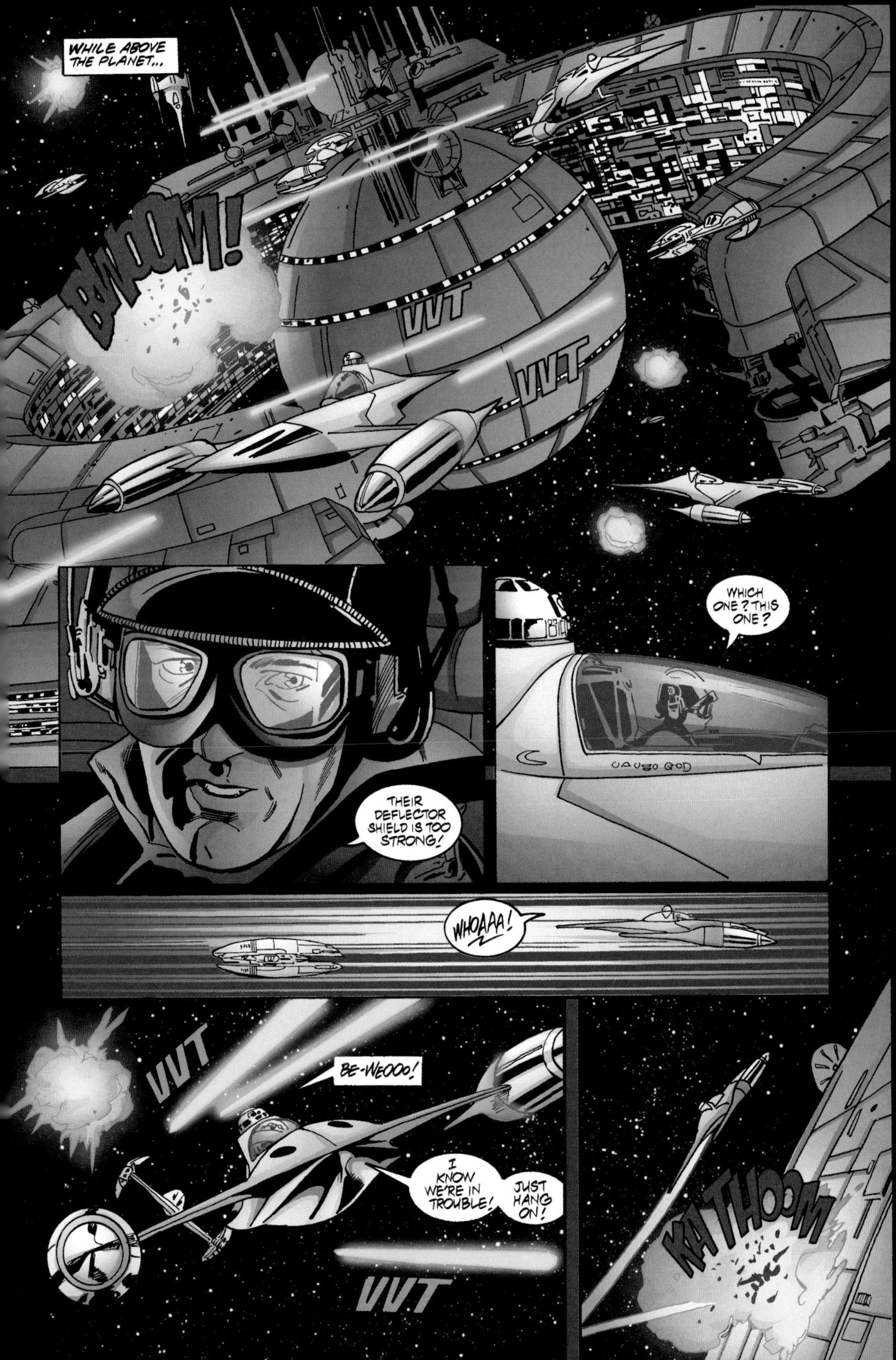
WHILE ABOVE THE PLANET...
BADOOM!
VVT
VVT
THEIR DEFLECTOR SHIELD IS TOO STRONG!
WHICH ONE? THIS ONE?
WHOAAA!
VVT
BE-WEOOO!
I KNOW WE'RE IN TROUBLE!
JUST HANG ON!
VVT
KATHOOM

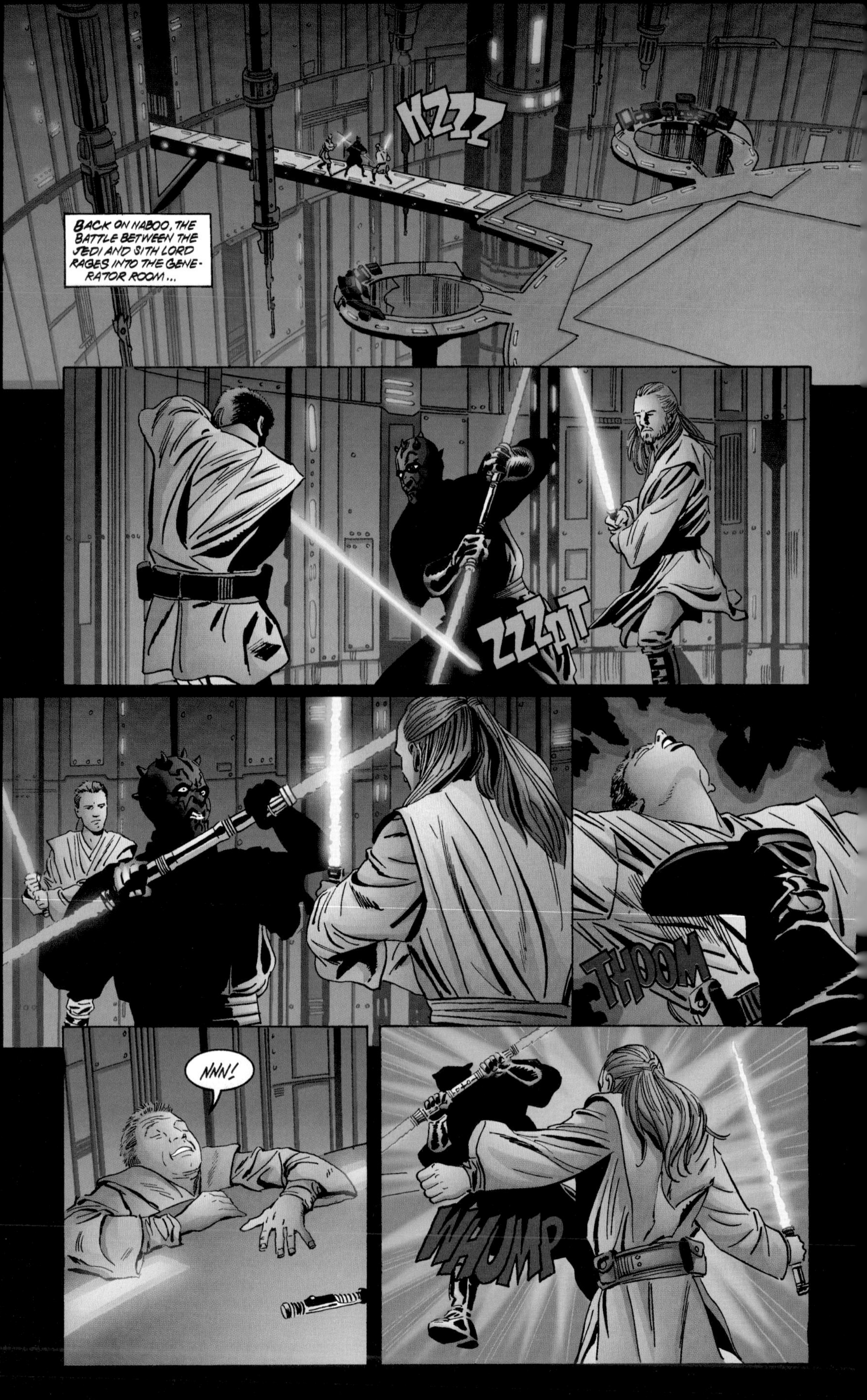
HZZZ
BACK ON NABOO, THE BATTLE BETWEEN THE JEDI AND SITH LORD RAGES INTO THE GENERATOR ROOM...
ZZZAT
THOOM
NNN!
WHUMP

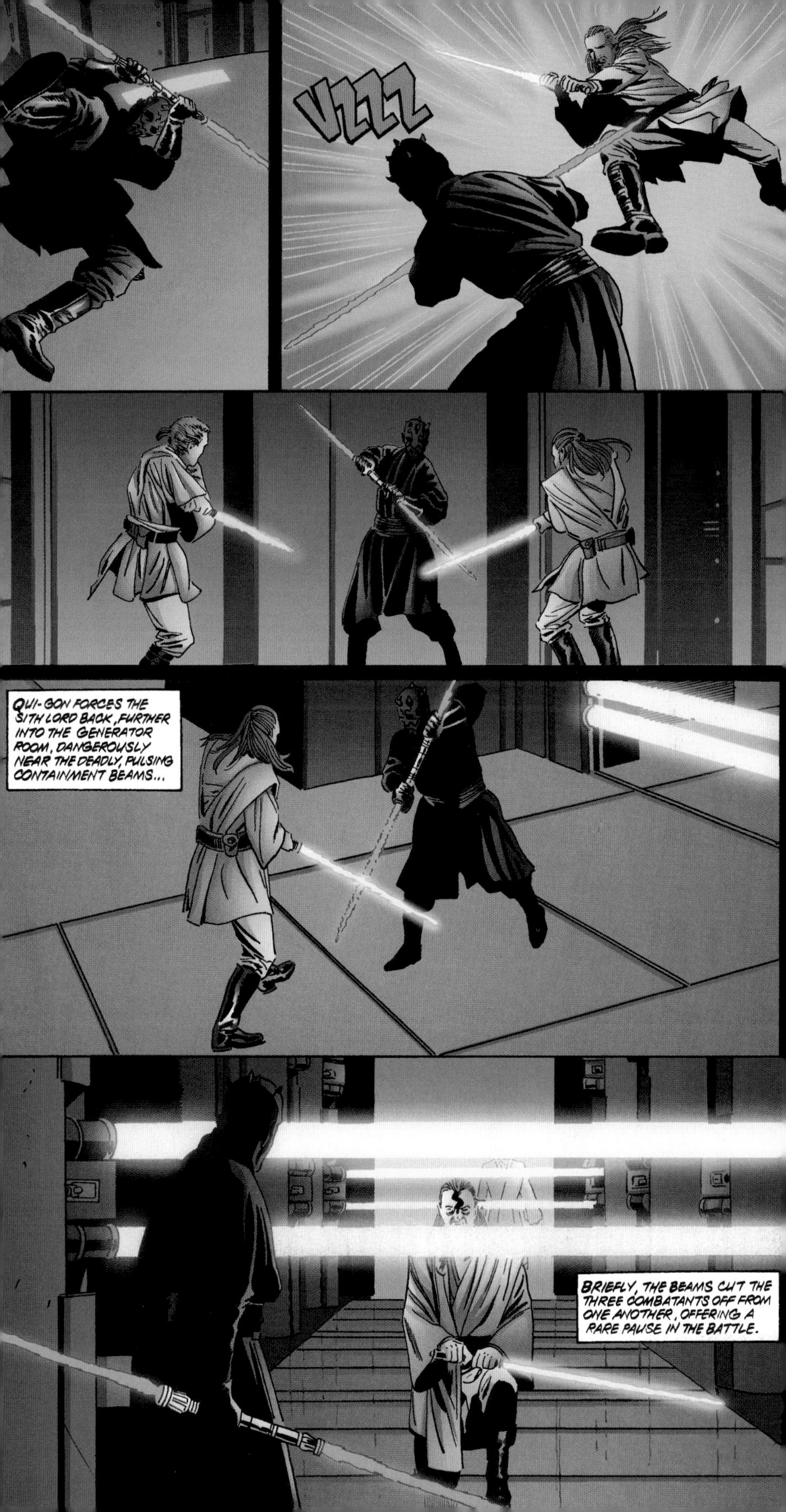
VZZZ
QUI-GON FORCES THE SITH LORD BACK, FURTHER INTO THE GENERATOR ROOM, DANGEROUSLY NEAR THE DEADLY, PULSING CONTAINMENT BEAMS...
BRIEFLY, THE BEAMS CUT THE THREE COMBATANTS OFF FROM ONE ANOTHER, OFFERING A RARE PAUSE IN THE BATTLE.

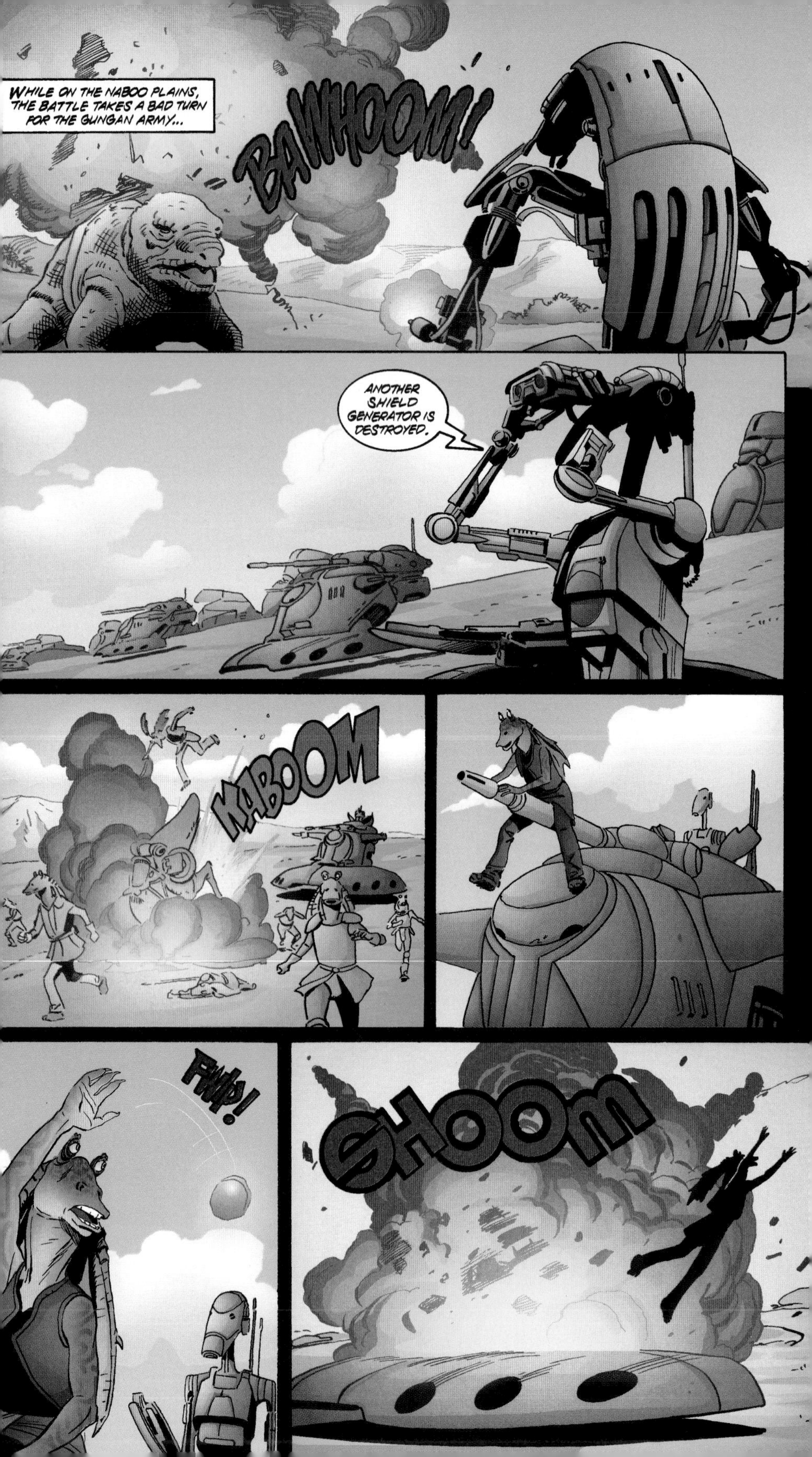
WHILE ON THE NABOO PLAINS, THE BATTLE TAKES A BAD TURN FOR THE GUNGAN ARMY...
BAWHOOM!
ANOTHER SHIELD GENERATOR IS DESTROYED.
KABOOM
FWIP!
SHOOM

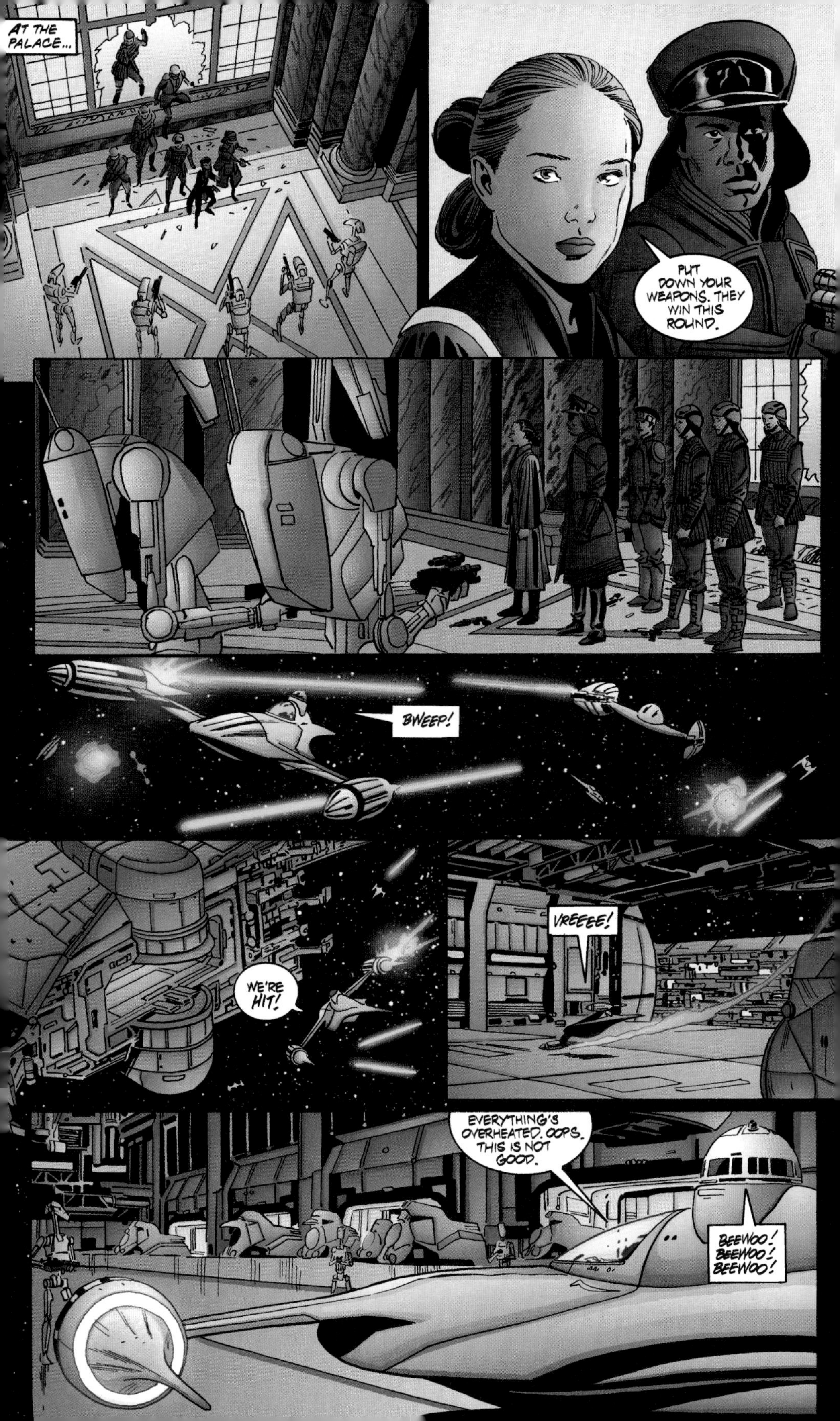
AT THE PALACE...
PUT DOWN YOUR WEAPONS. THEY WIN THIS ROUND.
BWEEP!
WE'RE HIT!
VREEEE!
EVERYTHING'S OVERHEATED. OOPS. THIS IS NOT GOOD.
BEEWOO! BEEWOO! BEEWOO!

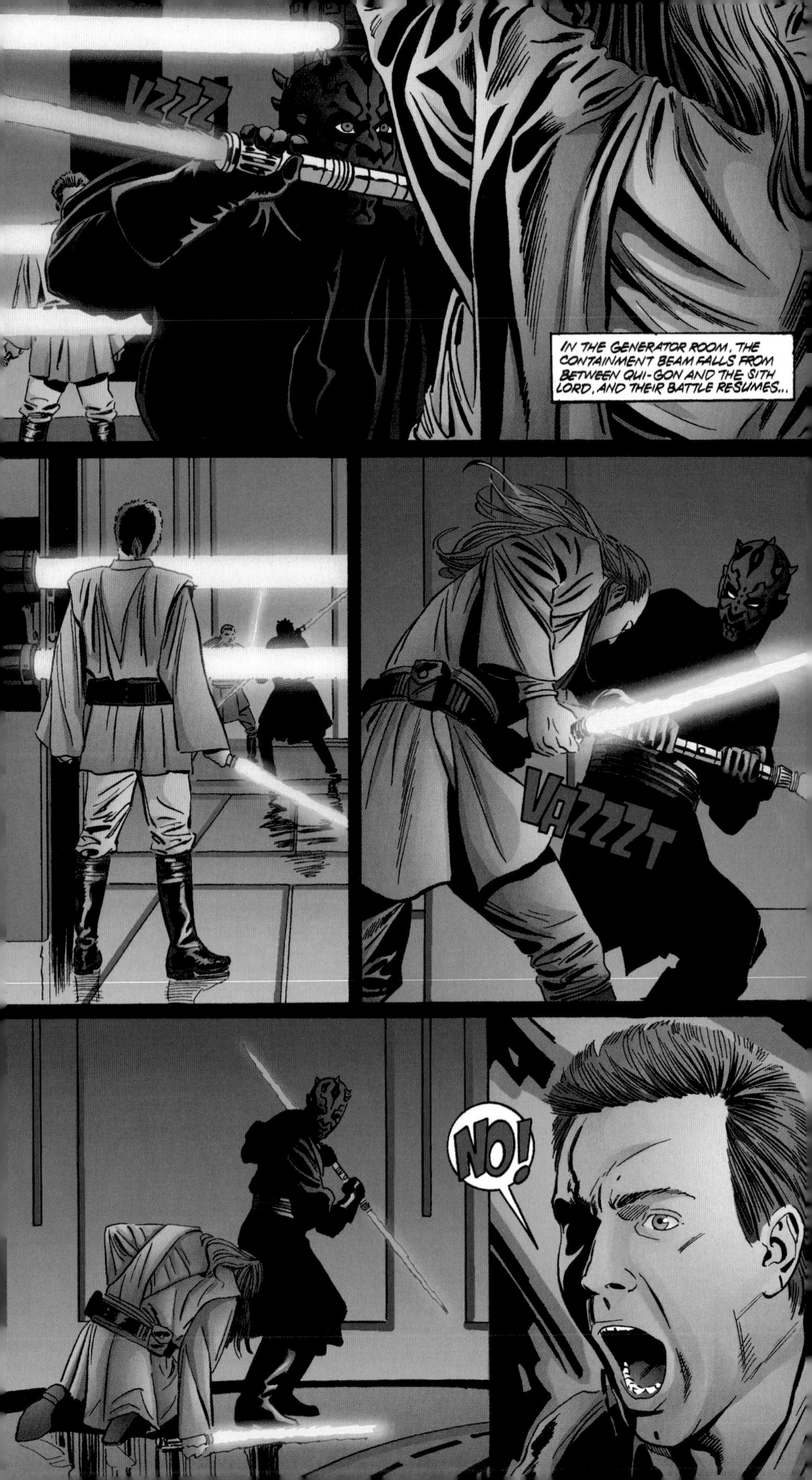
VZZZZ
IN THE GENERATOR ROOM, THE CONTAINMENT BEAM FALLS FROM BETWEEN QUI-GON AND THE SITH LORD, AND THEIR BATTLE RESUMES...
VAZZZZT
NO!

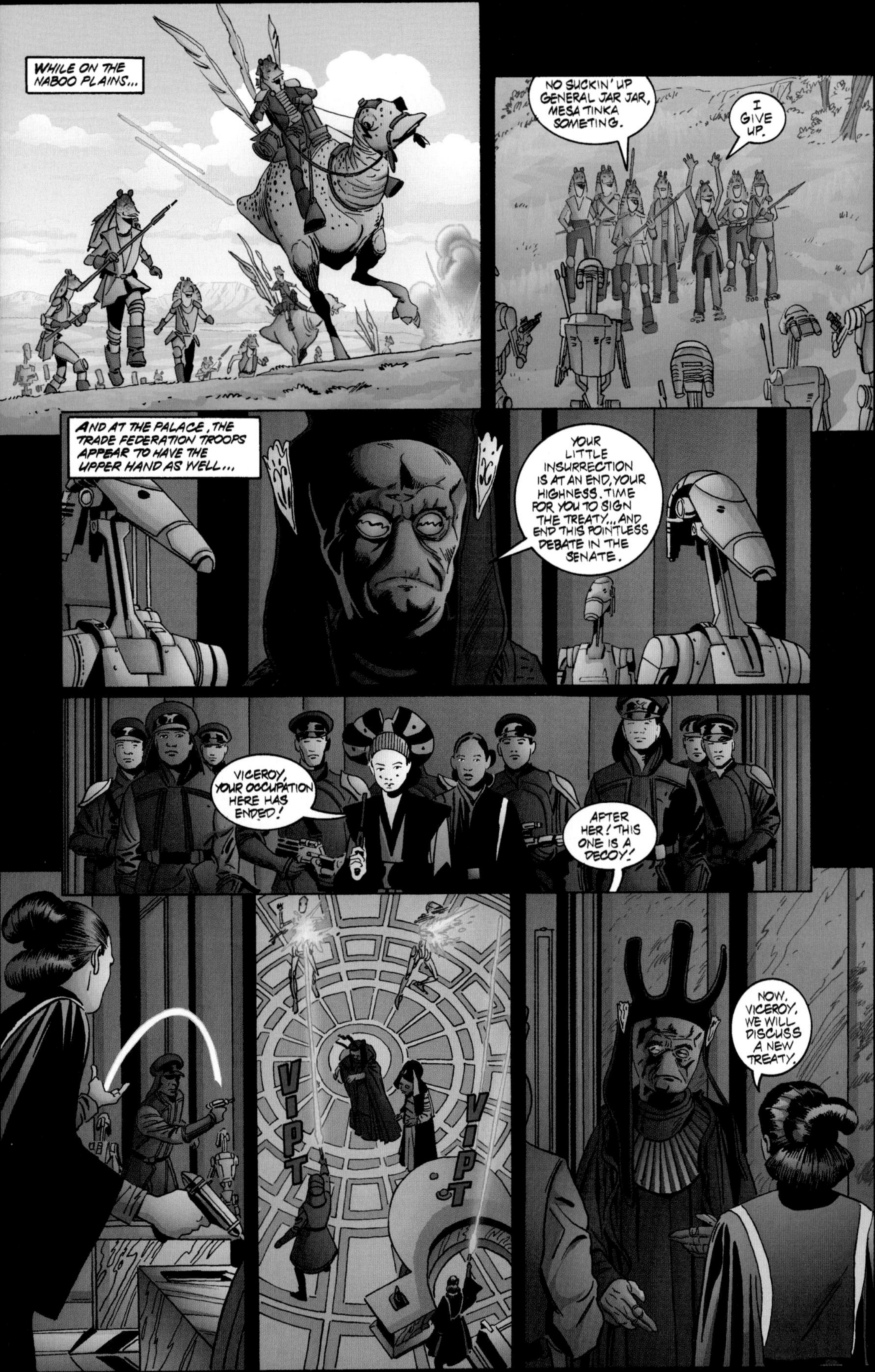

WHILE ON THE NABOO PLAINS...
NO SUCKIN' UP GENERAL JAR JAR, MESA TINKA SOMETING.
I GIVE UP.
AND AT THE PALACE, THE TRADE FEDERATION TROOPS APPEAR TO HAVE THE UPPER HAND AS WELL...
YOUR LITTLE INSURRECTION IS AT AN END, YOUR HIGHNESS. TIME FOR YOU TO SIGN THE TREATY... AND END THIS POINTLESS DEBATE IN THE SENATE.
VICEROY, YOUR OCCUPATION HERE HAS ENDED!
AFTER HER! THIS ONE IS A DECOY!
VIPT
VIPT
NOW, VICEROY, WE WILL DISCUSS A NEW TREATY.

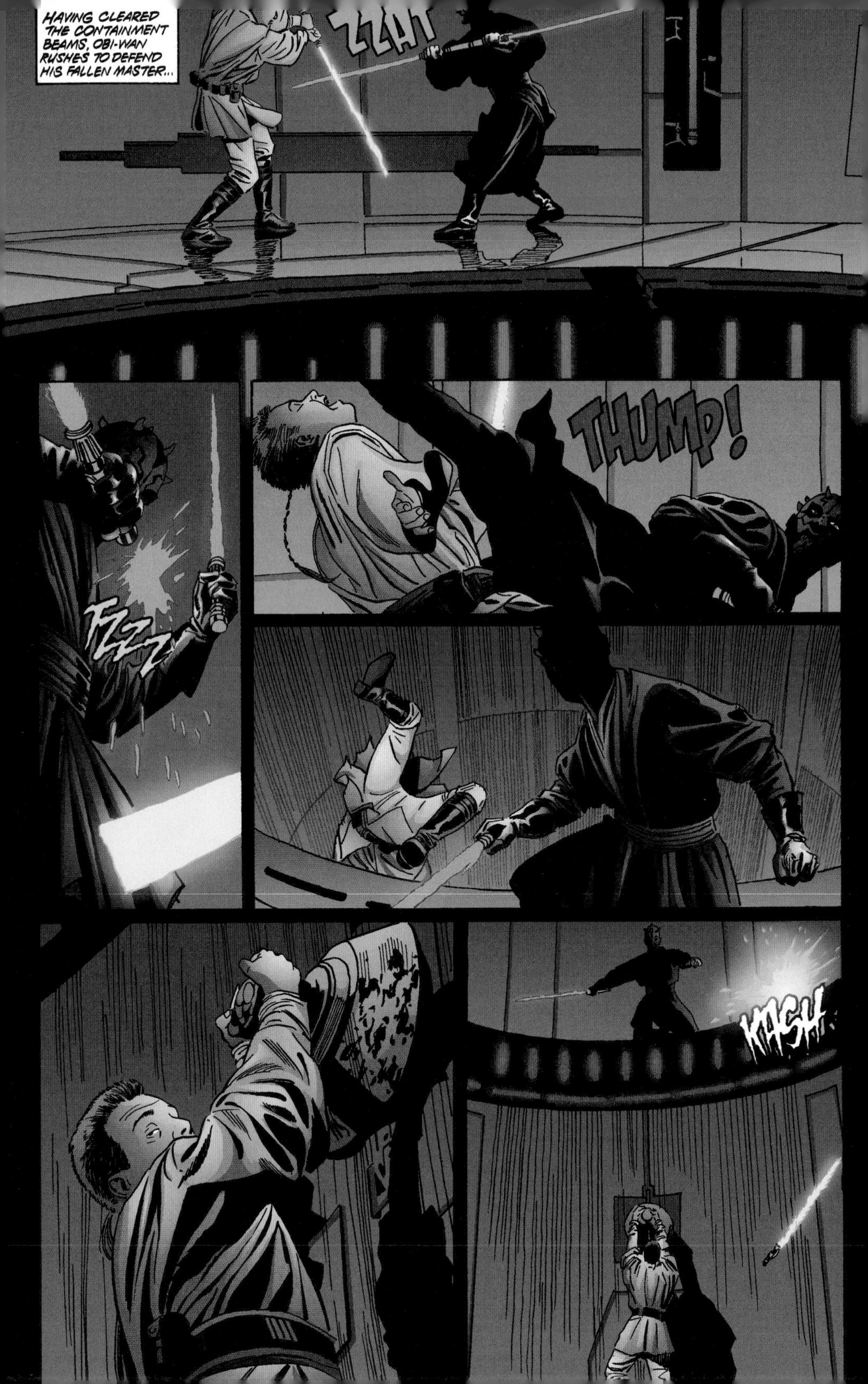
HAVING CLEARED THE CONTAINMENT BEAMS, OBI-WAN RUSHES TO DEFEND HIS FALLEN MASTER...
ZZAT
FZZZ
THUMP!
KASH

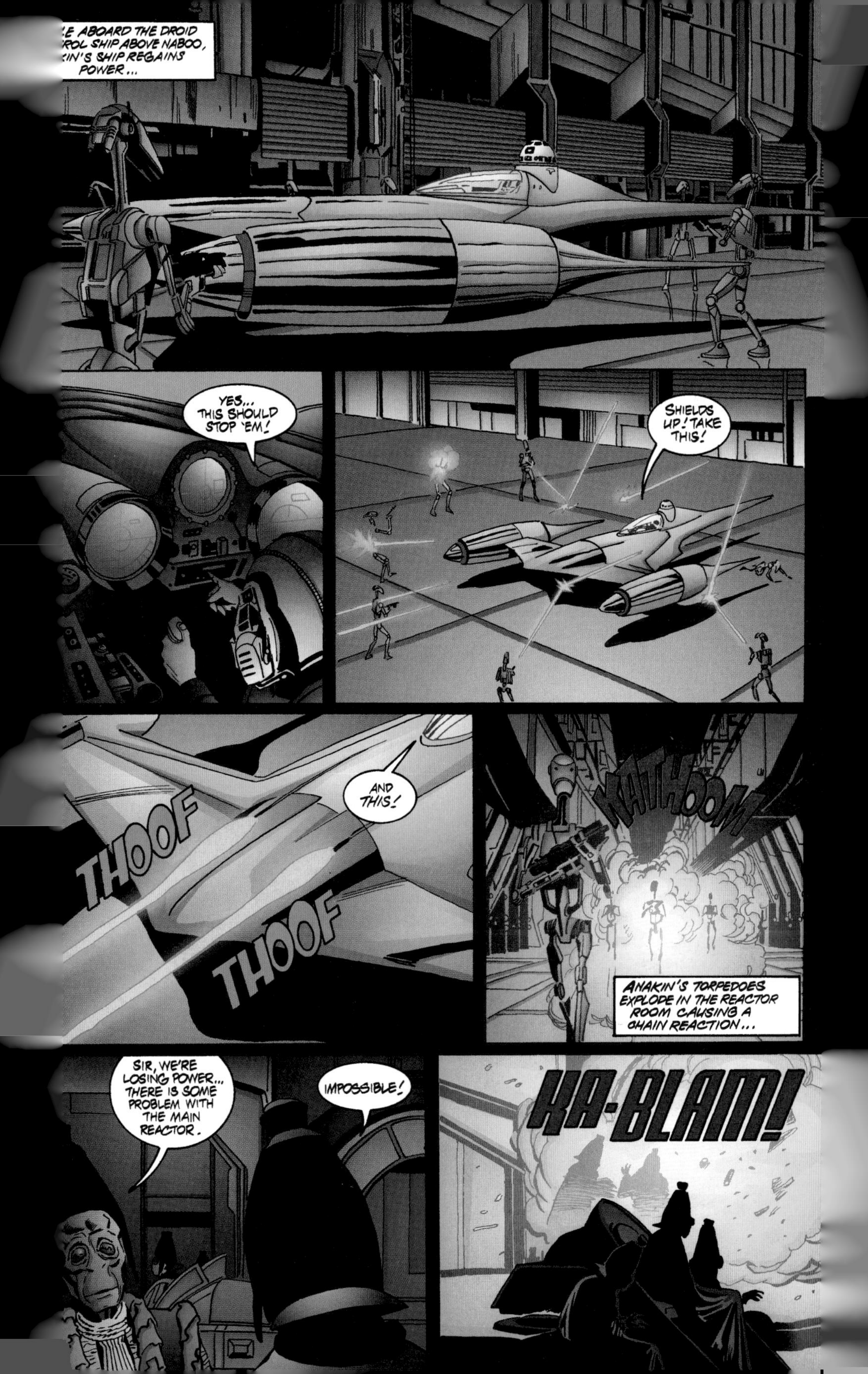

E ABOARD THE DROID
ROL SHIP ABOVE NABOO,
KIN'S SHIP REGAINS
POWER...
YES... THIS SHOULD STOP 'EM!
SHIELDS UP! TAKE THIS!
THOOF
THOOF
AND THIS!
KATHOOM
ANAKIN'S TORPEDOES EXPLODE IN THE REACTOR ROOM CAUSING A CHAIN REACTION...
SIR, WE'RE LOSING POWER... THERE IS SOME PROBLEM WITH THE MAIN REACTOR.
IMPOSSIBLE!
KA-BLAM!

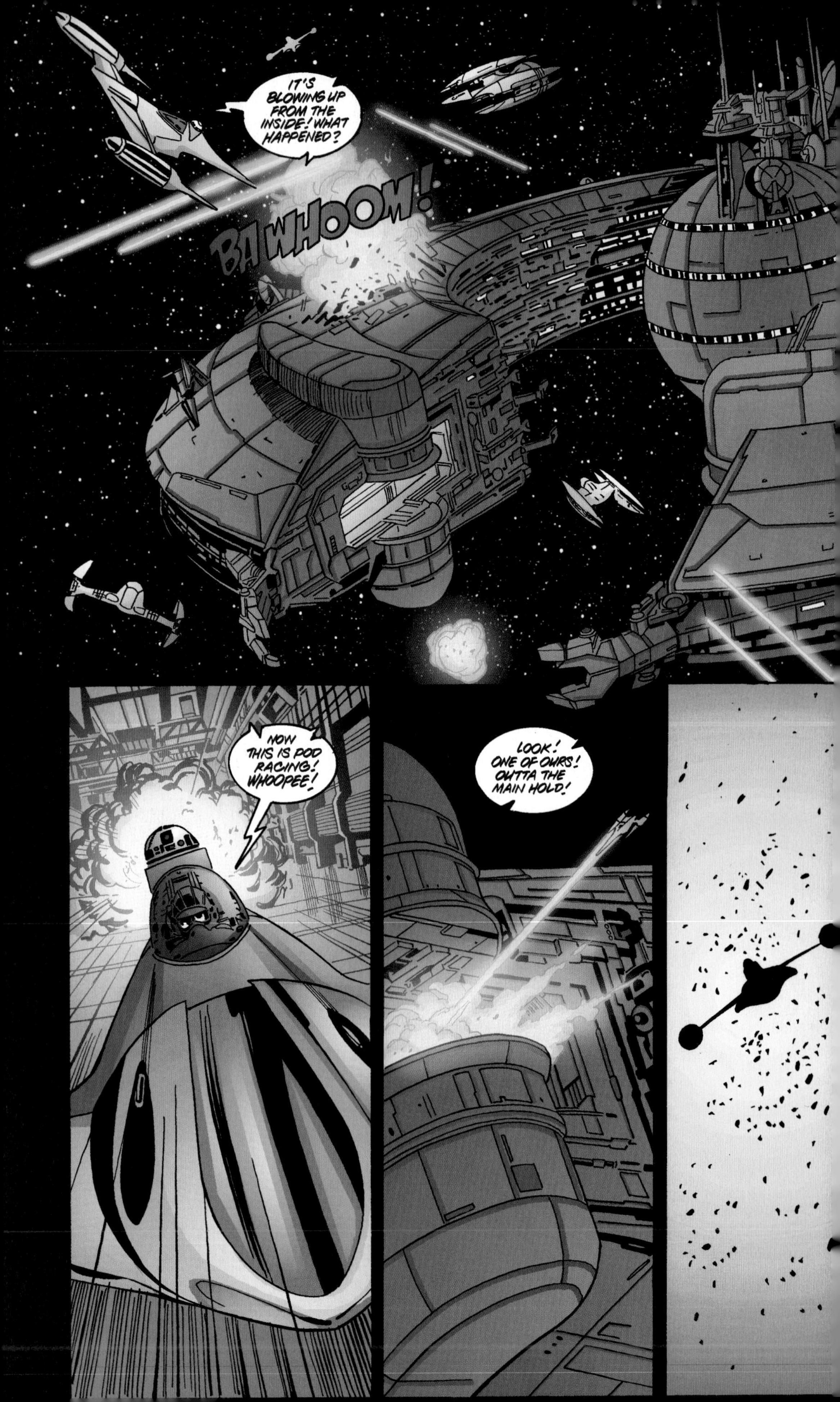
IT'S BLOWING UP FROM THE INSIDE! WHAT HAPPENED?
BA WHOOM!
NOW THIS IS POD RACING! WHOOPEE!
LOOK! ONE OF OURS! OUTTA THE MAIN HOLD!

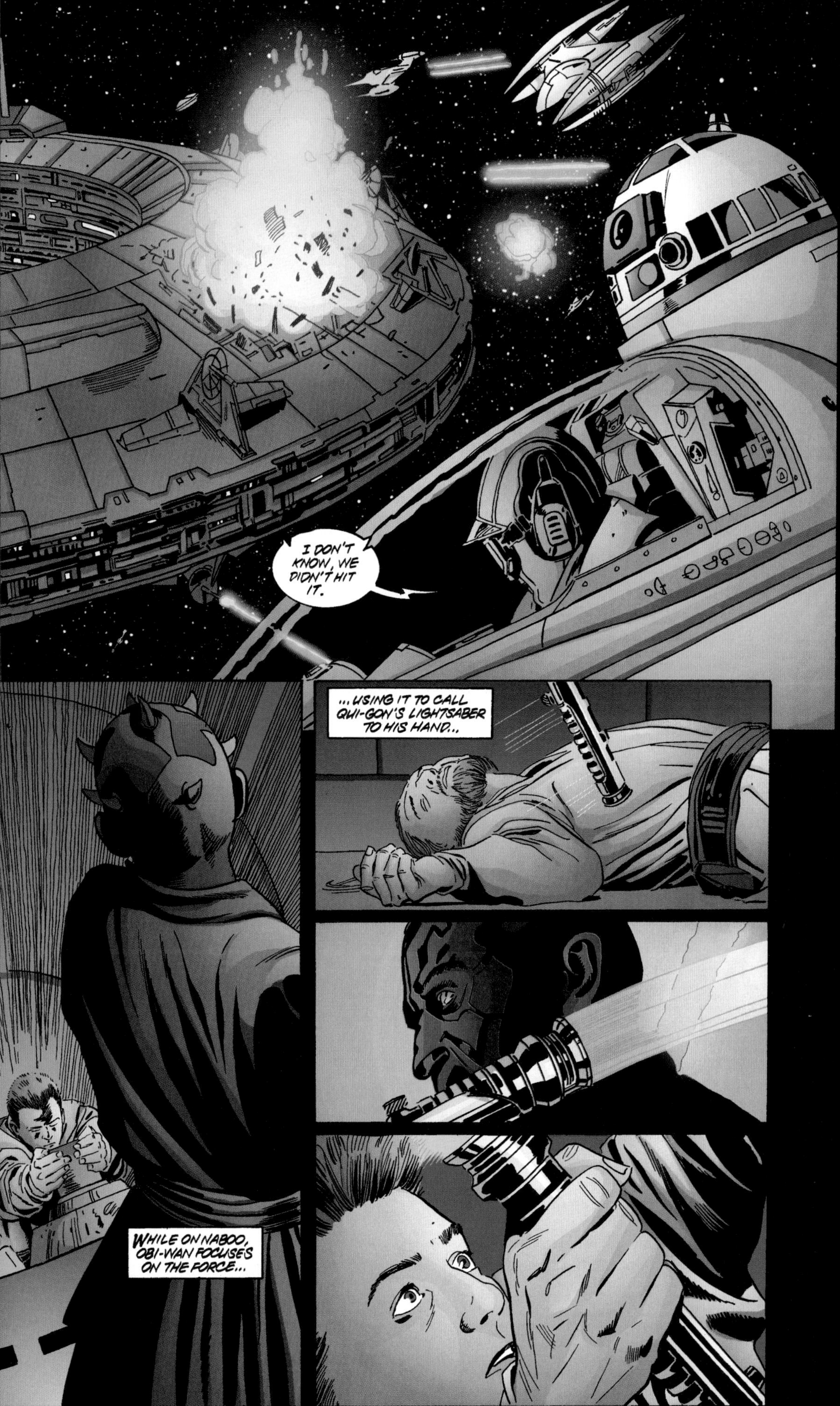
I DON'T KNOW, WE DIDN'T HIT IT.
...USING IT TO CALL QUI-GON'S LIGHTSABER TO HIS HAND...
WHILE ON NABOO, OBI-WAN FOCUSES ON THE FORCE...

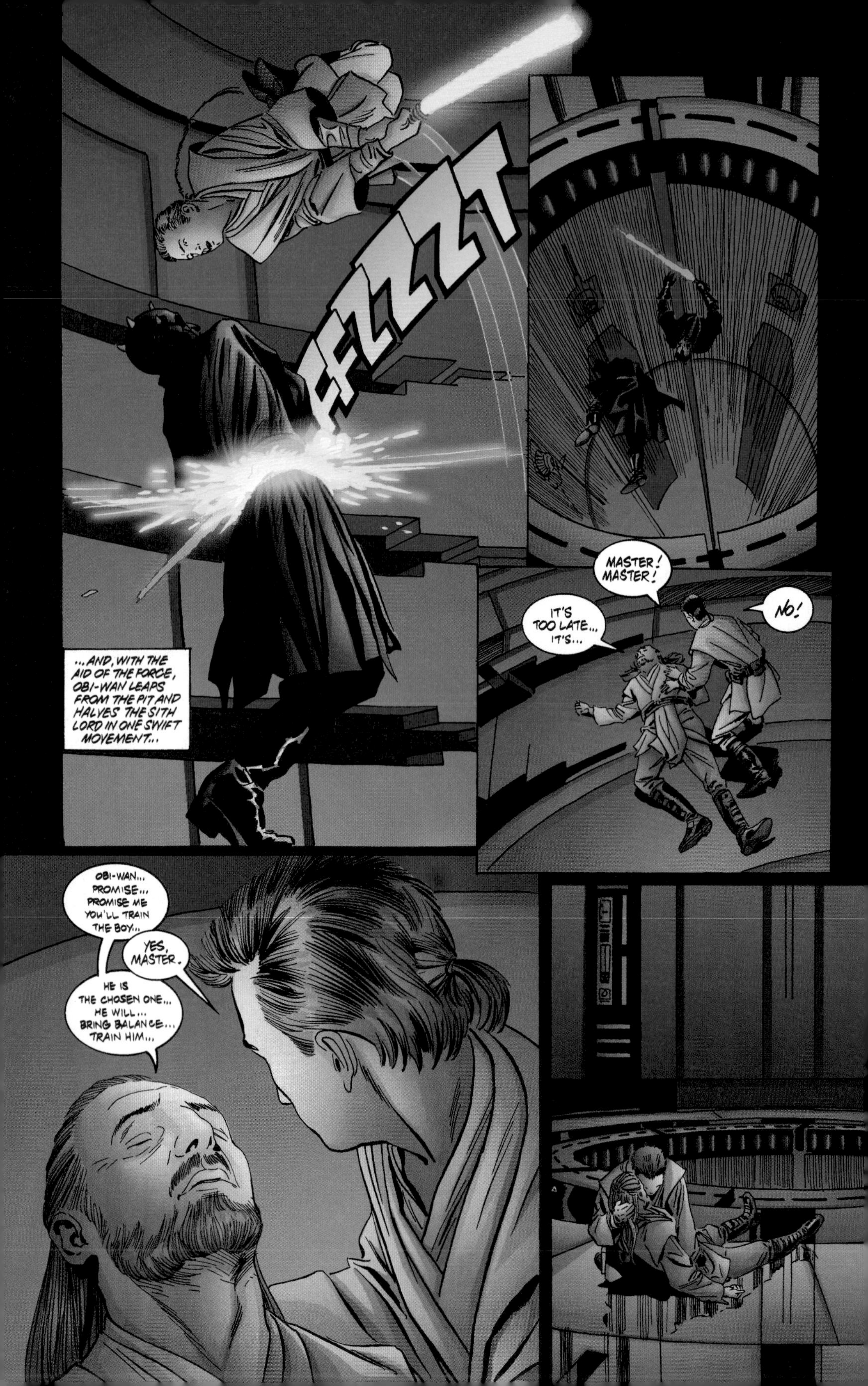
FZZZT
...AND, WITH THE AID OF THE FORCE, OBI-WAN LEAPS FROM THE PIT AND HALVES THE SITH LORD IN ONE SWIFT MOVEMENT...
MASTER! MASTER!
NO!
IT'S TOO LATE... IT'S...
OBI-WAN... PROMISE... PROMISE ME YOU'LL TRAIN THE BOY...
YES, MASTER.
HE IS THE CHOSEN ONE... HE WILL... BRING BALANCE... TRAIN HIM...

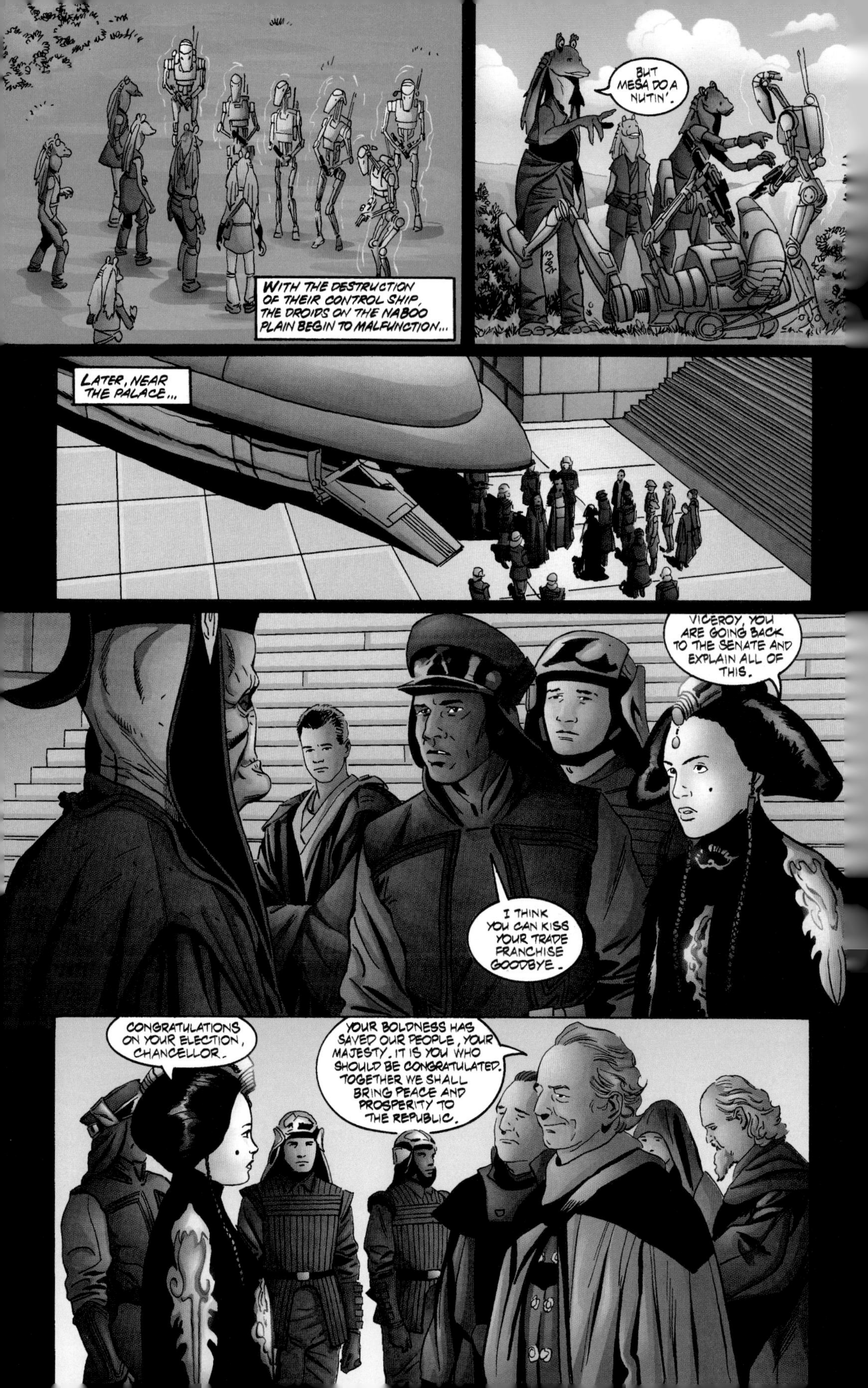
WITH THE DESTRUCTION OF THEIR CONTROL SHIP, THE DROIDS ON THE NABOO PLAIN BEGIN TO MALFUNCTION...
BUT MESA DO A NUTIN'.
LATER, NEAR THE PALACE...
VICEROY, YOU ARE GOING BACK TO THE SENATE AND EXPLAIN ALL OF THIS.
I THINK YOU CAN KISS YOUR TRADE FRANCHISE GOODBYE.
CONGRATULATIONS ON YOUR ELECTION, CHANCELLOR.
YOUR BOLDNESS HAS SAVED OUR PEOPLE, YOUR MAJESTY. IT IS YOU WHO SHOULD BE CONGRATULATED. TOGETHER WE SHALL BRING PEACE AND PROSPERITY TO THE REPUBLIC.

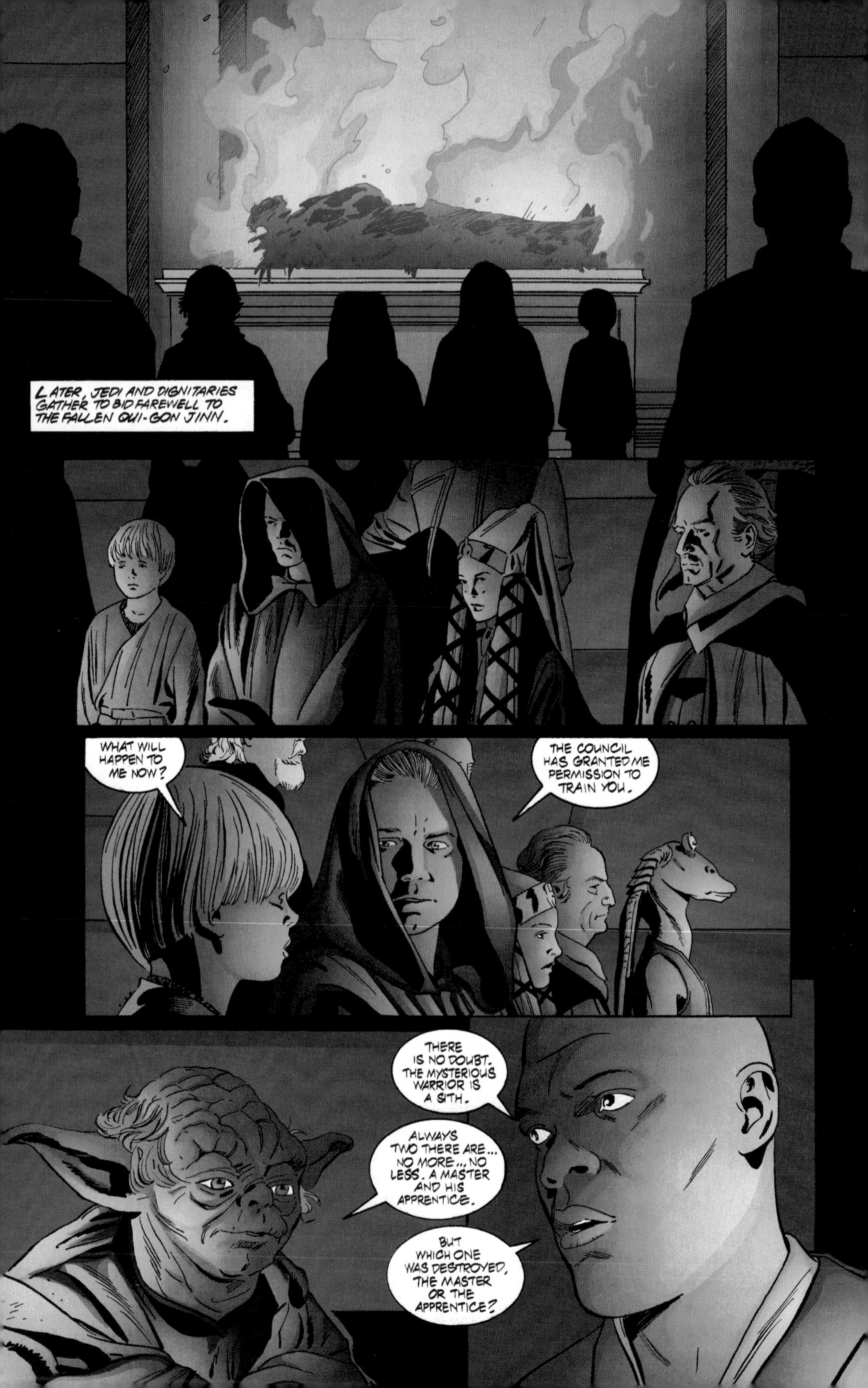
LATER, JEDI AND DIGNITARIES GATHER TO BID FAREWELL TO THE FALLEN QUI-GON JINN.
WHAT WILL HAPPEN TO ME NOW?
THE COUNCIL HAS GRANTED ME PERMISSION TO TRAIN YOU.
THERE IS NO DOUBT. THE MYSTERIOUS WARRIOR IS A SITH.
ALWAYS TWO THERE ARE... NO MORE... NO LESS. A MASTER AND HIS APPRENTICE.
BUT WHICH ONE WAS DESTROYED, THE MASTER OR THE APPRENTICE?

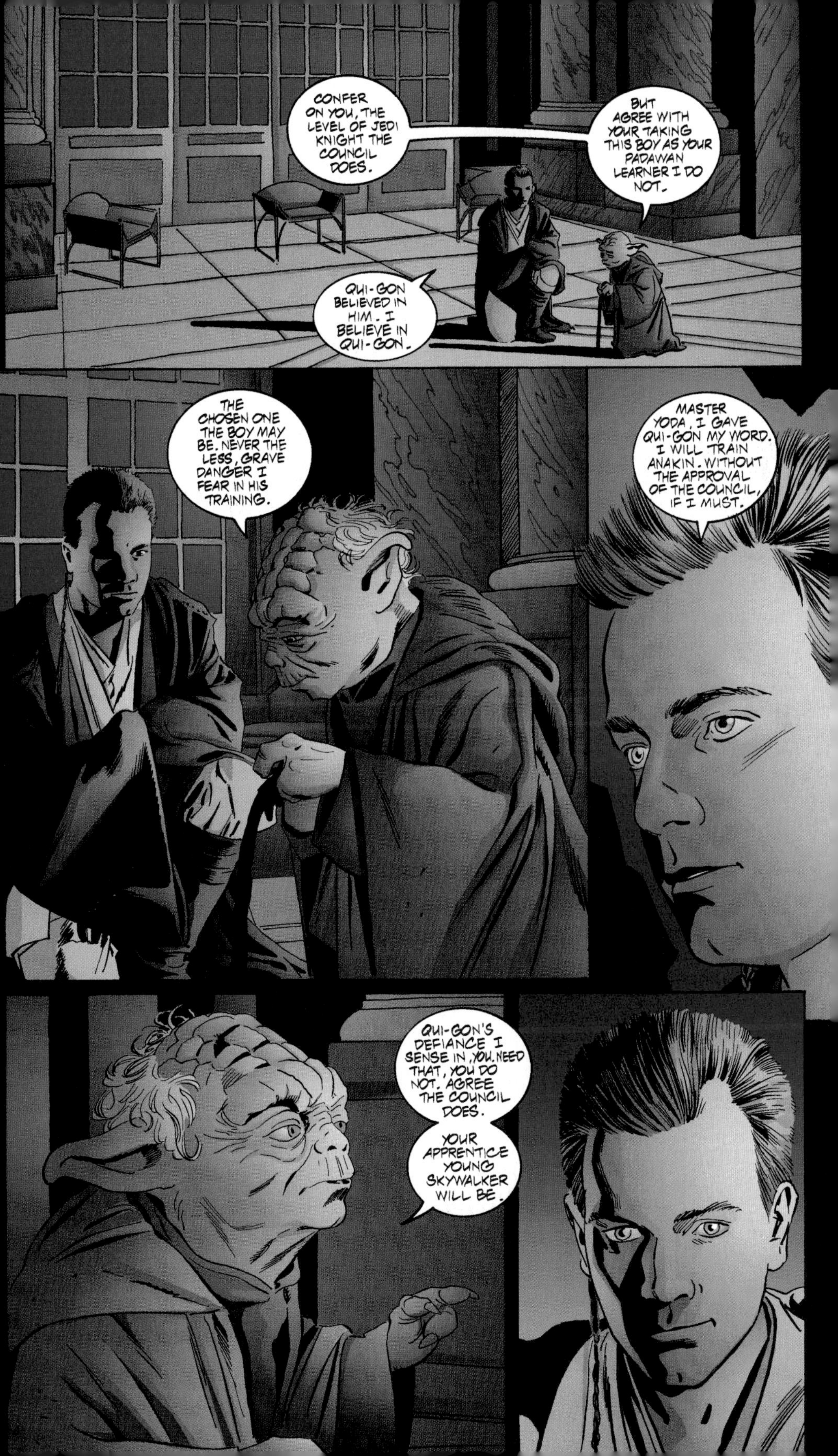
CONFER ON YOU, THE LEVEL OF JEDI KNIGHT THE COUNCIL DOES.
BUT AGREE WITH YOUR TAKING THIS BOY AS YOUR PADAWAN LEARNER I DO NOT.
QUI-GON BELIEVED IN HIM. I BELIEVE IN QUI-GON.
THE CHOSEN ONE THE BOY MAY BE. NEVER THE LESS, GRAVE DANGER I FEAR IN HIS TRAINING.
MASTER YODA, I GAVE QUI-GON MY WORD. I WILL TRAIN ANAKIN. WITHOUT THE APPROVAL OF THE COUNCIL, IF I MUST.
QUI-GON'S DEFIANCE I SENSE IN YOU. NEED THAT, YOU DO NOT. AGREE THE COUNCIL DOES.
YOUR APPRENTICE YOUNG SKYWALKER WILL BE.

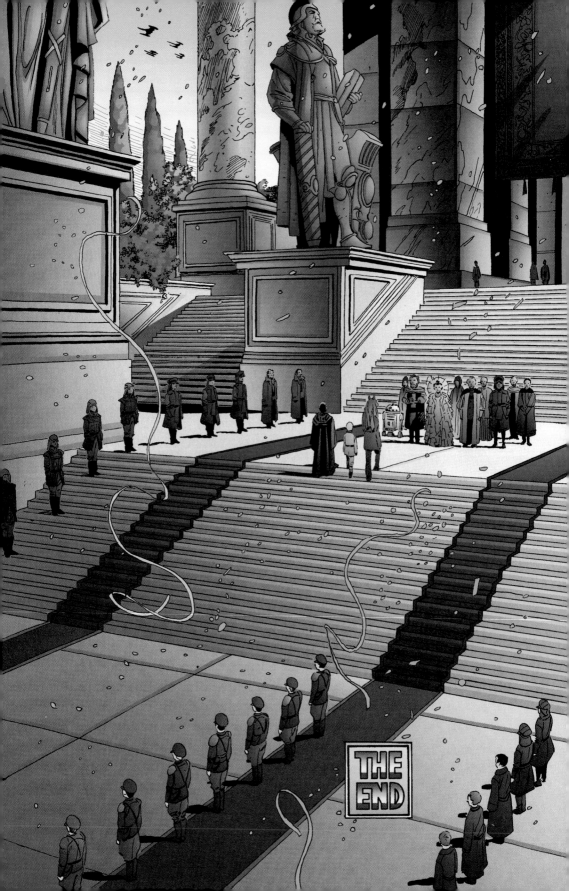

THE
END

COVER GALLERY

The following paintings by

HUGH FLEMING

appeared on the front

covers of the serialized

comics editions of

STAR WARS

EPISODE I

THE PHANTOM MENACE.

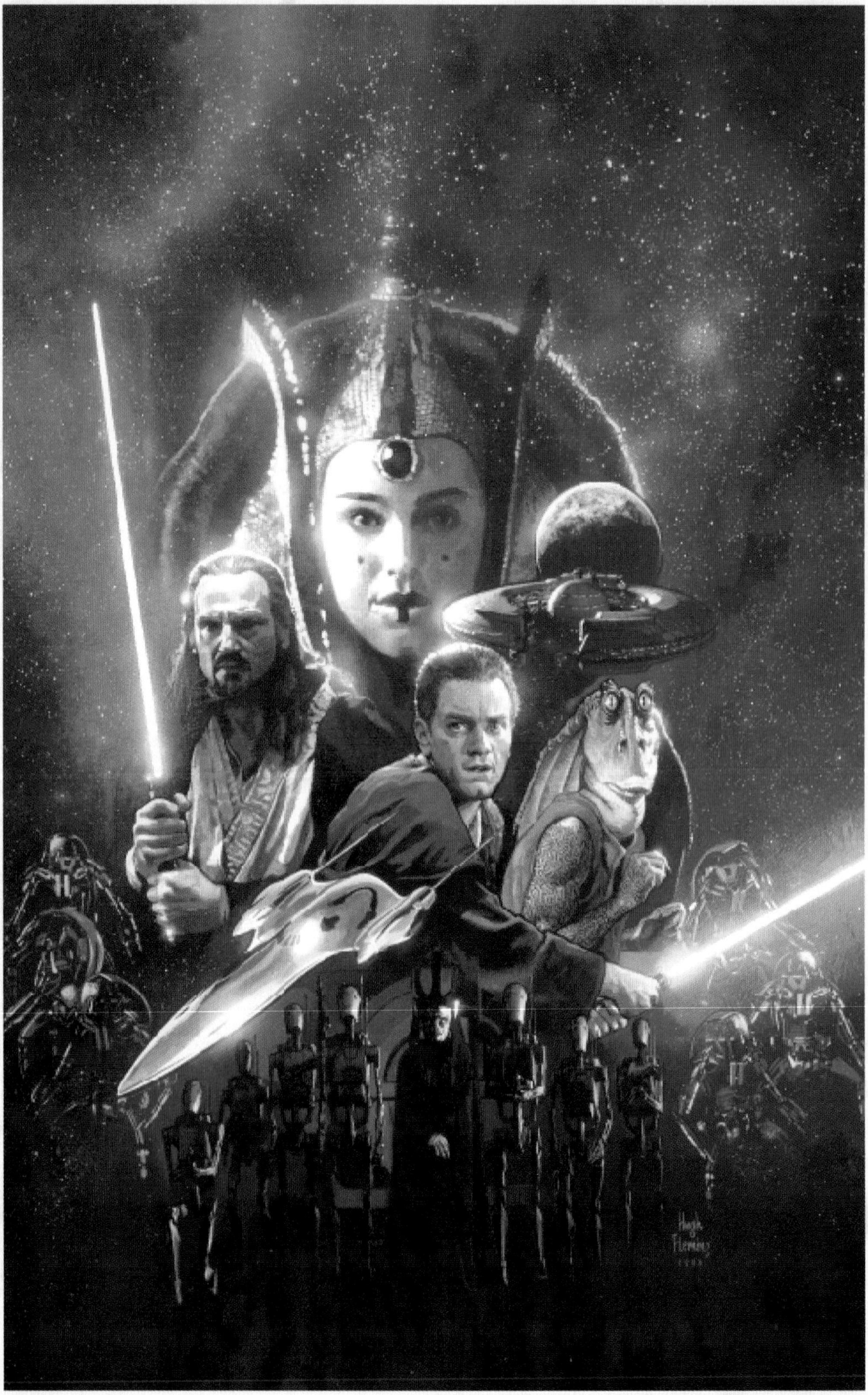

Issue One

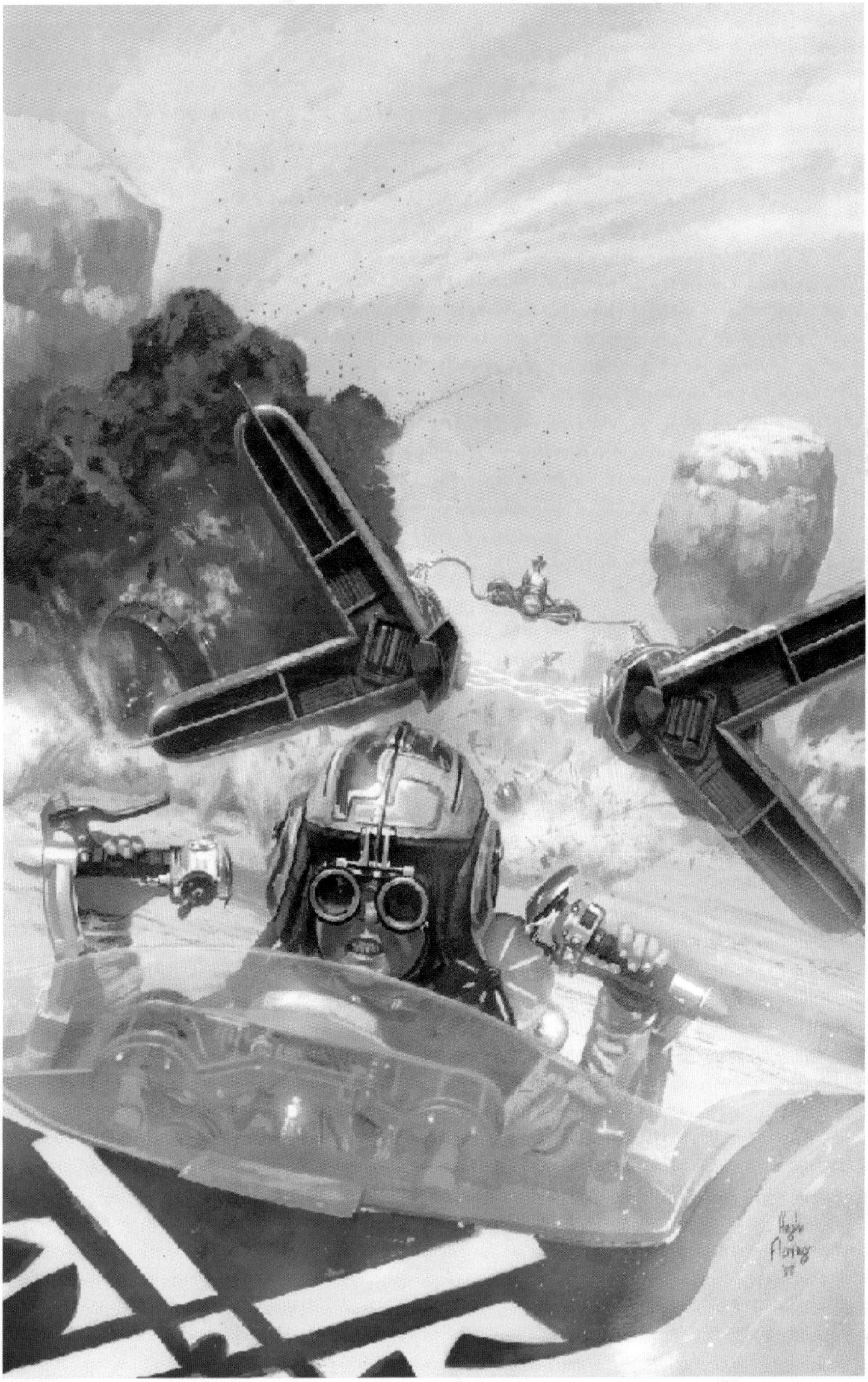

Issue Two

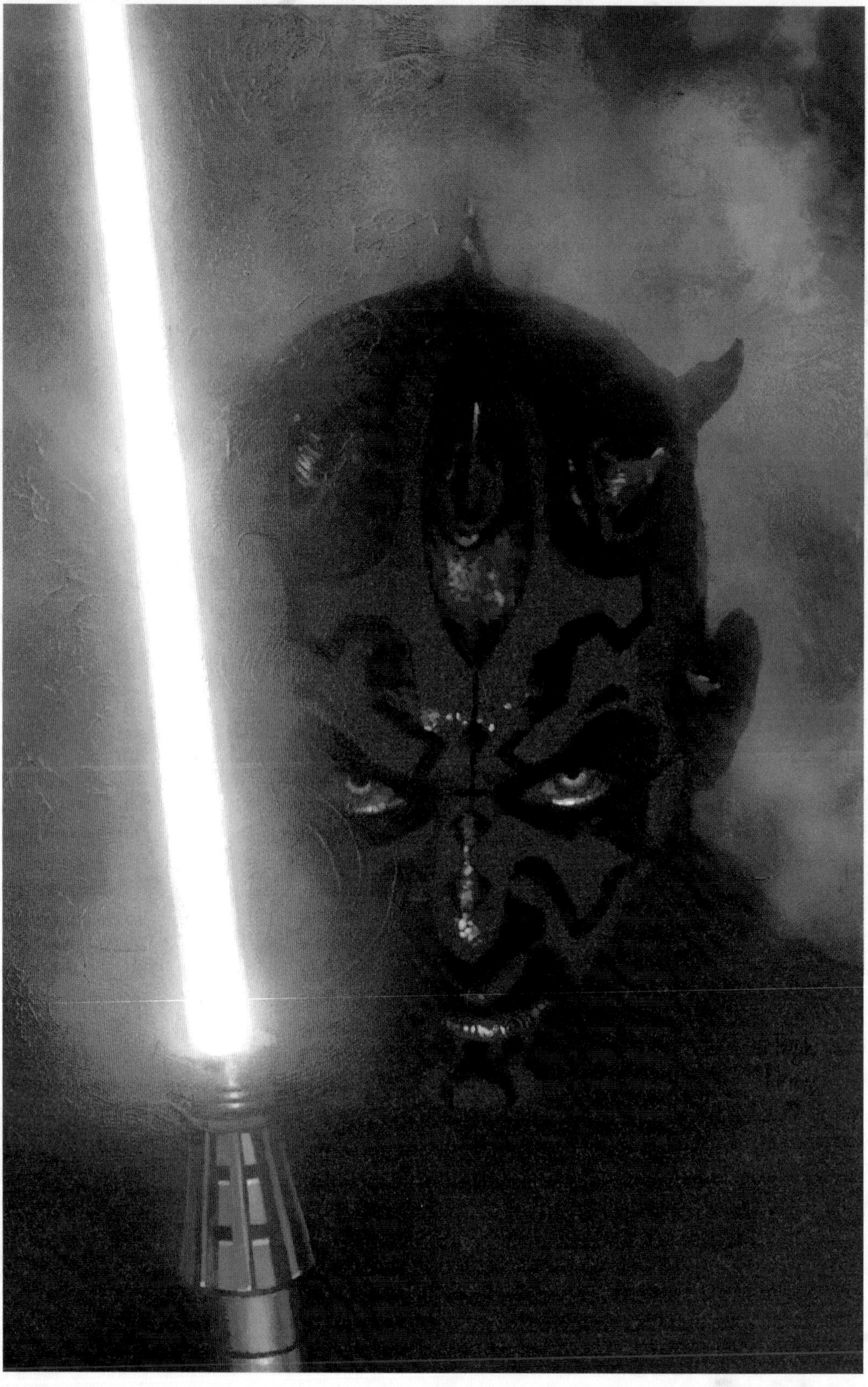

Issue Three

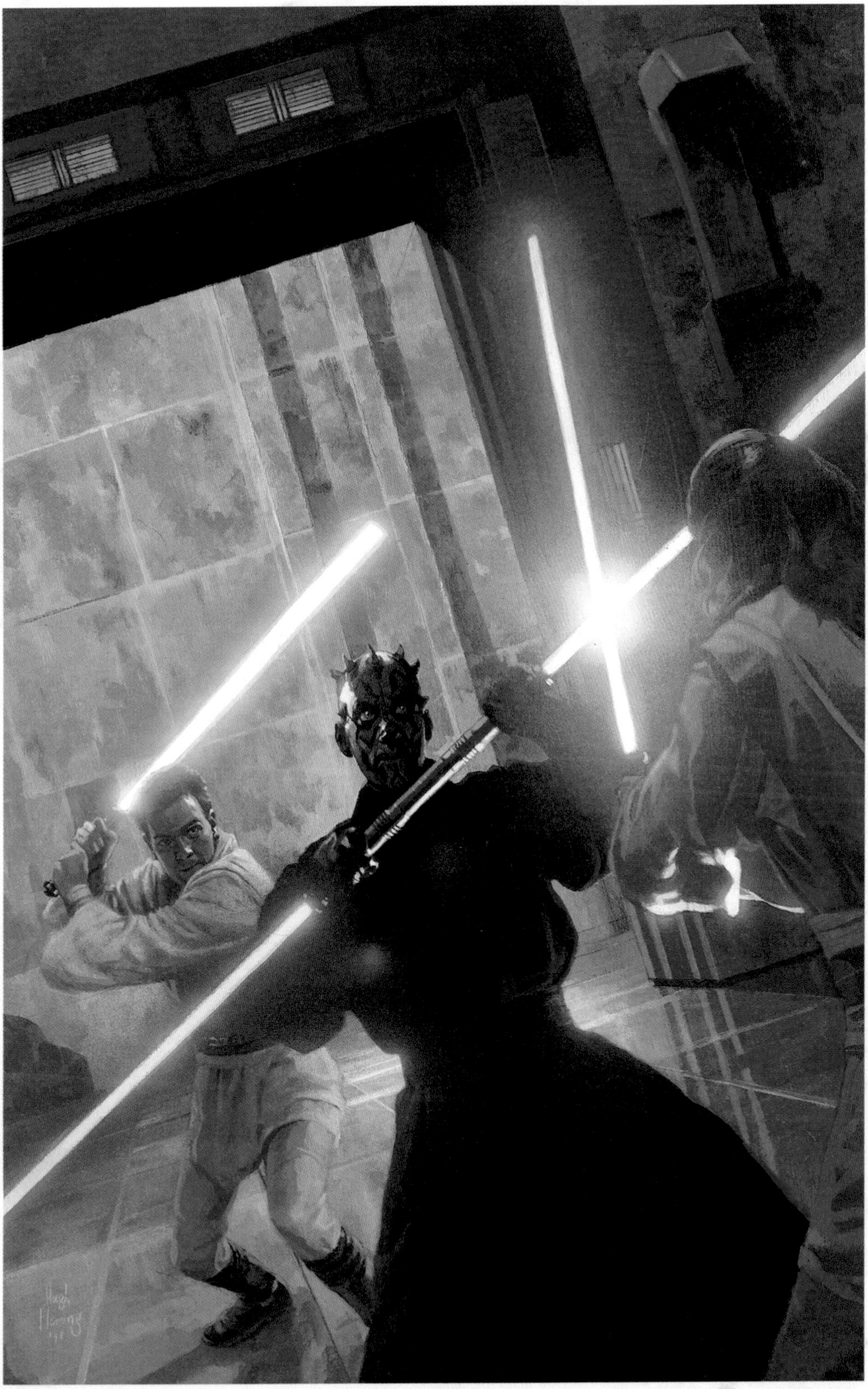

Issue Four

STAR WARS

EPISODE I

THE PHANTOM MENACE

Story
GEORGE LUCAS

Script
HENRY GILROY

Penciller
RODOLFO DAMAGGIO

Inker
AL WILLIAMSON

Letterer **STEVE DUTRO**

Colorist **DAVE NESTELLE**

Color Separator **HAROLD MacKINNON**

Cover Artist **RAVENWOOD**

Designer **MARK COX**

Editor **DAVID LAND**

Publisher **MIKE RICHARDSON**

Special thanks to **ALLAN KAUSCH** & **LUCY AUTREY WILSON** at
Lucas Licensing and **TINA MILLS** & **JUSTIN GRAHAM** at Lucasfilm

Published by
Titan Books Ltd.
42-44 Dolben Street
London SE1 0UP

First edition: May 1999
ISBN: 1-84023-025-8

2 4 6 8 10 9 7 5 3

Printed in the UK by Bath Press, Lower Bristol Rd, Bath.

OTHER TITLES AVAILABLE FROM **TITAN BOOKS**

ALIENS

FEMALE WAR
(formerly ALIENS: EARTH WAR)
Verheiden • Kieth
112-page color paperback
ISBN: 1-85286-784-1

GENOCIDE
Arcudi • Willis • Story
112-page color paperback
ISBN: 1-85286-805-8

HARVEST
(formerly ALIENS: HIVE)
Prosser • Jones
128-page color paperback
ISBN: 1-85286-838-4

LABYRINTH
Woodring • Plunkett
136-page color paperback
ISBN: 1-85286-844-9

NIGHTMARE ASYLUM
(formerly ALIENS: BOOK TWO)
Verheiden • Beauvais
112-page color paperback
ISBN: 1-85286-765-5

OUTBREAK
(formerly ALIENS: BOOK ONE)
Verheiden • Nelson
168-page color paperback
ISBN: 1-85286-756-6

ROGUE
Edginton • Simpson
112-page color paperback
ISBN: 1-85286-851-1

STRONGHOLD
Arcudi • Mahnke • Palmiotti
112-page color paperback
ISBN: 1-85286-875-9

ALIENS VS PREDATOR

ALIENS VS PREDATOR
Stradley • Norwood • Warner • Story • Campanella
176-page color paperback
ISBN: 1-85286-413-3

THE DEADLIEST OF THE SPECIES
Claremont • Guice • Barreto
320-page color paperback
ISBN: 1-85286-953-4

WAR
various
200-page color paperback
ISBN: 1-85286-703-5

APPLESEED
Masamune Shirow

BOOK ONE
192-page color paperback
ISBN: 1-84023-067-3

BOOK TWO
192-page color paperback
ISBN: 1-85286-821-X

BOOK THREE
224-page color paperback
ISBN: 1-85286-825-2

BOOK FOUR
224-page color paperback
ISBN: 1-85286-826-0

BATMAN VS PREDATOR

BATMAN VS PREDATOR
Gibbons • Kubert • Kubert
96-page color paperback
ISBN: 1-85286-446-X

BATMAN VS PREDATOR II: BLOODMATCH
Moench • Gulacy • Austin
136-page color paperback
ISBN: 1-85286-667-5

BATMAN VS PREDATOR III: BLOOD TIES
Dixon • Damaggio
136-page color paperback
ISBN: 1-85286-913-5

BUFFY THE VAMPIRE SLAYER

THE DUST WALTZ
Brereton • Gomez
80-page color paperback
ISBN: 1-84023-057-6

THE REMAINING SUNLIGHT
Watson • Van Meter • Bennett • Ross • Ketcham
88-page color paperback
ISBN: 1-84023-078-9

GHOST

GHOST STORIES
various
96-page color paperback
ISBN: 1-85286-711-6

NOCTURNES
various
96-page color paperback
ISBN: 1-85286-724-8

EXHUMING ELISA
Luke • Reis • Emberlin
160-page color paperback
ISBN: 1-85286-902-X

GODZILLA

AGE OF MONSTERS
various
256-page B&W paperback
ISBN: 1-85286-929-1

PAST PRESENT FUTURE
various
276-page B&W paperback
ISBN: 1-85286-930-5

PREDATOR

BIG GAME
Arcudi • Dorkin • Gil
112-page color paperback
ISBN: 1-85286-454-0

COLD WAR
Verheiden • Randall • Mitchell
112-page color paperback
ISBN: 1-85286-576-8

KINDRED
Lamb • Tolson
112-page color paperback
ISBN: 1-85286-908-9

SIN CITY
Frank Miller

SIN CITY
208-page B&W paperback
ISBN: 1-85286-468-0

A DAME TO KILL FOR
208-page B&W paperback
ISBN: 1-85286-574-1

THE BIG FAT KILL
184-page B&W paperback
ISBN: 1-85286-698-5

THAT YELLOW BASTARD
240-page black-and-white-and-yellow hardcover
ISBN: 1-85286-776-0
240-page black-and-white-and-yellow paperback
ISBN: 1-85286-842-2

FAMILY VALUES
128-page B&W paperback
ISBN: 1-85286-898-8

BOOZE, BROADS, & BULLETS
160-page black-and-white-and-red-and-blue paperback
ISBN: 1-84023-056-8

STAR WARS

CRIMSON EMPIRE
Richardson • Stradley • Gulacy • Russell
160-page color paperback
ISBN: 1-84023-006-1

EPISODE I—THE PHANTOM MENACE
Gilroy • Damaggio • Williamson
112-page color paperback
ISBN: 1-84023-025-8

TALES OF THE JEDI—THE GOLDEN AGE OF THE SITH
Anderson • Gossett • Carrasco • Heike • Black • Beckett • Woch
144-page color paperback
ISBN: 1-84023-000-2

X-WING ROGUE SQUADRON—THE WARRIOR PRINCESS
Stackpole • Tolson • Nadeau • Ensign
96-page color paperback
ISBN: 1-85286-997-6

X-WING ROGUE SQUADRON—REQUIEM FOR A ROGUE
Stackpole • Strnad • Erskine
112-page color paperback
ISBN: 1-85286-026-6

VARIOUS

BATMAN/ALIENS
Marz • Wrightson
128-page color paperback
ISBN: 1-85286-887-2

GHOST IN THE SHELL
Masamune Shirow
368-page color/B&W paperback
ISBN: 1-85286-889-9

PREDATOR VS JUDGE DREDD
Wagner • Alcatena
80-page color paperback
ISBN: 1-84023-021-5

STARSHIP TROOPERS
various
144-page color paperback
ISBN: 1-85286-886-4

SUPERMAN/ALIENS
Jurgens • Nowlan
152-page color paperback
ISBN: 1-85286-704-3

THE TALE OF ONE BAD RAT
Bryan Talbot
136-page color paperback
ISBN: 1-85286-689-6

TARZAN VS PREDATOR AT THE EARTH'S CORE
Simonson • Weeks
104-page color paperback
ISBN: 1-85286-888-0

All publications are available through most good bookshops or direct from our mail-order service at Titan Books. For a free graphic-novels catalogue or to order, telephone 01858 433 169 with your credit-card details or contact **Titan Books Mail Order, Bowden House, 36 Northampton Road, Market Harborough, Leics, LE16 9HE**, quoting reference SW1/GN.